BLACK IMAGES IN AMERICAN FILMS, 1896-1954

The Interplay Between Civil Rights and Film Culture

James R. Nesteby

UNIVERSITY PRESS OF AMERICA

Lanham • New York • London

4720 Boston Way
Lanham, MD 20706

3 Henrietta Street
London WC2E 8LU England

Printed in the United States of America

British Cataloging in Publication Information Available

Library of Congress Cataloging in Publication Data

Nesteby, James R.
Black images in American films, 1896-1954.

1. Afro-Americans in motion pictures. 2. Moving-pictures—United States. I. Title.
PN1995.9.N4N4 791.43'09'093520396073. 80-5697
ISBN 0-8191-2167-3 AACR2
ISBN 0-8191-2168-1 (pbk.)

All University Press of America books are produced on acid-free paper which exceeds the minimum standards set by the National Historical Publications and Records Commission.

For

Two Inspiring Teacher-Writers

Paul Vanderwood

and

James Baldwin

Acknowledgments

In the initial stages of research and writing, during the years 1973-1975, I was blessed with the genuine and encouraging assistance of Paul Vanderwood, Gene Wise, Fred Moramarco, Robert Redding, and Charles Cutter. In the final stages of rewriting and publishing, during the years 1980-1981, I have benefited from the generous and timely assistance of Lynn Adams, Mary Hébert, Janet Mandaville, and Anna Casey.

Those who have written on films and Afro-Americans before me are thanked for their contributions. Particularly influential have been the works of Peter Noble, Donald Bogle, Daniel Leab, Thomas Cripps, and Phyllis Klotman.

Semaj Betysen is the dedicated shadow who saw to it that this manuscript was typed and proofed.

Aleppo University
Aleppo, Syria
October 1981

Contents

"Credo" (1896)

I cannot find my way: there is no star
In all the shrouded heavens anywhere . . .
No there is not a glimmer, nor a call,
For one that welcomes, welcomes when he fears
The black and awful chaos of the night;
For through it all--above, beyond it all--
I know the far-sent message of the years
I feel the coming glory of the Light.

Edwin Arlington Robinson
Collected Poems

Chapter One

The Law of the Land: *Plessy* versus *Brown*

For Afro-Americans, 1896 was a very good year. Only eighty Afro-American men and women were lynched without trial in the United States of America; this was thirty-two less than the year before and forty-two less than the year following, according to the running count kept by W.E.B. DuBois in *The Crisis*.[1] Between the years 1896 and 1954, the "coming glory of the Light," of which Edwin Arlington Robinson wrote in "Credo" (1896),[2] was delayed for Afro-Americans though the culture of America experienced the shock waves of a dramatic evolution. Afro-American images heavily influenced by Anglo-Americans were present in the evolutions of both a gigantic film industry and a national consciousness of civil rights. The parallel changes which occurred in the film images and in the self-image of the civil rights leadership are traced in this study from the *Plessy versus Ferguson* Supreme Court decision on 18 May 1896 to the *Brown versus The Board of Education* Supreme Court decision on 17 May 1954.

The terms "Afro-American" and "Anglo-American" are most often used here when referring to "black" and "white" Americans. These are, it is acknowledged, polarizing terms but, today, more subtle distinctions are often necessary when referring to either the white community or the black community in America. Regardless of the terms chosen, someone is bound to protest. Within the last fifteen years "Negro" went out of fashion in favor of "black" or "Black" and now the trend seems to be directed once more toward "Afro-American." In the forties, the term "Aframerican" was cited as "felicitously designated" by one Afro-American civil rights publication. Along with "Anglo-American" have come the fashionable terms "Polish-American," "Italian-American," "German-American" and all other conceivable combinations; along with "Afro-American" have come "Indian-American" and "West Indian-American," to name but two more contemporary ethnic terms.

This difficulty goes far back in history, of course, and it has always been complicated by changing conceptions of group identity. The term "black" has been used for centuries, for instance, as has the term "negro"; only since the early decades of the twentieth century has the designation "negro" been regularly capitalized. In 1835, the Fifth National Negro Convention resolved to recommend that "Negroes remove the word 'African' from the names of their institutions and organizations."[3] Most early independent Afro-American film companies, if they referred to ethnic origins at all in their names, used the term "Colored." The largest distributing company for Afro-American films in the twenties, however, was called the "Afro-American Film Exhibitors, Inc." Another set of controversial terms among critics of the art--"movie," "film," "cinema," "motion picture" and so forth--are used interchangeably.

In this study, then, the terms "Afro-American" and "Anglo-American" shall be used to designate the two major cultures in America, that of black African origins and that of white European origins. These terms are intended neither to be exclusive nor all-inclusive of the national or racial origins of Americans. "Black images" rather than "Afro-American images" is used in the title of this study primarily because "black" is a currently acceptable generic term and, more importantly, because of the numerous culture-wide connotations, overwhelmingly negative, which Americans have for the word "black." "Black" is thus a forked-word used here intentionally on both a literal level, as a synonym for Afro-American and, as is oftentimes the case in American culture, on a symbolic level as a conjure-word for darkness, evil, and depravity.

Film stereotypes have evolved in western civilization from archetypal portrayals of Africans and Afro-Americans in which black has been equated with bad, inhuman or subhuman, and soulless and white has been equated with good, mature, pure, and civilized. Commonplace phrases reflect these connotations: "he has a black mark against him," "he has been blackballed or blacklisted," "buy it on the black market," "he is being blackmailed," "he is blackhearted," and "he believes in black magic." In films, the major character of *In the Days of Gold* (ca. 1911) is referred to as "a black sheep," although he is white. Similarly, a film about Anglo-Americans is titled *The Black Sheep* (1915), with the connotation being that there exists a negative asset to the family. President Theodore Roosevelt is cited by historian James Ford Rhodes as referring to the Afro-Americans involved in the "Brownsville Affray" (Rhodes' phrase), as being "guilty of a black and dastardly crime."[4] Thus, black is frequently representative of negative values and, by implication, black Americans are frequently representative of the same negative values.

For purposes of definition, the Afro-American image in films shall be tentatively considered as both a reflection of attitudes and as a mirror of the predominant traits of American culture such as those expressed by President Roosevelt. The static quality of these images through films from earlier and later years may have reinforced those attitudes from which the civil rights groups sought to break free. The civil rights groups, rather than the film medium, were the active agents of change. Afro-American input into the creation of their own images was severely limited throughout the period under investigation. One might therefore challenge I.C. Jarvie's general thesis that the film "image is not wilfully created, because it emerges from an interaction between the publicity, the film itself and the audience."[5] This may be true in the abstract, considering a homogeneous group within American culture, but it is not true in this instance when the disparate cultures of both Afro-Americans and Anglo-Americans were being put together competitively in the same films. It is the nature of the film medium to create fantastic and superficial images of the peoples and cultures it treats. But when it comes to race, American films went further by keeping the popular mind ignorant of Afro-Americans and their culture. The anti-humanistic and anti-intellectual strains in the American character produced a film culture in which Afro-Americans were denied even the most cherished of American ideals: liberty, justice, and equality.

Film images reflect and illuminate American culture in some specific ways. Popular films are geared for audience understanding and in this sense they must be reflections of what can be understood by people of the era in which the film was produced. The Afro-American image, though not always a reflection of cultural contexts, is frequently a reflection and illumination of cultural myths and fantasies. This is true of nearly all film images, but it is particularly true for Afro-Americans who have been negative values in American culture. To draw upon New Critical or subjective terminology, each film has a life of its own. It may be studied in the sociological or psychological sense, attempting to gauge subtle and oftentimes simply internalized audience reactions, which has previously resulted in a host of contradictory "provens." It may also be studied in the sense that each film is a multiple art form, emphasizing sound and sight, which captures and capsulizes a menagerie of cultural experiences on celluloid. The latter approach is essentially what this study has undertaken to show in relation to the black image in films. The result is referred to here as film culture. Based on the collective fantasies of the popular mind, film culture projects an idealized version of the way Americans want their culture to be.

This book will provide an overview of the black images in American film culture from 1896 to 1954. The first of two objectives is to impart a sense not necessarily of growth, for there was much stagnation along the way, but of the interrelationships between the civil rights movement and the influence of the film industry in the cumulative experience of Afro-Americans. Calling forth highlights from these experiences as they were reflected or molded by civil rights activities and films will permit insights into the attitudes and images which exist today in both Afro-American and Anglo-American communities. It should be remembered that it was predominantly for Anglo-Americans that the Afro-American image was projected on the screen; but it was predominantly to Afro-Americans that civil rights groups presented alternative images and the tactics and strategies through which the existing negative images of Afro-Americans could be changed.

The Afro-American image in films may have been the popular image of Afro-Americans in America, but this image had little or no basis in reality. Whether or not the image of Afro-Americans in films changed contextually or superficially over the years is essentially an unresolvable issue, though this study demonstrates that both forms of change occurred on a limited scale. The differences in opinion that arise over this issue are in the semantics of scholars and and critics, however, and not in matters of what the images actually represent or how myths and symbols serve as reinforcements for the images.

The second, more important objective of this book is to expose the myths about Afro-Americans which permeated the American popular mind through the film medium. Films featuring Afro-Americans, throughout the period from 1896 to 1954, purported to be films about Afro-Americans, about Afro-American themes and problems, and about Afro-American culture. The interplay between civil rights activities and American film culture will expose the myths about Afro-Americans still influential today, as many of the films supporting them remain in circulation. There were isolated attempts within the film industry itself to change the image of Afro-Americans. These efforts usually came about at the instigation of civil rights groups for whom the changing of the film image was only a component struggle in their battle to change both the image and status of Afro-Americans in America.

While not an either/or proposition for most Afro-Americans, it may have been easier to watch films than to join in a civil rights movement. The passivity of film--predominantly a one-way communication--rather than the activity of a cause which would require two-way communication, involves no long-term investment or commitment and little in the way of time or money. Perhaps most importantly, it did not present adequate alternatives for changes in either outlook or belief except in a negative fashion by objecting to the images the film culture was putting forth.

The Afro-American images captured on film present a valid historical document reflecting predominant attitudes, conscious or unconscious, in American culture during the era in which the film was produced. In the final analysis, however, a film cannot be looked at solely as an historical document any more than it can be looked at solely as a literary document. It requires study as a cultural document, as an artifact in the larger sense of being susceptible to both new and established investigatory techniques. In the present study, there is a difficulty in documentation, since most early films are no longer extant. Reviews, handbills, advertisements, still photographs from the films, and the works of film historians are relied upon when the films themselves are not available, thus mitigating to a degree this strong statement in favor of film as a reflector of culture. For the early period and for the instances in which the films have been lost or destroyed, it is primarily the documents describing the films that become the cultural reflectors. The languages of film and print, therefore, shall be interwoven in an attempt to bring these cultural attitudes and experiences into focus. Much seems to have depended upon the use to which a director could put language effects in the films themselves. Afro-Americans, regardless of class or educational distinctions, were most often expected to speak the least sophisticated forms of black English. A drawled "Yaa-Za" for "Yes, Sir," for example, was comical to Anglo-American audiences. Since the American public would not tolerate Afro-Americans speaking the more widely used Anglo-American English, such roles were imposed upon the Afro-American actors.

The term "popular mind" is used here to reflect the attitudes and images of the majority of filmgoers and is intended as a counterpart to the term "intellectual mind," redundant as the phrase is, with its perspectives in history and its search for explanation. The popular mind encompasses the most widely discussed issues communicated primarily by mass media. Popular mind is embodied in the sentiments which are normally associated with an era or a milieu for it cuts across such distinctions as working class and middle class, Afro-American and Anglo-American. For example, when American ideals were threatened during World War One, Afro-Americans enlisted in the military as quickly as Anglo-Americans; in the same vein, there were both Afro-American and Anglo-American intellectuals who refused to support the war effort. That the popular mind knew no substantial difference between black and white in terms of public reaction to American wars was the case also in World War Two and the Korean police action.

There are exceptions, segments of the population which are obviously not participating in the formation of the popular mind. These people are excluded either by location or by desire. The popular mind is relatively inaccessible to Native-Americans on reservations and Afro-Americans in kraals, or ghettoes. Certain ethnic or religious communities desire separate identities, and thus have their own institutions and media. Somewhere between those groups without access to media and those who deliberately choose alternative media are the Americans whose thoughts, ideals, and attitudes actually make up the popular mind.

It is postulated that the prevailing Afro-American image in the overwhelming majority of films, regardless of whether it got there intentionally or unintentionally, is to be accepted as visual evidence of the cultural conditions against which the civil rights groups were protesting. The leadership voices of the various civil rights groups will be used to express the representative thoughts of the Afro-American community. A description of their activities will be presented as evidence of their representative leadership. There are three overlapping reasons for this choice of civil rights spokespeople and activists to represent the major Afro-American viewpoints. The first is that at least until there is an authoritative and widely-accepted intellectual history of the Afro-American community available, the most vocal Afro-Americans are the most accessible sources of thoughts and attitudes in the Afro-American community. The second reason for looking most closely at civil rights spokespeople is that while other sources of legitimate leadership are considered to some extent, they are either local sources or specialized sources such as business people, publishers and artists. The third is that only the leadership of large civil rights groups, and a few of the outspoken Afro-American writers and actors, reach the same national audience reached by American films; this national leadership has been in the best position to counter the film images of Afro-Americans disseminated throughout American culture.

Some films along the way will be spotlighted for critical examination as individual entities when this approach can be of value in elucidating something more extensive than the intrinsic screen experience. This will normally mean an overview of highlights rather than an in-depth exploration of every nuance and change that affected Afro-Americans in this era's cultural history. What follows is but one perspective on an important cultural phenomenon which has, at least indirectly, influenced all living Americans throughout their lives.

This study proceeds on the premise that the single most dangerous flaw in the American character emanates from the failure to reconcile Anglo-Americans and Afro-Americans. The melting pot, an idealistic formulation with little basis in reality, may have served to distract interest in closer race relations. If the American popular mind believed the melting pot idea was working successfully, few Anglo-Americans actually attempted to make a contribution to its success. Films could have helped, but they did not. Instead, America's film culture served as positive reinforcement of negative attitudes toward Afro-Americans. It is the supremacist attitudes of Anglo-Americans toward Afro-Americans, based on ethnocentrism and prejudice rather than fact, that defines the racism found in America. It is not that the resulting racial discord kept America from becoming a great nation, but racial discord did keep America from becoming the consummate nation it once promised to be and could perhaps yet become if more avenues are opened for Afro-American participation. The loss to American culture prior to the *Brown* decision in 1954 is incalculable and is only partially revealed in the following discussion of how it took the first half of the twentieth century--the average lifetime for a person of that era--to reverse the *Plessy* decision of 1896.

Finally, the thesis about Afro-Americans in relation to Anglo-Americans to which this study attempts to adhere is that there is one gene pool for all humankind and that no persons or groups are inherently inferior or superior. The differences that have arisen are cultural and, therefore, this study is also an examination of the cultural biases which shaped the attitudes toward Afro-Americans found in American films from 1896 to 1954. The response to these attitudes, formulated primarily by Afro-American civil rights spokespeople, points up the grotesqueries which were fostered through the film medium. The overwhelmingly reactionary attitudes found in Hollywood films during this era were representative of culture-wide attempts to keep the images of blacks consistent with nineteenth-century notions. That this contrasted with the reality of Afro-American culture is made evident by reviewing the slow but ongoing progress made during the same period in the realm of civil rights.

Notes

[1] See particularly "The Burden," *The Crisis* (December 1914), pp. 94-95.

[2] Edwin Arlington Robinson, "Credo," *Collected Poems of Edwin Arlinton Robinson* (New York: Macmillan, 1929), p. 94.

[3] Irving J. Sloan, *The American Negro: A Chronology and Fact Book* (Dobbs Ferry, NY: Oceana, 1965), p. 14.

[4] James Ford Rhodes, *History of the United States: From the Compromise of 1850 to the End of the Roosevelt Administration*, vol. 9 (New York: Macmillan, 1928), p. 340.

[5] I.C. Jarvie, *Movies and Society* (New York: Basic Books, 1970), p. 189.

- plessy vs ferguson
- De Facto

Chapter Two

Blackfacing and Film Shorts

During 1896, the Olympic Games were revived as a gesture to increase international goodwill for all peoples; the Populists and the little man's candidate, William Jennings Bryan, went down in defeat in the national elections as the era of the Progressives began; and the Koster and Beal Music Hall in New York City featured its first motion picture short on Thomas Edison's Vitascope. Another historic change that year was the *Plessy versus Ferguson* Supreme Court decision. It differed from the other changes in that it was a step backward for the young and idealistic American republic preparing to take its place as a world leader; it differed because it legitimized at the dawn of the twentieth century the *de facto* segregation practiced in many areas of the United States. The second-class citizenship it bestowed upon Afro-Americans is apparent from the practice that developed of using blackface Anglo-Americans to impose the models for what Afro-Americans were to represent in early film shorts made in America before World War One.

Prior to the *Plessy versus Ferguson* "separate but equal public facilities" decision, the United States Supreme Court in 1883 struck down the Civil Rights Act of 1875, constricting once more the outward extension of the rights of Afro-Americans as American citizens. These rights had been established immediately following the Civil War by amendments to the United States Constitution. The Thirteenth Amendment prohibited slavery, the Fourteenth made citizens of the former slaves, and the Fifteenth outlawed infringements on the right to vote based on "race, color, or previous conditions of servitude." "Black Codes" designed to circumvent these amendments evolved in the South nonetheless. In what is known as the Compromise of 1876, Congress placed Rutherford B. Hayes in the presidency over the popularly elected William Tildon. The Era of Reconstruction ended then, and the "Black Codes" led to Jim Crow laws that effectively nullified the Thirteenth, Fourtheenth, and Fifteenth Amendments.

Extralegal activities after 1876 were aimed at making sure that the new Jim Crow laws enacted across the land were enforced and that the popular racist attitudes of the Anglo-American public were enforced. The impact of these extralegal activities was not so dramatic as earlier, in the generation following the American Civil War, or later, in the American racial riots during World War One. One cause of this relative lull in racial antagonisms was that the contrast was diminished between what mobs or marauders like the Ku Klux Klan did and what the law allowed, that is, separate but supposedly equal treatment of Afro-Americans. Racial separation became a legal reality with the *Plessy* decision and true equality remained an unobtainable ideal for Afro-Americans.

W.E.B. DuBois split the opinion of the Afro-American community, as well as of the Anglo-American community, just after the turn of the century. He did this by advocating a radical departure from the more docile Booker T. Washington's toleration of intolerance. While Washington and DuBois both expressed Afro-American views to the Anglo-American community in the linguistic style of Anglo-Americans, most Anglo-Americans were pacified by Washington's outward indifference to segregation of Afro-Americans and his acceptance of American economic ideals, symbolized by his efforts to create the National Negro Business League in 1900. DuBois' radical insistence upon equal opportunities for Afro-Americans was frightening, as was his stance that if integration was not feasible, then a politically, socially, and economically powerful Afro-American community was needed.

Booker T. Washington, however, saw his method as just that: a method. He too was personally anxious to acquire equality as well as liberty for Afro-Americans. But he felt the need to publicly promote gradualism and the proving of one's "blackself" first at the expense of political rights. His compromise in the "Atlanta Address" of 1895 came on the eve of the *Plessy* decision and reflected paternal sentiments similar to those which the Supreme Court interpreted into law the following year. The essence of the sentiments was Washington's metaphor of the hand: economically, Afro-Americans and Anglo-Americans should work together like one hand, while socially they should be as separate as the fingers. In effect, a second-class citizenship was being outlined.

The conflicts dealt with by Washington persisted in one form or another throughout the first half of the twentieth century. Others, including DuBois and Asa Philip Randolph, utilized Washington's preparation for both liberty and equality in the battles for political and economic, as well as social and spiritual, integration. Within the first decade of the twentieth century, at the height of Washington's influence, the time had already come to move beyond his efforts, including his vocational program at the Tuskegee Institute in Alabama. Alternatives were established. In 1901, William Monroe Trotter, like DuBois a graduate of Harvard University, founded the militant *Boston Guardian* which opposed Washington's policies. In 1905, the influential *Chicago Defender* was founded by Robert S. Abbott, and that same year DuBois and Trotter sponsored the equality seeking Niagara Movement.

DuBois and Trotter at first gained little popular support among members of the Afro-American community, but they did attract the attention and money of a small group of Anglo-American and Jewish-American liberals. In 1909, the Niagara Movement entered into an alliance with the Constitution League to create the National Association for the Advancement of Colored People (NAACP). DuBois was a volatile spokesperson in comparison to the pacifistic statements of Washington, who died in 1915. As editor from 1910 to 1934 of *The Crisis*, the NAACP's publication, DuBois was pounding out a pulsating call for Afro-American action which set in motion counteractions among Anglo-Americans. The resulting tensions concerning the status of Afro-Americans in reality and in the media have prevailed in the civil rights conflict to the present day.

The NAACP waged a bitter campaign against D.W. Griffith's *The Birth of a Nation* (1915) and William Fox's *The Nigger* (1915), films which appealed to Anglo-American racial hatreds and distrusts. The first big test for the NAACP came in 1917, however, when discord between Anglo-American and Afro-American soldiers at Fort Sam Houston in Texas resulted in twenty deaths. Despite the efforts of the NAACP, 118 Afro-American soldiers were indicted and all but eight were convicted. Sentences of life imprisonment were given to sixty-three. Nineteen more were hanged, thirteen of them prior to a review of the courts-martial could take place and before their sentences were made public.[1] A full pardon for those still living came in 1974. It was to take nearly this long for significant reversals in the Afro-American image in film to occur. Early in the century, "negro," "nigger," "darky," "colored," and "coon" were images used indiscriminately in films and other media, and "the literature of the day," writes Daniel Leab in *From Sambo to Superspade* (1975), "viciously lampooned the black, glorified the plantation tradition, rationalized lynchings, and explained away inequitable treatment of blacks."[2] Black faces sprinkled into the background of films were not difficult to spot, but prominant and dignified roles for Afro-Americans were scarce until the late sixties and early seventies.

For many American moviegoers, *The Birth of a Nation* in 1915 marks the beginning of Afro-American portrayals in film. But Leab has pointed out, in an article titled "The Gamut from A to B: The Image of the Black in Pre-1915 Movies," that a considerable influx of Afro-American minstrels and vaudevillians made the transition to film while many Anglo-Americans shunned the low pay and lack of prestige associated with the new medium.[3] These early stage and film images of Afro-Americans were linked to songs and dances suggestive of plantation slaves and riverboat oarsmen. Afro-American folk images were further popularized through both blackface minstrelsy and Negro minstrelsy. These stage entertainments found their way into early American film shorts, beginning with Edison's peep-show, *The Pickaninnies Doing a Dance* (1894).

The image of Afro-Americans in films, as well as the tradition of blackfacing, was thus well-established long before Griffith's masterwork. The Afro-American minstrel Tom Fletcher, writing in his autobiography just after the turn of the century, describes his part in the making of these short films:

> My partner Al Barley and I got leading comedy parts . . . I was the talent scout for the colored people. There were no types, just colored men, women and children. There were no script writers, no make-up artists, wardrobe mistresses . . . At the end of each day, I got

Blackfacing?

> eight dollars. We all considered it a lot of fun with pay.[4]

The fun-making did not continue for long, and neither did the lack of types, for the Afro-American image was early constituted as something which the film-viewer either laughed at, as in *Watermelon Contest* (1899), featuring "four grinning Negroes [who] wolfed melons and spat seeds with a will,"[5] or feared, as in *A Scrap in Black and White* (1903) in which the Afro-American youngster comes out on top. Other films made ambiguous use of black and white archetypes, as in George Méliès' blackface *Off to Bloomingdale Asylum* (French; 1903), a nightmarish piece in which four blacks become white and then turn into one huge black before disintegrating, and in the use of two versions of *Everybody Works but Father* (1905), one with Afro-Americans and one with Anglo-Americans.

Prior to the development of film narrative, credited to Edwin S. Porter in *The Great Train Robbery* (1903), a wide range of roles existed for Afro-Americans. This was the era of "the unformed image" for Afro-Americans in films, according to Thomas Cripps in *Slow Fade to Black* (1977).[6] These roles included the Afro-American comic, already familiar through minstrelsy and vaudeville, in films ranging from the blackface *Sambo and Aunt Jemima: Comedians* (ca. 1897-1900) to the appearance of Afro-Americans in *Chicken Thieves* (1897) and the pre-1900 films, *Interrupted Crap Game*, *Prize Fight in Coon Town*, and *A Night in Blackville*.

More genuine was the entertaining *Ballyhoo Cake-walk* (1903) and the portrayal of Afro-Americans as defenders of America during the Spanish-American War of 1898, in which twenty Afro-American regiments served. The latter films include *Colored Troops Disembarking* (1898), *The Ninth Negro Cavalry Watering Horses* (1898), and *Colored Invincibles* (ca. 1898). But in *The Rout of the Filipinos* (1899),

> white soldiers bang away at a retreating brown-skinned adversary. For blacks who could not find themselves in a campaign in which they actually took part, it was one of the first instances of white editorial control over a filmed racial statement.[7]

By 1905, the use of cutting to produce a narrative was

common in films made by Anglo-Americans. The new storylines for Afro-American characters were adopted from rural southern stereotypes, the most renowned of which came from Harriet Beecher Stowe's *Uncle Tom's Cabin* (1852). Still in circulation, the latest filming of *Uncle Tom's Cabin* was in Europe in 1964, starring the American, John Kitzmiller, as Uncle Tom.

White actors and actresses were blackened in Edwin S. Porter's production of *Uncle Tom's Cabin* (1903). Porter used Anglo-Americans in the major roles, whiteface or blackface, with a sprinkling of Afro-Americans in the minor roles. In the silent era, there were at least six other versions of Stowe's romance, coming in 1909, 1913, 1914, 1915, 1918, and 1927. Only the 1914 and 1927 versions of *Uncle Tom's Cabin* starred an Afro-American as Uncle Tom, played in 1914 by the revered and widely known Sam Lucas and in 1927 by the first Afro-American lead in a Hollywood studio film, James Lowe. With the exception of Lowe's principled and spirited portrayal, these film versions invoked little of the conscientious spirit of Stowe's romance, relying instead on melodramatic or tragic renderings of her characters which helped evolve several of the major film stereotypes for Afro-Americans: the comic stooge or pickaninny (Topsy), the faithful retainer (Uncle Tom), the brute (Sambo and Quimbo), and the tragic mulatto (George). These treatments attest to the fact that Americans were not anxious to face cultural realities reflected in Stowe's work; rather, they wanted to accept the myths about rural Afro-Americans inspired by it.

Biograph's *The Thirteen Club* (1903), for instance, presented a black waiter who "suddenly notices a death's head centerpiece; instantly he gets the shakes and the bugeyes."[8] In *A Bucket of Cream Ale* (1904), the joke was on the Anglo-American when a blackface maid threw the ale onto his head; in later films the roles were nearly always reversed with an Anglo-American trickster figure and an Afro-American recipient of the joke. Another Biograph short, *The Nigger in the Woodpile* (1904), presented the Afro-American as a lazy and dishonest comic figure who was both a deacon of the African Church and a thief. The degrading comic image was further fostered in one of the first all-black shorts, *Wooing and Wedding of a Coon* (1905), as well as in *The Pickaninnies* (1905), *A Georgia Wedding* (1909), *Uncle Tom Wins* (1909), *The Colored Stenographer* (1909), and *King Cotton* (n.d.).

In *The Fights of Nations* (1907), both the title and characterizations were similar to the later *The Birth of a Nation* (1915), and the image of the Afro-Americans was of fearsome razor-toting brutes. *The Dancing Nig* (1907)--produced the year in which the first Afro-American, Alain Locke of Harvard University, was selected to become a Rhodes Scholar--presented just what the title promised, a "dancing nig." An Anglo-American's revulsion over unexpectedly discovering an Afro-American woman where an Anglo-American woman was supposed to be, provided the storyline for both *The Masher* (1907) and *The Dark Romance of a Tobacco Can* (1911); in *The Masher* the discovery came when the woman was both literally and symbolically unveiled.

Other representative early film shorts include D.W. Griffith's *The Zulu's Heart* (1908), in which a Zulu turns on his fellows in order to aid the whites, Pathe's *For Massa's Sake* (1911), in which a freed slave sacrifices his liberty by indenturing himself on behalf of his financially strapped former master, and Triangle's *The Coward* (1915), in which an Afro-American servant kills a Yankee in defense of his young master. Similar slave imagery appears in *A Slave's Devotion* (1913), *Old Mammy's Charge* (1914), *The Littlest Rebel* (1914), and *Old Mammy's Secret Code* (1913). *In Slavery Days* (1913) presents a blackface mulatto attempting to "pass" for white. Miscegenation is placed in a comic context in *Black and White* (n.d.), racial identities are muddled in *The Valet's Wife* (1908), swapping for Afro-American babies takes place in *Mixed Colors* (1913), *Mammy's Child* (1913) and *Cause for Thanksgiving* (n.d.), and children of the two races are not allowed to become close in *Sonny Jim at the Mardi Gras* (n.d.). Among the exotic presentations of Afro-Americans are *Swami Sam* (1915), with a "classic ghetto hustler," and *Florida Enchantment* (1915) in which "black transvestism was the subject of a gaily mounted burlesque."[9]

There is an unpleasant irony in the fact that Afro-Americans actually played "Afro-American" roles only selectively in many of these films and others such as Griffith's *The Slave* (1909), Keystone's *Colored Villainy* (1915) and *A Colored Girl's Love* (n.d.), and Mack Sennett's *The Hunt* (1916). Before long, the pattern of values associated with Afro-Americans in their film roles were tied to negative values in the Anglo-American culture. Standardized roles, like the Afro-American maid in *His Last Laugh* (1916), were soon entrenched along with the passive Afro-American in the South in hundreds of films, claims Thomas Cripps in *Black Film as Genre* (1979), ranging from *The Soldier Brothers of Susannah* (1912), *The Empty Sleeve* (1914), *Days of War* (ca. 1914), *For the Cause of the South* (1914), to *A Fair Rebel* (1914).[10] Just as Afro-Americans were excluded from the American Dream in reality, Afro-Americans were soon excluded from the images of the American Dream in films.

Early images of blacks in jungles, which is where many Anglo-Americans thought Afro-Americans were from and should return to, appeared in documentaries like *Tuaregs in Their Country* (1909) and *Life in Senegal* (1910). Other documentaries, or quasi-documentaries, were based on the African safaris of Theodore Roosevelt, Paul J. Rainey and others: *Theodore Roosevelt in Africa* (n.d.), *Theodore Roosevelt's Camp in Africa* (n.d.), *Paul J. Rainey's African Hunt* (1912), *Capturing Circus Animals in the African Wilds* (ca. 1913), and *African Natives* (n.d.).

Big Game Hunting in Africa (1909) is a "documentary," filmed in Selig's Chicago studio, of Teddy Roosevelt's safar to Mombasa, Kenya, in 1909. Many viewers believed this film to be actual footage from Africa. Aside from the realism of using live animals, real Chicago natives acted as savage Africans should have acted. A review of this film in *Colliers* noted that when going into the bush after the lion, "the beaters became scared, but the ex-president was calm." The juxtaposition of the lowliest black and the highest--in the eyes of many Americans--achiever of the Anglo-American race, was illustrated further in the *Colliers* narrative: "The big native tracker, always on the job, burst through the underbrush and found the slain monarch [the lion] breathing his last. Again he raised his war-cry and wrapped his arms around his naked body, snake fashion. The other natives hurried up with Mr. Roosevelt and his son in the lead."[11]

The offspring of these films, all prior to the appearance of the first of a long string of Tarzan jungle films, include *Missionaries in Darkest Africa* (1912), *The Terrors of the Jungle* (1913), *Voodoo Vengeance* (1913), *The Military Drill of the Kikuyu Tribes and Other Native Ceremonies* (1914), *The Loyalty of Jumbo* (1914), *Forbidden Adventure* (1915), and *A Night in the Jungle* (1915). Though set in Africa, the themes were frequently similar to other American-made films with Afro-Americans in them, as with the comic situations of *The Zulu King* (1913) and *Queen for a Day* (n.d.), and the presentation of a black defending whites in *The Kaffir's Gratitude* (1915). By 1916, the genre was being parodied along with Darwinism in *Pa's Family Tree*.[12]

Reflecting what was to be the norm for another fifty years, one of the few all-black films made up to this time, *Darktown Jubilee* (1914) with Bert Williams, was an immediate failure with filmgoers. Early American film audiences rejected the Afro-American Williams, however talented, in a major role. In Brooklyn, in fact, a showing of *Darktown Jubilee* incited a riot. Earlier, a Civil War melodrama, titled *A Southern Girl's Heroism* (1911), drew Anglo-American protests for its variation from the black stereotype of Topsy the slave. This Topsy, spelled "Topsie," is kissed on screen by a Union officer and, in another scene, she appears on the Union officer's arm while his Anglo-American lover holds his other arm. Anglo-American protests were also registered after the appearance of *The Soldier's Ring* (1911), yet another Civil War story, in which a servant fails to carry out his duties in such a way as to project the idea that "he knows his place."

Advertisements for *Mystery of the Pine Tree Camp* (1913) claimed that the film used a real black convict in its bloodhound chase scene, correlating for all viewers the reality of the image on screen with the reality of the Afro-American off screen. A still from the 1913 film, *A Black Hand Elopment*, shows a man in blackface yawning and stretching in such a way that his hand crosses in front of a window. In the shadows of the window stands a frightened Anglo-American woman gazing at the black hand. Perhaps as a suggestion of potential violence or of sexual aggression, there is a knife stuck in the ground beneath the window (and beside the black). A reviewer, also in 1913, wrote that "our darker breathren never complain" about their image in film. There were complaints from Afro-Americans too, of course, but oftentimes they failed to penetrate the veil dividing Anglo-Americans and Afro-Americans.

Even the identity of black authors was often not

publicized. Selig's 1908 version of *The Count of Monte Cristo*, in keeping with early film practices of not including screen credits, failed to mention the name of the story's part-black author, Alexander Dumas. The 1912 version acknowledged Dumas as author. This was after the 1908 Supreme Court decision banning piracy of stories for use in films, which decision also inspired the creation of the first censorship boards, the National Board of Review in 1909, and state censorship boards shortly thereafter. Censorship of films was approved by the Supreme Court in 1915 when it determined that film is an entertainment and, therefore, not protected by the First Amendment; the result was that while "inciting to racial tension" was banned, caricatures of the Afro-American character and culture was not. No action was taken to insure that the creations of black artists were acknowledged. Adolph Zukor's first film was a successful version of *The Count of Monte Cristo* (1913) and Clarence Muse appeared in the 1934 version. Dumas' adventure stories, the most recent being the 1975 filmings of *The Three Musketeers* and its sequel, *The Four Musketeers*, have been among the most filmed and most enjoyed in an America which is largely unaware, even today, that Dumas, the creator of many American cultural myths, was black.

Popular exceptions to featured Afro-Americans like Bert Williams were the all-black casts which Sigmund Lubin used in his Sambo series, made between 1909 and 1911, and his Rastus series. Sambo, Rastus, and Remus were synonymous with black characters in many early shorts. For years, Lubin focused on one popular stock role for blacks, Rastus the coon, beginning with *How Rastus Got His Pork Chops* (1908). Amusement was the objective of the coon image, whether it was presented as buffoonery or as slapstick. Such efforts as *How Rastus Got His Turkey*, *Rastus' Riotous Ride*, *Rastus and Chicken*, *Chicken Thief*, and *Pickaninnies and Watermelon* (all ca. 1910), relied on the coon image. In Essanay's *C-H-I-C-K-E-N Spells Chicken* (1910), a similar plotline was spelled out for the viewer. The chicken-stealer stereotype of the coon included the characteristics of being childlike, foolishly pretentious, shiftless (except when it comes to chickens and gambling), clumsy and vulgar.[13] In 1917, by producing *Uncle Remus' First Visit to New York*, the Afro-American Independent Colored and Indian Film Company helped foster the black images being created by Anglo-Americans!

In Lubin's *Rastus in Zululand* (1910), a lazy Rastus dreams of being shipwrecked in Zululand, in Africa, and the storyline is premised on the Pocahontas/John Smith myth. There is a comic twist in that the princess is obese. An earlier variation on the Pocahontas plot is in Biograph's *The King of the Cannibal Islands* (1908). Here the comedy revolves around the rescue of a very fat black queen. These obese princesses and queens were pre-mammy figures. By the time the blackface version of Aristophanes' *Lysistrata* (1914) and Lubin's all-black *Coon Town Suffragettes* (1914) were filmed, the stereotype of the black mammy was fully developed.

In the same genre as the Rastus and Sambo series, but integrating both Afro-American and Anglo-American children, Hal Roach put together the silent *Our Gang* shorts during the early twenties, including a parody of *Uncle Tom's Cabin* titled *Uncle Tom's Uncle* (1926). A forerunner of *Our Gang*, states Donald Bogle in *Toms, Coons, Mulattoes, Mammies, and Bucks* (1973), was *Ten Pickaninnies* (1904), in which "nameless Negro children romped and ran about while being referred to as snowballs, cherubs, coons, bad chillun, inky kids, smoky kids, black lambs, cute ebonies, and chubbie ebonies."[14] In 1938, Metro-Goldwyn-Meyer purchased the rights to *Our Gang*. For six years, throughout the World War Two era, Farina, Stymie and Buckwheat carried on as *The Little Rascals*. These episodic encounters between Afro-American and Anglo-American children, first popularized by the Rastus and Sambo series, continued to use similar stereotypes. The tranquil laziness of the Afro-American children is interrupted by their antics and occasional terror, at which time their eyes go wide, their hair stands on end, and their voice boxes refuse to function.

Pejorative titles alone oftentimes were box office attraction enough for Anglo-American audiences. *The Nigger* (1915) portrayed hatred and intolerance toward Afro-Americans; the one Anglo-American sympathizer with "the nigger" turns out himself to have an Afro-American heritage. A similar sympathy had been shown to an Afro-American by an Anglo-American judge in *The Judge's Story* (1911). *The Nigger* and *Broken Chains* (1922) reflect images similar to those which Griffith utilized in *The Birth of a Nation* (1915); *The Nigger* was one of the first films to be campaigned against by the NAACP. The only significant results of the protest was that in some areas the title of *The Nigger* was changed to *The New Governor* and the release of another racist film, *Free and Equal* (1915) was delayed for ten years because of the furor. Other film shorts played on the color concept from different perspectives. As in James Weldon Johnson's novel, *The Autobiography of an Ex-Coloured Man* (1912), the themes of Afro-American identity crises and of "passing" were present in *The Debt* (1912) and *The Octoroon* (1913). In *The Debt*, an Anglo-American's wife and Afro-American lover both have children by him at the same time--an Anglo-American son and a mulatto daughter who grow up together. They decide to marry but are told that they are brother and sister and, to pile ruin upon ruin, that she is part Afro-American.

The threat the Afro-American exceller posed to Anglo-American manhood was carried out when Jack Johnson took the heavyweight boxing championship in 1908. For seven years, Anglo-Americans looked for a "great white hope." One of several parodies of Johnson's prowess was the blackface *The Night I Fought Jack Johnson* (1913), in which exaggerated fear is shown by the Anglo-American fighting the blackface imitation of Johnson. *Some White Hope* (1915) appeared the year Johnson lost the title; nonetheless, it was recalled shortly after its release because it was repugnant and embarrassing to the supremacist attitudes of Anglo-American sports fans. These films were precursors to the appearance of the Afro-American actor, James Earl Jones (whose father, coincidentally, was also an actor and a prizefighter), in *The Great White Hope* (1970).

Reminiscent of *Drawing the Color Line* (1909), similarly, is *Black Like Me* (1964). Both present the fantasy of an Anglo-American who experiences a change for the darker in his skin color. In *Drawing the Color Line*, an inebriated Anglo-American is blackfaced by his drinking buddies and sent out unrecognized among his Anglo-American acquaintances. The theme of *In Humanity's Cause* (1911) is a variation on the Jekyll-Hyde syndrome which remained in service into the sixties as a vehicle for Sidney Poitier in *All the Young Men* (1960). *In Humanity's Cause* concerns a wounded Confederate officer in the Civil War who, while unconscious, is given a life-saving blood transfusion from an Afro-American. The officer's personality is "brutalized" by the Afro-American blood, the plot suggests, and his revenge is consumated in his own death as well as the death of the Afro-American donor. In *All the Young Men*, the racial conflict is similar but the setting is the Korean War; the Anglo-American suspects a dire outcome and so refuses at first to accept the only available blood of his type from an Afro-American.

The coming of World War One speeded up migration from the South to the North by both Anglo-Americans and Afro-Americans who would fight economic as well as physical battles for the limited jobs and housing in urban areas. Excluded from unions, the migrant Afro-Americans were often used as strikebreakers or scabs during World War One. Anglo-American workmen rioted against Afro-Americans in 1919, but the worst incident occurred in St. Louis, Missouri, in 1917. Other migrations into America in the first decade of the twentieth century supplied the movie industry with its first mass audiences for film shorts. World War One and the restrictive Immigration Acts of 1921 and 1924 brought this era to a close. After 1915, the middle class began to supplant the lower class immigrants as the largest film audience. When the art of film thus began to appeal to the public as a form of family entertainment, the feature-length film was born.

By World War One, the nation's capitol city, Washington, D.C., was segregated. In a NAACP-sponsored march in New York City in 1917, the slogan was "Why not make America safe for Democracy?" Lynchings nonetheless increased to eighty-three in 1918. Some Afro-Americans were hanged while still in the uniform of the United States Army. It was a disgusting hypocrisy: Afro-Americans were being asked to defend America abroad, but at home they were defenseless against the same Anglo-American culture they helped defend. The war experience did not change the image of Afro-American soldiers or civilians in the new feature-length films, although the two men first decorated for heroism in American Army units in France were Afro-Americans. The Afro-American community made an outstanding, though largely unacknowledged, contribution to the war effort. Over one-third of a million Afro-Americans served in the Army, six hundred of them as officers.

The Income Tax Amendment to the United States Constitution passed in 1913, establishing a regressive national tax that adversely affected mostly poorer people like Afro-Americans. Horatio Alger's "luck and pluck" books were no longer the rage, but America quickly adopted the "business equals success" idea and, by the time World War One began, movies were on their way to becoming one of the largest businesses of all. New York City bankers financed the development of Hollywood, California. Prior to World War One, Italian feature-length films gave American producers their greatest competition overseas. After the war, trade embargoes and the necessity for reconstruction in other film-producing countries allowed Hollywood to quickly dominate the world market, spreading America's peculiar institutionalizing of the images of Afro-Americans far beyond the borders of the United States.

As purveyor of films to the world, Hollywood was placed in a minor dilemma concerning its portrayal of Afro-Americans. The desire on the part of foreigners to learn more about the Afro-Americans they had come in contact with during the war led some producers to include more Afro-Americans in their films, but always it was done with an eye to the effect which increased Afro-American exposure might have on the domestic market in the South. The dilemma of which audience to appeal to, foreigners or Southerners, was most often balanced in favor of the Southerners. Not coincidentally, it happened that the most successful American film producer in the first third of the twentieth century was D.W. Griffith, a Southerner, whose career was instrumental in evolving the feature film out of film shorts.

Notes

[1] Jack D. Foner, *Blacks and the Military in American History: A New Perspective* (New York: Praeger, 1974), p. 115.

[2] Daniel J. Leab, *From Sambo to Superspade: The Black Experience in Motion Pictures* (Boston: Houghton Mifflin, 1975), pp. 7-8.

[3] Daniel J. Leab, "The Gamut from A to B: The Image of the Black in Pre-1915 Movies," *Political Science Quarterly*, 88 (March 1973), passim. A revised

version of this article appears as chapter one of Leab's *From Sambo to Superspade* (1975).

[4] Eileen Landay, *Black Film Stars* (New York: Drake, 1973), pp. 13-14.

[5] Thomas Cripps, *Slow Fade to Black: The Negro in American Films, 1900-1942* (New York: Oxford Univ. Press, 1977), p. 12.

[6] Cripps, p. 10. Cripps' new insights in his chapter on "The Unformed Image" are relied upon in this and several other paragraphs particularly.

[7] Cripps, p. 12.

[8] Leab's *From Sambo to Superspade*, p. 17.

[9] Cripps, p. 24.

[10] Thomas Cripps, *Black Film as Genre* (Bloomington: Indiana Univ. Press, 1979), pp. 14-15.

[11] Kalton C. Lahue, ed., *Motion Picture Pioneer: The Selig Polyscope Company* (New York: A.S. Barnes, 1973), p. 52.

[12] Cripps' *Slow Fade to Black*, pp. 19, 23, and 135 particularly.

[13] Leab's *From Sambo to Superspade*, p. 14.

[14] Donald Bogle, *Toms, Coons, Mulattoes, Mammies, and Bucks: An Interpretive History of Blacks in American Films* (New York: Viking, 1973), p. 7.

Chapter Three

World War One and David Wark Griffith

In his long career, primarily in Hollywood, David Wark Griffith developed the prototypes of the most influential Afro-American images and simultaneously carried them to their farthest frontiers. In later years the full range of emotion which the Griffith images evoked was rarely surpassed; usually filmmakers retreated from them, so vicious and sterile were they. Griffith often felt compelled to reiterate his belief that he was not anti-black, that his film stories had their bases in history. Griffith's rhetoric has been small compensation for three generations of Americans who, Afro-American and Anglo-American, find Griffith the most consistently racist film producer America has had.

Griffith, to complicate the cultural perspective, was also the most talented film producer in America during the era covered by this study. His greatness was in his artistry and in his technical mastery of the film medium. The content of his films exhibit an obsession with the themes of ethnic purity, idealized Anglo-American women, and hard-fought battles. His views were influenced primarily by the romanticism of his southern background. A producer of racist films, he was also an idealist who felt the motion picture industry could become the panacea for the ills of the world. A lover of battle epics, he felt that a brotherhood of man created out of the moving unity of pictures would eliminate wars. He was a portrayer of the cult of chivalry in which Anglo-American goddesses were glorified, though he was a believer in the equality of humankind. The contradictions in his mind were also the contradictions in the popular mind of America.

Griffith reflected the obsession of filmmakers with Afro-Americans from the rural South at a time when many Afro-Americans were creating an entirely different life style in the urban centers of the

North. *The Confederate Spy* (ca. 1910), for instance, was a non-Griffith film which, like most of the popular Civil War genre films, reflected the white supremacist attitudes of Reconstruction historians William Archibald Dunning and James Ford Rhodes. About the turn of the century another Reconstruction historian, John W. Burgess, wrote that

> there is something natural in the subordination of an inferior race to a superior race, even to the point of the enslavement of the inferior race, but there is nothing natural in the opposite. It is entirely unnatural, ruinous, and utterly demoralizing and barbarizing to both races.[1]

For the supporters of these popular Reconstruction historians, there was nothing inconsistent with the image of Old Uncle Daniel, in *The Confederate Spy*, spying in the North for the South. Uncle Daniel is executed by a firing squad, "but he is content, happy that he 'did it for massa's sake and little massa.'"[2] Since most Anglo-Americans had little knowledge of Afro-American life or culture, they accepted the southern stereotypes on film. The tension was felt in the Afro-American community, however, where the southern orientation of Booker T. Washington was challenged by the northern views of W.E.B. DuBois; the emphasis on Afro-American duty was slowly being replaced by the emphasis on Afro-American rights.

Political agitation, first clearly demonstrated in the NAACP's challenge to Griffith's *The Birth of a Nation* (1915), overrode the political apathy of Washington who recounted his conversations with President Roosevelt in the following manner:

> . . . it is, I believe, not an exaggeration to say that one-half of the time we were discussing methods for keeping out of office, and out of all political power, the ignorant, semi-criminal, shiftless Black Man who, when manipulated by the able and unscrupulous politician, Black or White, is so dreadful a menace to our political institutions.[3]

In a negative rather than positive fashion, Washington and Roosevelt were in agreement on critical issues concerning the place of Afro-Americans in politics. In 1907, the year before Griffith began his film career, President Roosevelt wrote the following to his friend, Owen Wister: "Now as to the negroes! I entirely agree with you that as a race and in the mass they are altogether inferior to the whites."[4] Such views were generally accepted by Anglo-Americans and they were most strikingly played out on film by Griffith, for stereotypical imagery of Afro-Americans had become part of the language and culture by 1915. "The cinema is a Topsy 'dat jes' growed," reported a reviewer in 1915.[5] The images of film blended together easily with the norms of culture as Vachal Lindsay demonstrated in his review of *The Birth of a Nation*:

> The Reverend Thomas Dixon is a rather stagy Simon Legree: in his avowed views a deal like the gentleman with the spiritual hydrophobia in the latter end of *Uncle Tom's Cabin*. Unconsciously Mr. Dixon has done his best to prove that Legree was not a fictitious character.[6]

Dixon was probably quite conscious of what he was doing, for he and other racist authors were aware that the American culture was absorbing the southern myths about Afro-Americans and that the first generation of American films was reflecting these distortions.

The extremes to which the image of Afro-Americans could be pushed were demonstrated in the popular genre of literary history which included the novels of Thomas Dixon. Dixon's father was a member of the original Ku Klux Klan and this family interest was carried to its summit in his "Southern Trilogy," written in response to the still popular *Uncle Tom's Cabin*: *The Leopard's Spots: A Romance of the White Man's Burden, 1865-1900* (1902), *The Clansman: An Historical Romance of the Ku Klux Klan* (1905), and *The Traitor* (1907). Ray Stannard Baker reported in *Following the Color Line* (1908) that a play version of Dixon's *The Clansman* contributed to the racial unrest in Atlanta in 1906, just prior to the mayhem which left twelve dead.[7] It was Dixon, a former classmate of Woodrow Wilson's at Johns Hopkins University, who arranged the epic showing of *The Birth of a Nation* at the White House, to which a sympathetic President Wilson responded, "It is like writing history with lightning." *The Clansman* served as the basis of the latter half of *The Birth of a Nation*, just as former Professor Wilson's widely read history of the United States served as the basis of the first half. Dixon was one of the most successful propagandists of racism and violence in this era, not just through *The Birth of a Nation* but in such films as his pro-war *The Fall of a Nation* (1916).

Like many living in the era of his films, Dixon excluded, Griffith also embraced an idealism which was too far removed from reality to have a substantial impact on his activities and day-to-day beliefs. He was an outstanding artist and an outstanding propagandist; he demonstrated the potential heights as well as the potential depths to which the new medium of films could be taken. Like others in his generation, including President Woodrow Wilson, Griffith was dedicated to both artistry and propaganda, diametrically opposed as they might be. He was able to maintain his credibility with Anglo-Americans even though he portrayed Afro-Americans in superderogatory scenes in his films and maintained a plea for humanism and equality in his speeches. Paul Robeson, one of the most influential independent Afro-American voices in the twentieth century, felt that President Wilson did the same during the years 1913 to 1921 by advocating "democracy for the world and Jim Crow for America."[8] Jim Crow was synonomous with segregation. In its most vicious form, Jim Crow meant a legal as well as a social segregation of Anglo-Americans and Afro-Americans; it meant not only that in some areas of America Afro-Americans could not legally elect others or be elected themselves to official positions, but that Afro-Americans could not drink from the same water fountain, eat at the same lunch counter, or sleep in the same hotel beds used by Anglo-Americans.

One of the ideals to which Griffith and most Americans of his era clung was that Americans were responsible for their fellow human beings both at home and across the world. This idealistic notion did not dissipate until America rejected the reality of the League of Nations in 1920. By then, Americans were unwilling, apparently, to be strapped tighter into the role of responsible citizens who must acknowledge both rights and duties for themselves as well as for others. Light-minded passing off of contradictions remained current throughout the twenties and is reflected in the casual view--still idealistic rather than realistic--Americans took toward the Kellogg-Briand Pact in 1928, a pact which "outlawed" the use of warfare forever and has yet to be repealed. America and most other nations signed this pact midway between World War One and World War Two.

As the finest of America's early filmmakers, notwithstanding the social commentary which most Americans today find unacceptable, Griffith still looms as impressive and enduring. His films were statements. He also foresaw and predicted the saturation of ideas which would take place through the film medium in the lives of Americans. The grand theatrical palaces which he envisioned fulfilling this public function did not appear on a wide scale, but in the early fifties the television medium fulfilled his prognostication of saturation by entering the province of American homes. His belief that movies should never be accompanied by voice--an innovation which was, he first felt, impossible, but one which even if it were possible would dilute the artistic integrity of the cinematic art form--caused him to leave filmmaking in 1930, just after the beginning of film's sound era.

In 1915, Griffith's most famous film, retitled *The Birth of a Nation* by Dixon because he felt *The Clansman* too tame, epitomized the racial antagonisms and intolerance present in America. It was among the most racist films ever produced. As a racist epic for America it would never again be equaled, even by *Gone with the Wind* (1939). It was a film in the tradition of glorious battle epics, this one commemorating the fiftieth anniversary of the end of the Civil War. The genre of romantic war films would survive, but it would not thrive so heartily after the war which came almost immediately upon the heels of the production of *The Birth of a Nation*. This film was among the most outlandish presentations of the flawless Anglo-American female, as well. The cult of the vagina, through which the virginal Anglo-American woman was held up as a symbol of racial purity, was one of Griffith's favorite themes. The image was battered in the liberating post-war era when women were granted the right to vote and, socially, when changes occurred like previously all-male saloons becoming movie houses with mixed company.

The Birth of a Nation capitalized on the periodic American hysteria over subversion occasioned by supposed menaces both internal and external, by Afro-Americans in America and by "Huns" or "Boches" from aggressive Germany. In this climate of hostility toward anything unorthodox, or just out of the ordinary, the new Ku Klux Klan was conceived in 1915, just in time to give a premier showing of *The Birth of a Nation* in celebration of its reorganization meeting on Stone Mountain near Atlanta, Georgia. The Klan again would take it upon itself to expand the governmental persecution of minorities in an atmosphere of holy war that Griffith portrayed in films about struggles with Afro-Americans.[9]

The new Klan was rather indiscriminate in its discrimination. By converting community leaders like local officials and ministers who in turn converted the populace, the Klan directed its vindictiveness against the Catholics and Jews in America, and then against Afro-Americans, the Japanese-Americans, and the Mexican-Americans when they or any other ethnic minority populated the regions in which the Ku Klux Klan organized. The Klan also found, in addition to its pro-war work, energies to expend upon labor agitators, whores, idlers, draft-dodgers, evolutionists, modernists and spies. Behind its oppressive views and tactics were values to which the Klan laid claim. The Klan's role as the protector of an unsharable domain led them to extoll the virtues of (Anglo-) Americanism, (Protestant) Christianity, the (southern) Cult of Chivalry, (secretive) Fraternity, the idolization of (Anglo-American) Motherhood, and the chastity of (Anglo-American Womanhood. Obviously most human beings in America and the world have always been excluded from what the Klan's definition is of America's ideology.

Various branches of the post-Civil War Ku Klux Klan were known as the Knights of the Golden Circle; the two names were often used synonymously following the war. The major precepts of the Kights of the Golden Circle, which originated long before the Civil War, influenced an imperialistic scheme to quest after an empire of slave states throughout the Caribbean, including Cuba and the other West Indies, Mexico, Central America and the northern part of South America. Thus, the anachronistic "golden circle" constituted a larger concern of the Klan for an empire dominated by the master race of Anglo-Americans. The Klan's techniques of American Nazism, most conspicuously its method of scapegoating those not in a position to retaliate, were incorporated into America's National Socialist White Peoples Party, known also as America's Neo-Nazi Party, after World War Two. Even today, the National Socialist White Peoples Party remains much stronger in some areas like Los Angeles and Chicago than does the periodically revived Klan. For many Anglo-Americans, the values of the nineteenth century remain viable.

The psychological draw which the values of the Klan had for Anglo-Americans in 1915 was evidenced by the rebirth of the Klan and *The Birth of a Nation*. The pervasiveness of prejudice in America was mocked by H.L. Menckin and G.J. Nathan in their satiric "defense" of the Ku Klux Klan on the basis that the Klan represented no more and no less than the values of all upstanding American institutions and citizens including, deep down, themselves:

> Not a single solitary reason has yet been advanced for putting the Ku Klux Klan out of business. If the Klan is against the Jews, so are half of the good hotels of the Republic and three-quarters of the good clubs. If the Klan is against the foreign-born or the hyphenated citizen, so is the National Institute of Arts and Letters. If the Klan is against the Negro, so are all of the States south of the Mason-Dixon line. If the Klan is for damnation and persecution, so is the Methodist Church. If the Klan is bent upon political control, so are the American Legion and Tammany Hall. If the Klan wears grotesque uniforms, so do the Knights of Pythias and the Mystic Shriners. If the Klan conducts its business in secret, so do the police, the letter-carriers and firemen. If the Klan's officers bear ridiculous names, so do the officers of the Lamb's Club. If the Klan uses the mails for shaking down suckers, so does the Red Cross. If the Klan constitutes itself a censor of private morals, so does the Congress of the United States. If the Klan lynches a Moor for raping someone's daughter, so would you or I.[10]

Griffith, furthermore, effectively presented the Klan as a substitute for anarchy, a glorifier of war, a savior of the Anglo-American race, and an agency to protect the vaginas of southern belles. The duality of meaning which the title *The Birth of a Nation* expressed was significant, for it spoke to both the birth of the Anglo-American Union in America, North and South, and to the birth of the original Ku Klux Klan, meanings which were synonymous to Anglo-American supporters of the film's themes.

Griffith had glorified the Old South or the Civil War in many pictures, including *In Old Kentucky* (1909), *Honor of His Family* (1910), *House with Closed Shutters* (1910), and *The Battle* (1911). He followed with *The Battle at Elderberry Gulch* (1913) and *The Massacre* (1914), which dealt with the terrible hindrances Anglo-American settlers experienced in their conquest of Native-American lands. *The Birth of a Nation* outdid all the numerous war-oriented battle films which preceded World War One. The national psyche was still fighting the wars of Manifest Destiny. Energies recently channeled to America's post-continental imperialist era, which included the confinement, degradation or genocide of the Native-American population, were rechanneled by the news of European imperialists seeking to redefine their colonial boundaries in Africa and Asia. Like his Afro-Americans, Griffith's Native-Americans were more savage than Anglo-Americans and both groups represented a menace to Anglo-American women.

Griffith's nearly flawless Anglo-American women were often queens of perfection who swooned behind the veiled symbolism of the Old South's cult of chivalry. The chivalric knighthood of medievalism was the facade of a Protestantism directed toward political ends as the Ku Klux Klan imbibed, ironically, the Catholic fervor of the crusades. No sacrifice was too high to protect these Anglo-American goddesses, for whom love was both an abstraction and a social obligation similar to the courtly love of medieval days. Should it prove impossible to protect them in this life, then the Anglo-American men were only too willing to send the Anglo-American women to another, cleaner and safer world through death. An equation with which the audiences were expected to identify in a Griffith film was that the capture of an Anglo-American woman by Afro-Americans or Native-Americans meant automatic ravishment by the "savages."

In *The Battle at Elderberry Gulch* an unidentified Anglo-American male prepares to shoot the young heroine, played by Lillian Gish, as the Native-Americans appear to be overwhelming the stronghold. No gun is raised, however, over the head of a crusty old Anglo-American settler woman who is attempting to comfort Lillian. In *The Birth of a Nation* a similar scene takes place with Afro-Americans storming the cabin. When the Anglo-American males can no longer hold off the assailants, the heroine's father dramatically raises a pistol butt aimed at her temple in anticipation of the final charge by the Afro-Americans. The heroine's father ignores his old wife altogether. In both cases, of course, the pretty heroine's head is rescued by the organized militia in the form of the United States cavalry or, in *The Birth of a Nation*, by the Ku Klux Klan vigilantes.

Another Griffith extravaganza, *Judith of Bethulia* lends additional insight into Griffith's complex over the purity of the Anglo-American woman and of the Anglo-American race. A review written by L.R. Harrison characterizes Judith as a splendid piece of womanhood who "dares be all and do all that revolts her finer nature from a deep hatred of injustice and wrong meted out to her peace-loving kindred and friends." She does all this "from a noble desire to preserve her country and the destinies of her race."[11] Griffith's fanatical defences of Anglo-American women were explicit if not exquisite by today's standards.

Overreaction to ethnic incidents involving Anglo-American girls are integral themes in both *The Birth of a Nation* and *The Battle at Elderberry Gulch*. In *The Birth of a Nation* a Ku Klux Klan kangaroo court and then murder are used--justifiably if one accepts Griffith's viewpoint--to revenge a negligent homicide committed by a male Afro-American. *The Battle at Elderberry Gulch* presents a similar overreaction to ethnic incidents when the Anglo-American men automatically shoot the Native-Americans on the assumption that they are attacking the Anglo-American girl. In actuality, the Native-Americans are carrying off two puppies which happened to belong to the girl. The entire plot evolves from the fact that the two ignorant puppies cannot keep themselves out of trouble; the troublesome puppies in the film are meant to be associated with the immaturity of the "savages." In *The Birth of a Nation* the ethnic situation in the South is presented as one of harmony until the advent of outside influence from Northerners. The harmony, however, clearly means a willingness on the part of Afro-Americans literally to dance to the Anglo-American tune. Two puppies appear once again in a scene predating the Civil War. The puppies are lazy, contented, and lovingly cared for, just as are the Afro-Americans.

A different projection of Anglo-American fantasies was in the persistent film image of the

Afro-American as devoted servant. The loyalty in the midst of the Civil War of the Afro-American slaves in *The Birth of a Nation* was foreshadowed in a two-part serial Griffith produced in 1911, *His Trust* and *His Trust Fulfilled*. Not confined to Afro-Americans, Griffith's version of the devoted servant stereotype appears in the characterization of a trustworthy Mexican who makes himself a hero through a dangerous ride to secure aid for the Anglo-Americans in *The Battle at Elderberry Gulch*. In *The Massacre* it is the Native-American scout who would not desert the Anglo-Americans in their battle with other Native-Americans.

Among the implications of *The Birth of a Nation's* image-making message was that renegades like Gus, the Afro-American brute who forces Little Sister to protect her honor by leaping from the cliffs into "the sweet gates of death," did not exist before the death of Abraham Lincoln; that mature Anglo-American women never enjoyed the company of Afro-American men other than as servants and certainly not as lovers; and that Anglo-American men were chaste in the presence of Afro-American women. The loaded sexual-racial content of Griffith films greatly inhanced their power as image-makers for minorities in the period. As a contemporary reviewer put it, concerning *The Birth of a Nation*, "Having painted this insanely apprehensive picture of an unbridled, bestial, horrible race, relieved only by a few touches of low comedy, 'the grim reaping begins.'"[12]

Attempts to answer or dilute Griffith's impact through further films were unsuccessful: Triangle-Kay Bee's *The Bride of Hate* (1916) treated the South without the Civil War; Colin Campbell's *The Crisis* (1916), an adaptation of Winston Churchill's novel, simply exchanged the southern perspective for a northern one; Booker T. Washington and Emmett J. Scott's attempt to interest Universal in the filming of *Up from Slavery* was not followed through with; and Scott's *Lincoln's Dream*, later retitled and reformatted as *The Birth of a Race* (1918), was an artistic and financial disaster. Yet, "beginning in 1915,"

> Afro-Americans became the only racial minority capable of mounting a campaign against this force. The social struggle to shape cinema into a democratic art form became theirs. Negroes fell between Indians and immigrants in American

racial arrangements--ambivalent, caught between slavery and freedom. Unlike Indians, they had already absorbed American culture; unlike immigrants, they could not expect to be absorbed by it.[13]

As Thomas Cripps has pointed out, *The Birth of a Nation's* southern values contrasted with both the traditional rural and new urban realities for Afro-Americans. Because of its epic stature, the NAACP and Urban League set out on their first major crusade to censor the Afro-American film images created by Anglo-Americans. The result of their bitter campaign was a few scenes being cut before showings in Los Angeles, New York, and Boston and the banning of the film in several smaller cities. More significant than these immediate concessions were the creation of a NAACP lobby in Hollywood, the demonstration that civil rights groups could come together in common causes, and the raising of Afro-American consciousness concerning the power of film culture to miscontrue the Afro-American experience.

The overdone racism which Griffith extracted from his casts saturated the film genres in which he worked. As a silent film, *The Birth of a Nation* exaggerated the presentation of the Afro-American in ways that survived to 1954 and beyond. Violence was part of that image. Already ethnic riots were taking place in various areas of the country, many spawned by the dislocation from South to North of Afro-Americans and Anglo-Americans, both with prejudices deeply instilled already. A boll weevil blight and extensive floods in 1914, and then the labor exodus to serve the demands of the war industry up north and abroad, set in motion an agricultural depression in the South which was to last until the late thirties. The paradox of Afro-Americans defending America overseas during World War One was a sacrifice in which more and more Afro-Americans were unwilling to participate. A reaction to the extremism expressed by Griffith was in the making. It was, surprisingly, to come in part from Griffith himself.

Griffith's second classic, *Intolerance* (1916), appeared the same year as his *American Aristocracy* (1916). Although replete with a Civil War setting and the Ku Klux Klan, *Intolerance* was surprisingly subdued. It was much more tolerant than the earlier attitudes in his films toward Afro-Americans, for his theme was a call for brotherhood in the days preceding America's entry into World War One; unfortunately, the version being distributed today under the title *Intolerance* includes only the Babylonian segment of the original film, a segment with only stock representations of loyal black guardians of the empire. In *The Greatest Thing in Life* (1918), Griffith indulged himself in a war-effort propaganda film which emphasized brotherhood and de-emphasized his earlier propagandistic stance against Afro-Americans. Continuing his occasional departure from previous representations of Afro-Americans, Griffith produced *One Exciting Night* in 1922. Afro-Americans were introduced for comic relief, a technique Griffith exploited in his early film shorts as well. The result was a toned-down but still degrading image of the Afro-American as fool.

With the exception of *The White Rose* (1924), throughout his long career Griffith employed Anglo-Americans in blackface far more often than Afro-Amerians unless it was for minor roles in crowd scenes, native gatherings, or clichéd situations in films like *The Idol Dancer* (1920) and *His Darker Self* (1923). His career ended with the production of *Abraham Lincoln* (1930), an appropriate film finale in the context of his Civil War mania. Griffith always had an appreciate audience of Anglo-Americans, some of whom viewed his films as creative art, some of whom experienced entertainment, some of whom found an acceptable social commentary and some, perhaps, who developed an appreciation for each of these three major characteristics of his filmic talents as artist and propagandist.

D.W. Griffith's films, particularly *The Birth of a Nation*, were technically the most original of the early film productions. He experimented continually with his photographer, G.W. (Billy) Bitzer, devising multi-reel films and the "close up," refining film tinting and toning, making use of elaborate detail and elaborate recreations of battles. Of great importance to the development of plot and suspense in longer films, he developed the iris diaphragm which made it possible to include the split-second darkness which has come to be an unconscious expectation of a change of scene. Griffith also utilized parallel action by developing separate, unrelated scenes which were later tied into the picture's theme. Manipulation of this technique allowed for the creation of suspense. Parallel action was a device used to make the viewer desire to return to the theater for a continuation of the weekly serial. It was effective as well in the early days of one projector but several reels, for it kept the audience in the theater during those awkward moments when the reels were being exchanged. As his most masterful achievement, *The Birth of a Nation* brought all of this together to mark the end of the first generation of American film shorts and the launching of the new generation of feature-length films.

The catalytic year 1915 saw the birth of a new Ku Klux Klan as well as *The Birth of a Nation*. But it also saw the end of an era of relative passivity on the part of Afro-Americans. Booker T. Washington passed away and the eminence of the radical voice of W.E.B. DuBois was on the rise, despite the continuation of Washington's conservative approach by the new head of Tuskegee Institute, Robert Russa Morton. The Supreme Court's one significant civil rights decision of the teens, *Guinn versus The United States*, nullifying the racist "grandfather clauses" in two state constitutions, also came in 1915. The necessary factors were already present in embryo for an Afro-American consciousness, though it was not to flower, unfortunately, until another decade had passed. Meanwhile, the thoughts of DuBois simmered as he strove to find a means to overcome the stagnation in the status of civil rights for Afro-Americans:

> With the ascension of Woodrow Wilson to the presidency in 1913 there opened for the American Negro a period lasting through and long after the World War and culminating in 1919, which was an extraordinary test for their courage and a time of cruelty, discrimination and wholesale murder.[14]

These social stresses of the World War One era produced an increase in Afro-American cultural awareness and a corresponding increase in the willingness of Afro-Americans to take civil and political action. A particularly rankling incident occurred during the war when the United States Army forced the retirement of West Point graduate Colonel Charles Young, an Afro-American, on medical grounds. Sixth in line for promotion to brigadier general, Young was recalled to active duty only with the signing of the Armistice.[15]

Despite this blatant denial of a generalship for an Afro-American, and incidents like the occurrence at Fort Sam Houston in 1917, DuBois called for a suspension of the domestic struggle for the duration of the war. Other elements of the Afro-American community disagreed. Asa Philip Randolph's labor organ, *Messenger*, protested both American and Afro-American involvement in the war. This split was quickly reconciled at war's end when DuBois stated starkly that "We return. We return from fighting. We return fighting." Essentially the Anglo-American response was to adopt policies of covert racism, both in the North and the South, emanating from the long-standing Jim Crowism in America.

Overt racism continued to be perpetuated by governmental agencies which promoted the infamous United States Attorney General Palmer's raids, by the extralegal activities of the self-anointed superpatriots like the Ku Klux Klansters, and by filmmakers like Griffith, whose films both reflected and inflamed the prevailing national sentiments. These factors worked against the groundswell of significant developments which were preparing the way for the Harlem Renaissance, the greatest Afro-American cultural resurgence since Reconstruction. Within a decade the sentiment of the Afro-American community, previously captured in the title of Booker T. Washington's *Up from Slavery* (1901), was shifting significantly toward the emphasis explicit in the title of W.E.B. DuBois' *The Souls of Black Folk* (1903).

Notes

[1] John W. Burgess, *Reconstruction and the Constitution: 1866-1876* (New York: Charles Scribner's Sons, 1905), p. 245.

[2] Donald Bogle, *Toms, Coons, Mulattoes, Mammies, and Bucks: An Interpretive History of Blacks in American Films* (New York: Viking, 1973), p. 6.

[3] Emmett J. Scott and Lyman Beecher Stowe, *Booker T. Washington: Builder of a Civilization* (Garden City, NY: Doubleday, Page and Co., 1916), pp. xiii-xiv.

[4] Owen Wister, *Roosevelt: The Story of a Friendship, 1880-1919* (New York: Macmillan, 1930), p. 253.

[5] Stanley Kaufmann, ed., *American Film Criticism: From the Beginnings to Citizen Kane* (New York: Liveright, 1972), p. 92.

[6] Nicholas Vachel Lindsay, *The Art of the Motion Picture*, rev. ed. (New York: Macmillan, 1922), p. 48.

[7] Ray Stannard Baker, *Following the Color Line: American Negro Citizenship in the Progressive Era* (New York: Harper and Row, 1964), p. 4.

[8] Eileen Landay, *Black Film Stars* (New York: Drake, 1973), pp. 13-14.

[9] For an extended discussion of the issues at stake see my article, "Tarzan and the Ku Klux Klan: Anglo-Americanism in the Twenties," *Journal of English*, 6 (September 1979), 79-109.

[10] David M. Chalmers, *Hooded Americanism: The First Century of the Ku Klux Klan, 1865-1965* (Garden City, NY: Doubleday, 1965), p. 1. Chalmers begins his absorbing book by placing the context in the context just quoted; the quoted material appeared originally in a 1923 issue of *Smart Set*.

[11] Louise Reeves Harrison, Review of *Judith of Bethulia*, in Kemp R. Niver's *D.W. Griffith's The Battle at Elderberry Gulch*, ed. by Bebe Bergsten (Los Angeles: Locare Research Group, 1972), pp. 32 and 38-39. The review appeared originally in *The Moving Picture World* (7 March 1914).

[12] Francis Hackett, Review of *The Birth of a Nation*, in Kaufmann, p. 91. Hackett's review appeared originally in *The New Republic* (20 March 1915).

[13] Thomas Cripps, *Slow Fade to Black: The Negro in American Films, 1900-1942* (New York: Oxford Univ. Press, 1977), p. 37.

[14] W.E.B. DuBois, *Dusk at Dawn* (New York, 1940), p. 235.

[15] Jack D. Foner, *Blacks and the Military in American History: A New Perspective* (New York: Praeger, 1974), p. 113.

Chapter Four

Civil Rights and the Harlem Renaissance

A rejuvenated post-war America sped into the twenties with the hope of catching some of the glamor which the budding film medium dreamily offered. Unlike a generation before, Chautauqua tent shows, showboats, vaudeville, nichelodeons, Toby shows, and the Barnum and Bailey circuses were no longer the grand popular entertainments. Only a few troupes like the Ringling Brothers were holding on to supply the diminishing market for live performances. Immobile movie theaters, sports stadiums, amusement parks, and concert halls were quickly replacing the travelling shows and the grand and realistic spectacles filmed from trains known as Hale's Tours. The resurgence of Afro-American culture and artistry, the Harlem Renaissance, occurred at the same time. Inroads into American culture generally were still limited, but there were breakthroughs like folksinger Roland Hayes becoming the first Afro-American to join a big-city symphony when he signed with the Boston Symphony Orchestra in 1924.

Cecil B. DeMille began his career in the new popular entertainment market for film spectacles the same year that Griffith made *The Birth of a Nation*. Fantasies of the post-war era and concern over the Russian Revolution in 1917 were reflected in DeMille's *Male and Female* (1919). DeMille, it seems, played on these immediate cultural concerns for the film is based on James M. Barrie's play, *The Admirable Crichton*, written in 1914, the year World War One began and three years prior to the Russian Revolution. The wreck of a British aristocrat's yacht leads to the survival of the fittest and the butler becomes king of an island. But a fantasy within this fantasy of *Male and Female* reveals even more about the Anglo presence of mind. In a dream sequence after the shipwreck, two black slaves force an unrepentent Anglo slave to her death in the marble lion's pit; the victim had refused to submit to the butler-king and the savageness of his retribution is starkly represented by jungle lions and black men.

The negative context in which the images of blacks were placed would continue into the twenties.

Early in the twenties, for instance, Will Rogers appeared in Edward Venturini's version of a Washington Irving story, *The Headless Horseman* (Hodkinson, 1922). In this film a young Afro-American, not listed in the credits, saves Ichabod Crane from a tar and feathering. The symbolic overtures of this film suggest both promise and dismay. Promise, because obviously no one, black or white the film suggests, wishes to be tarred and feathered in one of America's traditional ways of punishing Afro-Americans. Dismay, because the standard presentation of an Afro-American as a loyal supporter of Anglo-Americans is carried into the twenties from films like the early short, *Uncle Pete's Ruse* (n.d.), in which an Afro-American slave protects a Confederate soldier, and D.W. Griffith's *Swords and Hearts* (Biograph, 1911), in which faithful Old Ben saves the Anglo family's treasure from the Yankees. Dismay also because, like American culture as a whole, the Afro-American in the film was not credited. This exclusion from the twenties' dreams of betterment took its toll on Afro-Americans in the public eye like Jack Johnson who went into self-exile in Europe, a course which Josephine Baker, Paul Robeson, and Johnny Kitzmiller were all to follow in the ensuing decades. The social realities were no less stark for other Afro-Americans, and this starkness was unintentionally recorded in the Hollywood film fantasies of the twenties.

By the late twenties, America was at the height of its abandon, it appeared, and Hollywood was preparing to express it to the world in more than moving pictures. Phonofilms used a recording with film in the musical short, *Sissle and Blake* (1925), starring the two well-known Afro-American syncopators, Noble Sissle and Eubie Blake. Warner Brothers experimented with the Vitaphone process in the feature film, *Don Juan* (1926), and in several shorter films like *Noble Sissle and Eubie Blake* (1927). The technology was applied to news reels as well when the touted launching of Charles Lindberg's famous flight was recorded on film with some sound, including the roar of the engine on take-off. Then Al Jolson coated his face with charcoal and sang "Mammy" on his way into history books with the first popular application of sound to a movie, Warner Brothers' *The Jazz Singer* (1927). His voice was sweet, but it was a pernicious imitation of an Afro-American. The film brought large audiences of

Afro-Americans as well as Anglo-Americans into the theaters, though, and other Hollywood studios quickly embraced the innovation of sound tracks. Unfortunately, Hollywood took the attitude that although an Afro-American culture exists it should not be conceded that Afro-Americans are capable of interpreting it on the screen in much other than flippant, comic, or entertaining contexts.

Sound tracks in films led primarily to Afro-American appearances in musical shorts, like Mamie Smith's singing in *Jailhouse Blues* (Columbia, 1929), and feature-length musicals like Ethel Waters' singing "Am I Blue?" in *On with the Show* (Warner Brothers, 1929). And Anglo-American attitudes toward Afro-Americans would not change significantly, as Elmer Anderson Carter of the Urban League rightly sensed when he pointed out in *Close Up* (August 1929) that "motion picture producers will hesitate long before they attempt anything in the nature of a new evaluation of the Negro."[1] The Afro-American community, however, had been exploring other avenues of redress for the image of blacks in films. These developments in the twenties were to have mounting influence in opposition to Hollywood's images of Afro-Americans.

The twenties witnessed the meteoric rise in prestige of a vanguard Afro-American intelligentsia. The energies of this vanguard were directed primarily toward the arts, as with the writers Claude McKay and Langston Hughes, but in 1921 the first three Afro-American women were granted Doctor of Philosophy degrees. Hollywood mimicked some of the creations of this vanguard but, for the most part, the contributors themselves were not given access to the mass media. Exceptions occurred in the publishing industry and to a lesser extent on the stage with the all-black Broadway productions of the musicals *Shuffle Along*, beginning in 1921, *Blackbirds* in 1927, *Porgy* in 1928, and *The Green Pastures* in 1930. One intermediary was the Anglo-American Carl Van Vechten, author of the popular twenties' novel about Harlem titled *Nigger Heaven*, who aided talented young Afro-Americans in their attempts to make use of the media controlled by Anglo-Americans.

Young civil rights groups continued to organize and to pursue social and economic redress. The most important of these Afro-American civil rights groups were the National Association for the Advancement of Colored People, the National Urban League, and the short-lived Universal Negro Improvement Association. A fourth group was the influential labor union, the Brotherhood of Sleeping Car Porters. In 1917, Asa Philip Randolph began publication of *Messenger*, a socialist journal through which the ideas for the Brotherhood of Sleeping Car Porters, founded in 1925, were developed. The tactics and strategies emphasized by these four movements varied considerably. Taken together they mirrored the diversity of Anglo-American attitudes as much as they mirrored the Afro-American attitudes toward conditions in America.

The National Association for the Advancement of Colored People (NAACP) was founded in 1909. During its early life it was most closely identified with the intellectual W.E.B. DuBois who, ten years later, organized the first Pan-African Conference. By far the most influential of the four groups, the NAACP emphasized both social and legal avenues of change and redress through which it sought to implement social and political integration. In the early twenties, the NAACP established an office in Hollywood with the hope of encouraging standards for the presentation of minorities. While this unofficial watchdogging produced only a few significant results, the NAACP was to have remarkable success in its arguments before the United States Supreme Court beginning in the early forties. The NAACP, in fact, won forty-three of the forty-seven cases it brought between the years 1941 and 1963. The most prominent figure behind this remarkable record was Thurgood Marshall, an Afro-American attorney who began his career with the NAACP in 1933. Marshall was to argue the watershed case of *Brown versus the Topeka Board of Education* in 1954. He later became the first Afro-American to be appointed as a justice to the United States Supreme Court.

The National Urban League (NUL) was founded in 1911, two years after the founding of the NAACP, as an offspring of the Tuskegee Industrial Welfare League. From the leadership of the NUL came formulations of economic strategy which were to influence the radical unionism of the Congress of Industrial Organizations in the thirties. While Charlie Chaplin mocked the dehumanization of the machine age in *Modern Times* (1936), the NUL lamented the fact that all too few Afro-Americans had or could get machine jobs which for them would have been, at that time, a humanizing step forward in America's increasingly abundant material culture. To Chaplin the issue was a moral one and to the

NUL the issue was a material one, as reflected in the title of its official publication, *Opportunity*. Both the NAACP and the NUL memberships included Anglo-Americans. The NAACP, in fact, had primarily Jewish leadership and financial base. No Afro-American rose above the rank of Executive Secretary in the NAACP during the period under study.

The Universal Negro Improvement Association (UNIA) was founded in 1914 by Marcus Garvey, a West Indian. As a movement it peaked in 1921 when Garvey appointed himself the Provisional President of "The Republic of Africa." Presenting what has been a recurrent proposition from both Afro-Americans and Anglo-Americans, Garvey called for the implementation of a program to return Afro-Americans to Africa to resettle their ancestors' homeland. Garvey publicly supported the racist Mississippi Senator Theodore G. Bilbo's Back-to-Africa Bill; politically powerful at the time, the Ku Klux Klan supported Garveyism. Put forth by many abolitionists and President Lincoln over a half century before, the program in fact goes even further back to when John C. Calhoun and Henry Clay helped establish the American Colonization Society in 1816 to return free Afro-Americans to Africa. The Republic of Liberia in West Africa was founded by the society in 1820, but only 20,000 Afro-Americans actually emigrated to Liberia. Essentially the same program was still being called for by the National Socialist White Peoples Party and the Black Muslims more than fifty years after Garvey's unsuccessful trials.

A uniquely Afro-American organization, the UNIA's membership was limited to blacks in America. The failure of the UNIA, as well as of the abolitionists, Lincoln, the National Socialist White Peoples Party, and the Black Muslims to attract more than faddish support for this program through the years highlights an assumption basic to the psychology of most Afro-Americans: their desire to become an integral part of American culture. As far back as the founding of Liberia in 1820, there were large-scale Afro-American protests against this effort to "exile us from the land of our nativity,"[2] protests echoed in the twentieth century by spokespeople like Richard Wright, James Baldwin, and Malcoln X. Wright and Baldwin did, ironically, impose self-exile in Europe on themselves, but their exile was for artist reasons. It was to take forty years from the time of the founding of the UNIA for the efforts of these four civil rights groups to resolve in the *Brown* decision the issue of whether most Afro-Americans would leave America, stay separate within America, or be integrated into American culture. Each of the groups had demonstrated in its own way that the majority of the Afro-American community wanted neither to destroy nor leave America nor, more importantly, to be left out of American culture and the American Dream. Demonstrating both commitments in the twenties, Randolph's Afro-American Brotherhood of Sleeping Car Porters applied for and was accepted into the American Federation of Labor in 1929. In Hollywood, too, there was no significant acceptance of Afro-Americans into American film culture until 1929. Instead, blackfacing, bit roles as menials or exotics, and a continuation of the stereotypes from *Uncle Tom's Cabin* were the rule.

The blackface tradition continued to be strong in the twenties. Coming from minstrelsy and vaudeville, it had found a place in the films of the major producers in such early comedy shorts as Edison's *The Gator and the Pickaninny* (1903), in which a blackface actor cuts open an alligator to save a pickaninny. D.W. Griffith was in the forefront of this means of misrepresenting Afro-Americans with films like *The Curtain Pole* (1909), a comedy short starring Mack Sennett which includes blackface actors in "darky" town contending with a tipsy Frenchman. Mack Sennett, when he in turn made the Keystone Comedies, used a blackface barber with a razor in *Barber of Darktown* (1915) and presented "coontown lovers" in *A Dark Lover's Play* (1915). Typical of theme, setting, and blackfacing was Edison's *Hearts and Flags* (1916) with its blackface servant, Uncle Wash, loyally serving his master during the Civil War. Fox's epic film about young Sam Houston, *The Conqueror* (1917), made use of blackface mammy. Through World War One, Griffith continued the tradition with films like *Romance of Happy Valley* (Art Craft, 1919), with a blackface farm hand, and *The Greatest Question* (First National, 1919), with a blackface coon.

After World War One, Griffith saw no reason to change, and he used Anglo-American Porter Strong in blackface in *Dream Street* (United Artists, 1921). Other filmmakers did the same. Anglo-American Jules Cowles appears in blackface in the feature film about soldiers of fortune in Panama, Famous Players-Lasky Corporation's *The Ne'er Do Well* (1923). In Harry Pollard's *California Straight Ahead* (Universal, 1926), Sambo the valet is Anglo-American Tom Wilson in blackface. Similar caricatures show up in the World War One farce, Warner Brothers' silent *Ham and Eggs at the Front* (1927), in which Myrna Loy in blackface is a Senegalese seductress and other actors in blackface, including Tom Wilson again, present a mock-serious view of war by cheating fate at cards when they cannot cheat fate on the battlefield.

Aside from Al Jolson, the last actors to consistently use blackface were the Anglo-American vaudeville team of George Moran and Charles Mack. Known as the "Black Crows," their comedies ranged from the Paramount feature films, *Why Bring that Up?* (1929) and *Anybody's War* (1930), to Mack Sennett's feature, *Hypnotized* (1933), which also included Hattie McDaniel. Educational Pictures did an animated cartoon, *Hot Hoofs* (1932), and a comedy short, *Two Black Crows in Africa* (1933), which also portrayed Moran and Mack in blackface. While blackfacing would continue, it was a dying tradition because Afro-Americans themselves appeared more frequently in films and because vaudeville was fading away.

How to present Afro-Americans in Hollywood films, however, was a question which blackfacing circumvented. Some studios did not employ Afro-Americans in the twenties because they felt Anglo-Americans were better actors, a view which changed dramatically with the introduction of sound films. Others did not use Afro-Americans out of preference, like D.W. Griffith, or simply concluded that Afro-Americans did not fit into the images they wanted to project in films. There was also the factor of the ubiquitous images in film culture emanating from a recurrent resort to *Uncle Tom's Cabin* as a means of portraying Afro-Americans.

The various attitudes concerning the use of Afro-Americans in films was manifested in the way *Uncle Tom's Cabin* was presented in the twenties. Early in the twenties, a performance of *Uncle Tom's Cabin* by Anglo-Americans appeared in George Baker's *Little Eva Ascends* (1922) and again in the feature film, *The Restless Sex* (1925). Walter Lantz did an animated cartoon titled *Dinky Doodle in Uncle Tom's Cabin* (1925) and, the same year, Universal did a short titled *Uncle Tom's Gal* (1925) which was a film about the filming of *Uncle Tom's Cabin*, a task which Universal undertook in reality with the last major production of *Uncle Tom's Cabin* (1927). Uncle Tom was pushed to the background in other films of this nature, as in the Topsy and Eva act included in Tiffany Productions' version of a Zane Grey story, *Lightning* (1926). The emphasis was shifted to Topsy, the comic pickaninny in the worst sense, who steals, lies, and is unconscionably superstitious. Noble Johnson was cast as Uncle Tom in Feature Productions' *Topsy and Eva* (1927), but it was a slight role. A silent feature film directed in the latter stages by D.W. Griffith, *Topsy and Eva* was made to compete with Universal's *Uncle Tom's Cabin* (1927). The film was adapted from the Duncan Sisters' stage production and it concentrated on the Topsy and Eva friendship with Anglo-American Rosetta Duncan playing Topsy in blackface. At the end of the decade, *Uncle Tom's Cabin* was again used as a show within the show in MGM's *The Girl in the Show* (1929).

In retrospect, from out of these flounderings by the film industry to bring Harriet Beecher Stowe's classic into the twentieth century, no forthright presentation of the book's issues emerged except in the dramatic performances of Afro-Americans James Lowe and Gertrude Howard in Universal's silent *Uncle Tom's Cabin* (1927). More than any other single film of the twenties, it revealed the potential of Afro-American actors. For just this reason, *Uncle Tom's Cabin* was never again filmed by Hollywood. After the sound era began, in other words, Hollywood would not provide a springboard for drama as intense as *Uncle Tom's Cabin* might be with the majestic voice of a Paul Robeson. Instead, with a few exceptions, Hollywood turned to Afro-American entertainers rather than to Afro-American drama in the first generation of sound. The offerings were more like the purely entertaining musical comedies *Mayor of Jimtown* (MGM, n.d.) and *Jimtown Speakeasy* (MGM, n.d.) with Afro-Americans Aubrey Lyles and Flourney E. Miller.

As the grotesque portrayals of an adulturated Topsy signaled, Afro-Americans in the twenties were most often cast in the extremes of stupic and lazy comics, exotic natives, or as despicable wards of Northerners. Noble Johnson, for instance, appears with the cannibals on an isolated island in Buster Keaton's *The Navigator* (MGM, 1924). Blackface characters, including one of the "aspiring brides-to-be" of the white hero and a "witless lethargic messenger," appear in Keaton's *Seven Chances* (Metro, 1925).[3] In Keaton's farce titled *The General* (Allied Artists, 1927), the Southerners win against the "stupid Yankee 'Nigger lovers.'"[4]

More developed interracial activities found refuge only in films for children. Pre-*Our Gang* formats were used in *Ten Pickaninnies* (1904) and Dave Fleisher's *Busting the Show* (1920). In the latter, a blackface actor appears in a show titled "The Grate Nigger Bucking Wing Dancer." Also similar to the *Our Gang* films was Marshall Neilan Productions' *Penrod* (1922) in which the young Afro-Americans, Ernest Morrison and Florence Morrison, are involved in a mixed boy's club. Florence made no other films, but Ernest went on to play Sunshine in the *Our Gang Series* the same year.

The first of over two hundred of these two-reeler comedies was the one which gave the series its name, Hal Roach's *Our Gang* (1922).[5] Among the names made famous by the series, which ran until 1944, are Ernie Morrison as Sunshine Sammy, Allen Hoskins as Farina, Jannie Hoskins as Mango, Matthew Beard as Stymie, and Billie Thomas as Buckwheat. The series also attracted Will Rogers, who played Jubilo in *Jubilo, Jr.* (1924), Tom Wilson in blackface as "Uncle Tom" in *Bring Home the Turkey* (1927), Clarence Muse and Louise Beavers in *Election Day* (1929), and Beavers and Willie Best in *General Spanky* (1936). Topically, *Uncle Tom's Cabin* was parodied in *Uncle Tom's Uncle* (1926) and *Spanky* (1932). Even the Ku Klux Klan came in for parody when the gang formed its own Cluck Cluck Klams in *Lodge Night* (1923). As with other films of this nature, though, the close involvement of Afro-Americans and Anglo-Americans had to be through children rather than adults, and it had to be through comedy rather than drama.

Rivals appeared, like the *"Baby Marie" Osborne Series* (n.d.), starring the Afro-American youth, Joffre Pershing Johnson, who was often listed in the credits as "Sambo." And prior to directing the all-black Christie Comedies in Hollywood, Anglo-American Octavious Roy Cohen made the all-black "blackface humor" films called *The Florian Slappey Series* (1925-1926). Typically, these comedy shorts with children involved no serious questioning of the status quo. In fact, often the Afro-Americans who appeared in films were "just there."

They continued to appear as background in films of the twenties just as they did in Civil War films like Griffith's *In the Border States* (1910). In the twenties' version of *Big City* (n.d.), for example, Afro-Americans provided atmosphere in a Harlem nite club scene. In United Artists' parody of *The Three Musketeers*, titled *The Three Must Get Theirs* (1922), there is an inexplicable but suggestively brief appearance of a black man in a bedroom. Afro-American jazz musicians were used only as back ups for a white singer in Robert Z. Leonard's *Circe the Enchantress* (Metro Goldwyn, 1924). And Afro-American children and an aged Afro-American man provided the setting for the MGM short, *Man, Woman, and Sin* (1927). Thus, the difference between reality in American culture and fantasy in American film culture was often minimal.

A similar set of examples involves an Afro-American who appeared in only a few films, all by Paramount. Oscar Smith went from valet in real life to Djikh, a Senegalese valet, in the French Foreign Legion film starring Gary Cooper and Noah Beery, *Beau Sabreur* (1927). In *The Canary Murder Case* (1928), Smith had a small role before appearing the following year with dozens of other Afro-Americans, including Madame Sul-te-Wan, Nathan Curry, Mosby's Blue Blowers, and S.S. Stewart in Joseph von Sternberg's *Thunderbolt* (1929). A crime melodrama, *Thunderbolt* featured two Anglo-Americans, one of whom was a boyfriend of a Harlem nite club singer played by Afro-American Teresa Harris.

There were other bit roles for Afro-Americans, some quite impressive, like the following: Douglas Carter as a porter in Owen Moore Film Corporation's *Love Is an Awful Thing* (1922); George Reed as a porter in Clarence Badger's *Red Lights* (1923); Sam Baker in a small role in the twenties' version of *Louisiana* (n.d.) as well as in the role of Queequeg in Warner Brothers' *The Sea Beast* (1926), which starred John Barrymore as Captain Ahab in an early filming of Melville's *Moby Dick* (1851); George Godfrey, a former boxer, as a ship's cook who helps with the fighting at Tripoli in DeMille's *Old Ironsides* (Paramount, 1926); Zack Williams as the ship's cook in Rupert Julian's *The Yankee Clipper* (1927); Rex Ingram as a faithful southern servant in King Vidor's *The Big Parade* (MGM, 1925); and both Rex Ingram and Noble Johnson in Paramount's *The Ten Commandments* (1923) and DeMille's *The King of Kings* (1927). Johnson played the bronze man in *The Ten Commandments* and a charioteer in *The King of Kings*.

Noble Johnson's thirty-year film career included roles in both all-black independent and Hollywood films. He founded Lincoln Motion Picture Company in the teens with his brother, starred in three of their films, and

and then worked in Hollywood and independent films through the late silent period and well into the sound era. His last film appearance, in fact, was as Red Shirt the Indian in John Ford's *She Wore a Yellow Ribbon* (1949).[6] Some of his small roles in the twenties include appearances in three films for Universal, *Red Ace* (n.d.), *Red Feather* (n.d.), and *Bull's Eye* (n.d.); similar bit parts were in *The Courtship of Miles Standish* (1923) and *Manon Lescaut* (1926). Johnson appeared as Conquest, one of the four plagues in Metro Pictures' *Four Horsemen of the Apocalypse* (1921), as a charioteer in MGM's *Ben Hur* (1925), as an Indian in Warner Brothers' *When a Man Loves* (1927), and as a ship's cook, Bimbo, in DeMille's *Vanity* (1927). He showed up in numerous jungle films and, Thomas Cripps adds, he was an exotic in *Son of India* (n.d.) and *Moby Dick* (n.d.),[7] "a thug in *The Murders in the Rue Morgue*" (n.d.), and "a Nubian in *The Mummy*" (n.d.).[8]

Like several other Afro-Americans, Noble Johnson also worked in westerns. In two Hoot Gibson westerns, Universal's *The Loaded Door* (1922) and Paramount's *The Flaming Frontier* (1926), Johnson played Blackie Lopez and then Chief Sitting Bull in the latter's reenactment of Custer's last stand. In the same era, a little-known Afro-American actor named Martin Turner played in sixteen Hollywood films ranging from westerns to melodramas.

Martin Turner started as a servant named Cellar in New Era Productions' *They're Off* (1923) and as Uncle Rose in Universal's *The Family Secret* (1924). In Harry J. Brown Productions' *Super Speed* (1925) he was a valet, and in Harry Webb Productions' *Silent Sheldon* (1925) he was Ivory, Sheldon's valet. In Otto K. Schreier Productions' *Midnight Faces* (1926), also titled *Midnight Fires*, he was again a valet, this time named Trohelius Snapp. He was Uncle Lude in Davis Distributing Divisions' *Three Pals* (1926), George Washington Jones in J.P. McGowan's *The Lost Express* (1926), and George in Trem Carr Productions' *On the Stroke of Twelve* (1927). Little additional information is available concerning his roles in these films, but he also appeared in Rayart-Imperial Photoplay's *The Cruise of the Hellion* (1927) and Harry J. Brown Productions' *The Royal American* (1927).

In his westerns, Turner played Luke Mosby in Independent Pictures' *Western Vengeance* (1924), Romeo in Ben Wilson Productions' western comedy, *Sell 'Em Cowboy*

(1924), and "Snowball," the hero's valet, in Harry Webb Productions' western comedy, *The Knockout Kid* (1925). His best roles were in William Steiner Productions' comedy westerns: In *Rainbow Rangers* (1924), he was Barbecue Sam, the cook, before being promoted to the sidekick of Anglo-American Pete Morrison in two more of Steiner's comedy westerns, *A Ropin' Ridin' Fool* (1925) and *The Ghost Rider* (1925). Yet another "sidekick to a white cowboy" in the twenties was James Lowe in Universal's *Blue Streak Series* (n.d.). There were few other pairings in the twenties beyond the exceptionally good roles of Afro-American Edgar "Blue" Washington and Anglo-American Richard Arlen in one suspense film, *Beggars of Life* (1928), in which they are hoboes aiding a young girl in trouble.

Other positive presentations of Afro-Americans were of questionable intent, like the Afro-American who, as frequently is the case in Hollywood films, is seen saving an Anglo-American from a murky death in the Williamson Brothers' *The Submarine Eye* (1917). Unusual in this regard was Cosmopolitan Productions' *The Woman God Changed* (1921) which was presented through the flashbacks of Afro-American Lillian Walker's memory as a maid. Roles for Afro-American women in Hollywood films were scant until the latter years of the decade. Madame Sul-te-Wan did appear as a house keeper in *Narrow Street* (1925), however, and Carolynne Snowden made all of her films in the twenties.

Snowden's first appearance was in Erich von Stroheim's comedy, *The Merry Widow* (MGM, 1925), which also had Zack Williams playing a dandy. She was a "nonchalant maid" in Fox's *The First Year* (1926), and she appeared briefly as a dancer in *The Gilded Butterfly* (n.d.) and von Stroheim's *The Wedding March* (1928). Her finest roles were in John M. Stahl's *In Old Kentucky* (1927) and David Butler's *Fox Movietone Follies* (1929). Paired with the new Fox star Stepin Fetchit in both films, Snowden and Fetchit had one of the few Afro-American love affairs in Hollywood films of the twenties in *In Old Kentucky*, and in *Fox Movietone Follies* they sing and dance several numbers together.

Even as he demonstrated his skills as a dancer, however, Stepin Fetchit was being groomed by the Fox studio as a comic coon in films like Kenneth Hawks' *Big Time* (1929), Lew Seiler's *The Ghost Talks* (1929), and John Ford's *Salute* (1929). While Fetchit's future image as a coon was determined in 1929, the image of

Louise Beavers as a mammy was not yet formulated though she made her first small film appearances in the Our Gang film *Election Day* (1929) as well as in *Barnum Was Right* (Universal, 1929), *Coquette* (United Artists, 1929), and *Glad Rag Doll* (Fox, 1929). Through Stepin Fetchit and Louise Beavers and others, the coon and the mammy would flourish in the films of the thirties. Additional established stereotypes like the Uncle Tom and the tragic mulatto did not dissipate either.

Another favorite was the portrayal of Afro-Americans as inferior Southerners. Reginald Baker's *Dixie Handicap* (Metro-Goldwyn Pictures, 1924), for instance, includes a "stupid colored man." Typical of this southern race consciousness was First National Pictures' *The Love Mart* (1927), a silent film in which Afro-American Raymond Turner is the servant, Poupet. The plot develops when

> the so-called belle of the South is rumored to have Negro ancestry and is sold as a slave. Her owner does not believe the rumor and forces the person who started the rumor to confess and then marries the girl.[9]

The obession with pure Anglo blood had not abated. It could have still been pre-World War One with Anglo-American Myrna Loy playing the mulatto in David Belasco's *The Heart of Maryland* (1915) or building a film around the "tragedy" of being a mulatto in Frank Hall and Edgar Lewis' *The Bar Sinister* (1917). When Hollywood filmmakers were not covering the same ground in terms of the image of Afro-Americans--as they would in competing with all-black musicals in 1929--they were backsliding.

Foreign films had not been as hesitant to present a diversity of black images in films. Early in the century, Pathe Freres' *Un Reve de Dranam* (French, 1905), showed a black woman who keeps taking the place of a white prostitute. In the teens, two Italian feature-length films presented major black heroes in *Cabiria* (Italy, 1914) and *Salambo* (Italy, 1915). In the twenties, Jean Renoir's *Charleston*, or *Sur un Air de Charleston* (Epinay Studios, 1927), featured black actor Johhny Higgins in a combination science fiction and jungle film for the French:

> Set in the year 2028, a black explorer flies from Central Africa (the seat of civilization) to visit

> Europe which he thought was not inhabited. He discovers in Paris a "primitive" girl dancing the Charleston. Entranced, he gets back into his space craft with her goes back to Africa.[10]

While Hollywood made great progress in the incrustation of stereotypical images of Afro-Americans, the French and Germans cooperated on a silent feature film directed by August Bruckner for Munchener Lichtspielkunst Emerlka and Compangnie Coloniale du Film. Titled *Samba* (Germany, 1928), it was "the first Negro film conceived and realized by French blacks; it is a faithful rendering of the life of Samba and Fatou made with nonprofessional actors."[11] In the country which produced the Harlem Renaissance and the revolutionary *The Jazz Singer* (1927), Hollywood would establish only one new precedent which, compared with the possibilities offered in foreign films, was miniscule.

This precedent, based on the abandon which sound brought to the screen, did not extend byond giving an added dimension to the stereotype of the Afro-American as entertainer in Hollywood films. Dramatic roles for Afro-Americans remained elusive. The first of these entertainment spectacles was Harry A. Pollard's *Show Boat* (Universal, 1929), one of three filmings of Edna Ferber's book. Starting as a silent film based on the popular Broadway production, sound was added and Afro-American Jules Bledsoe sang "Ol' Man River" while Stepin Fetchit and Gertrude Howard played Joe and Queenie. Unlike the all-black casts of the Hollywood studios' *The St. Louis Blues* (RKO, 1929), *Hearts in Dixie* (Fox, 1929), and *Hallelujah* (MGM, 1929), Universal's *Show Boat* had a mixed cast with Anglo-Americans Joseph Shildkraut and Laura La Plante, as the mulatto Julia, also playing prominent parts.

Prior to these musicals at the end of the decade, the participation of Afro-Americans in Hollywood films was obviously slight compared to the number of films produced. But the impact of the Garveyites "Back to Africa" call for separatism, the northward migration of millions of Afro-Americans, the writings inspired by the numerous riots and attendant conflicts, and the diverse energies of the Harlem Renaissance did shock Anglo-American publishers into producing books for an Afro-American market. Claude McKay's *Harlem Shadows* (1922) and Jean Toomer's *Cane* (1923), while not widely popular, were acclaimed during the Harlem Renaissance by black writers looking for Afro-American literary models. Other young Afro-American writers like Countee Cullen, Jessie Fauset, Nella Larson, Walter White, and Langston Hughes found outlets for their works. The disappointing parallels to the publishing breakthroughs were the cycle of Hollywood musicals produced in 1929.

As disparaging as it was discouraging, the United States Supreme Court seemed mute during the twenties on civil rights issues concerning Afro-Americans. The only exception was the significant case in 1927 which ruled that Afro-Americans could vote in the previously all-white Texas primary elections. Although there were over eighty lynchings and several dozen major riots between Anglo-Americans and Afro-Americans in 1919, the country was in no mood to ameliorate the substandard conditions which existed for Afro-Americans both in the laws and in the popular mind. The public was more concerned with the May Day bombings in 1919. These bombings were attributed to the radical Reds or Communists. The labor strikes which idled millions of workers set off riots between Anglo-Americans and Afro-Americans during the same year.

By 1924, the Prohibition and Women's Suffrage Amendments were added to the United States Constitution, as was an Amendment granting citizenship to Native-Americans. Prohibition encouraged the large-scale organization of crime. Bootlegging became a national sport while rackets and drugs became a familiar part of dialy life in the Afro-American *kraals* or ghettoes. A decade later the gangster and crime melodramas, including Afro-American Oscar Micheaux's *Underworld* (1936) as well as the Hollywood films, would being reflecting the hollow underside of the glittering twenties.

Afro-American legal and economic movements were not yet powerful enough to do more than shower anguished protests upon the many unsympathetic ears in America. Only in Illinois during the two decades to follow were Afro-Americans elected to state-wide or national offices. The first was Adelbert H. Roberts, elected in 1925 to the state legislature in Illinois. The twenties produced only one Afro-American United States Congressman, Oscar De Priest from Chicago in 1928; he was also the first Afro-American Congressman from a non-southern state. In 1934, De Priest was defeated by another Afro-American, Arthur Mitchell. And again in 1942, Chicago sent an Afro-American to Congress, William L. Dawson. Dawson in 1949 became the first Afro-American to chair a standing committee in the Congress, the House Expenditures Committee. Outside of Chicago, though, the social and political stalemate was circumvented preeminently by the Harlem Renaissance which had little or no affect on the films made in Hollywood until 1929.

The Harlem Renaissance was given an initial boost by Anglo-American playwrights Eugene O'Neill and Paul Green. O'Neill's 1920 Broadway production of *The Emperor Jones* was instrumental in opening doors for talented Afro-Americans. The play starred Charles Gilpin, the well-known Afro-American actor, and was immediately acclaimed a classic by Anglo-American critics. Focusing on Afro-Americans, the play marked the beginning of the Afro-American Renaissance centered in Harlem and New York City. It was a breakthrough of limited value, however, for the images of blacks in *The Emperor Jones* are still among the most derogatory in American literature. Through the medium of the stage, nonetheless, Afro-American performers did have more frequent and more critical exposure to the metropolitan Anglo-American public in the all-black Broadway musicals of the twenties. These early roots in drama and music caused many Afro-American writers to bend their talents toward the Broadway stage as a rebuff to a generally unreceptive Hollywood film community.

Afro-American artists also gathered together throughout America, particularly in the black belt of Harlem, to publish little magazines like the angry *Fire*, many of which lived for only a few issues. Many more Afro-American artists started their publication careers in DuBois' *The Crisis* which sought a fusion of art and propaganda. DuBois stated that "I do not care a damn for any art that is not used for propaganda."[12] Similar sentiments of D.W. Griffith have already been discussed. Outlasting all the purely literary journals which came and went during the twenties was Alain Locke's *Stylus*. The first Afro-American journal established at a college, *Stylus* was published sporadically at Howard College before becoming an annual publication in 1929.

Nourished from the roots of their own traditions and culture, the artistic themes of the Harlem Renaissance were exuberantly defined by Alain Locke in his famous essay, "The New Negro" (1925). The Harlem School capitalized on the popular and folk culture--traditionally transmitted through almanacs, Bibles, and song and dance--helped bring to the fore other Afro-American writers, including Jean Toomer, Claude McKay, Wallace Sherman, Rudolph Fisher, Zora Neale Hurston, and Langston Hughes. A significant following of Anglo-Americans made their way to Harlem, a suburb of New York City, for their first taste of Afro-American culture. Some Anglo-American writers, like Carl Van Vechten, fashioned a new genre of novels based upon the novelty of white encounters with black culture.

To the dismay of many civil rights leaders, whose influence on national issues during the twenties and thirties was not as strong as was the influence of the representatives of the Harlem Renaissance, much of the black literature after the Great Depression was written as literature of protest and revolt. Some of the renaissance writers reached too far in their rhetoric, the civil rights groups felt, creating a detrimental image of the Afro-American community as a whole. A singular example of this was Claude McKay's now-famous radical poem, "If We Must Die," which addressed itself both to World War One and the war in American between blacks and whites:

> If we must die, let it not be like hogs
> Hunted and penned in an inglorious spot,
> While round us bark the mad and hungry dogs,
> Making their mock at our accursed lot.
>
> If we must die, O let us nobly die,
> So that our precious blood may not be shed
> In vain; then even the monsters we defy
> Shall be contrained to honor us though dead!
>
> O kinsmen! we must meet the common foe!
> Though far outnumbered let us show us brave,
> And for their thousand blows deal one death-blow!
> What though before us lies the open grave?
>
> Like men we'll face the murderous, cowardly pack,
> pressed to the wall, dying, but fighting back!

Reflecting the pre-Harlem Renaissance attitudes in America, this inspiring sonnet was deleted by the publisher from McKay's collection, *Spring in New Hampshire* (1919). Belated vindication, so frequent in the history of Afro-Americans, came on the eve of World War Two when Winston Churchill, then British Prime Minister, used "If We Must Die" as a stirring conclusion to his plea for support before the United States Congress. In this vein, too, is the more revolutionary strain of late renaissance writing done by Richard Wright, whose literature of protest like *Uncle Tom's Children* (1938) and *Native Son* was perhaps the most sustained indictment of racism in America by a man of letters prior to James Baldwin.

By speaking their controversial minds, Langston Hughes in the late twenties and Paul Robeson in the decades of the thirties, forties, and fifties may have failed to help the Afro-American cause as that cause was represented through the civil rights movements. "Put one more S in the U.S.A.," sang Langston Hughes,

> To make it Soviet.
> One more S in the U.S.A.
> Oh, we'll live to see it yet.
> When the land belongs to the farmers
> And the factories to workingmen--
> The U.S.A. when we take control
> Will be the U.S.S.A. then.

Many of these writings by Afro-American artists were popularized by the multifarious Harlem Renaissance which stretched from approximately 1920 to 1945, though its peak years were the decade preceding the Great Depression. The majority of Afro-American independent filmmaker Oscar Micheaux's were produced at the height of the Harlem Renaissance and his career will be discussed in the following chapters.

In direct opposition to the flowering of the Harlem Renaissance, the Hollywood genre of jungle films was popularized in the twenties by films like the comic serial, *The Adventures of Tarzan* (1920). The dubious increment in filmed visibility Afro-Americans received was that the jungle films employed many extras for local color. In the thirties and forties, even this source of employment dwindled. In such films as *Tarzan Escapes* (1936) and *Tarzan and the Amazons* (1945), the producers of the jungle films threw off all pretense of verisimilitude and employed Anglo-Americans to play the Africans, often without bothering to blackface them! This development, too, will be taken up shortly in the chapter titled, "America, the Dark Continent."

The decade of the twenties also had its share of equally bigoted films set elsewhere than Africa. Shot in 1915, but not released until 1924, *Free and Equal* concentrated, contrary to its flighty title, on intolerance and the inferiority of Afro-Americans. The makers of such films, and those who revived them for the audiences of the twenties, were perpetrating the images which Griffith previously propagated. It is clear that the silent movie had some exciting advantages, for "audiences amused themselves by shouting warnings or advice to the screen characters, whistling at the heroines, hissing the villains and supplying appropriate bits of dialogue."[13] For many Anglo-Americans, *The Birth of a Nation* and its imitators in the twenties must have been quite stimulating with their array of black villains, comic "darkies," and subservient porters, valets, and mammies. A technical revolution in cinema, the soundtrack, appeared in the twenties, but no revolution of import in the Afro-American image came with it. Challenges to the stranglehold Anglo-Americans had on film production and distribution in America were feeble if prolific, for during the Harlem Renaissance Afro-American film-makers did present some alternatives to the entrenched Hollywood movie machine and its assembly line of interchangeable black images.

Notes

[1] Daniel J. Leab, *From Sambo to Superspade: The Black Experience in Motion Pictures* (Boston: Houghton Mifflin, 1975), p. 86. The statement appears in Elmer A. Carter, "Of Negro Motion Pictures," *Close Up*, 5 (August 1929), p. 119.

[2] Irving J. Sloan, *The American Negro: A Chronology and Fact Book* (Dobbs Ferry, NY: Oceana, 1965), p. 11.

[3] Phyllis Rauch Klotman, *Frame by Frame: A Black Filmography* (Bloomington: Indiana Univ. Press, 1979), p. 460.

[4] Klotman, p. 197.

[5] The extent of the impression made by the Our Gang films on three generations of Americans--the post-World War One generation, the World War Two generation, and the first generation of television watchers--is

incalculable. Usually just good fun in a stereotypical setting, the series did reinforce the image of inferiority for Afro-Americans in all contexts not solely involving the kids. For instance, in *General Spanky* (1936), set during the Civil War, Buchwheat voluntarily becomes a slave to Spanky. Despite the stereotypes, as well as because of them, the series is worth further study. Phyllis Rauch Klotman's filmography of black films is the most complete listing of the series, summarized here by years from her book:

1922: *Fire Fighters; One Terrible Day; Our Gang* [the original of the series]; *A Quiet Street; Saturday Morning;* and *Young Sherlocks.*

1923: *Back Stage; The Big Show; Boys to Board; The Champeen; The Cobbler; Derby Day; Dogs of War; Giants vs. Yanks; July Days; Lodge Night; No Noise; A Pleasant Journey; Stage Fright;* and *Sunday Calm.*

1924: *Big Business; The Buccaneers; Commencement Day; Cradle Robbers; Every Man for Himself; Fast Company; Tire Trouble; High Society; It's a Bear; Jubilo, Jr.; The Mysterious Mystery; Noisy Noises; Seein' Things;* and *The Sun Down Limited.*

1925: *Ask Grandma; Better Movies; The Big Town; Boys Will Be Boys; Circus Fever; Dog Days; The Love Bug; Mary, Queen of Tots; Official Officers; One Wild Ride; Shootin' Indians;* and *Your Own Back Yard.*

1926: *Baby Clothes; Buried Treasure; The Fourth Alarm; Good Cheer; Monkey Business; Telling Whoppers; Thundering Fleas; Seeing the World; Shivering Spooks; Uncle Tom's Uncle;* and *War Feathers.*

1927: *Baby Brother; Bring Home the Turkey; Chicken Feed; Dog Heaven; The Glorious Fourth; Heebee Jeebees; Love My Dog; The Old Wallop; Olympic Games; Ten Years Old; Tired Business Men;* and *Yale versus Harvard.*

1928: *Barnum and Ringling, Inc.; Crazy Horse; Edison, Marconi and Co.; Fair and Muddy; Growing Pains; The Old Gray Hoss; Playing Hookey; Rainy Days; School Begins; The Smile Wins; The Spanking Age;* and *Spook Spoofing.*

1929: *Bouncing Babies; Boxing Gloves; Cat, Dog, and Co.; Election Day; Fast Freight; The Holy Terror; Lazy Days; Little Mother; Moan and Groan; Railroading; Saturday's Lesson; Small Talk;* and *Wiggle Your Ears.*

1930: *Bear Shooters; The First Seven Years; Pups Is Pups; School's Out; Shivering Shakespeare; Teachers' Pet; A Tough Winter;* and *When the Wind Blows.*

1931: *Bargain Day; Big Ears; Fly My Kite; Helping Grandma; Little Daddy; Love Business;* and *Shiver My Timbers.*

1932: *Birthday Blues; Choo-Choo; Free Eats; Free Wheeling; Hook and Ladder; A Lad an' a Lamp; The Pooch; Readin' and Writin';* and *Spanky.*

1933: *Bedtime Worries; Fish Hooky; Forgotten Babies; The Kid from Borneo; Mush and Milk;* and *Wild Poses.*

1934: *The First Round-Up; For Pete's Sake; Hi' Neighbor; Honkey Donkey; Kiddie Care; Mama's Little Pirate; Mike Fright; Reunion in Rhythm* (ca. 1934)*; Shrimps for a Day;* and *Washee Ironee.*

1935: *Anniversay Trouble; Beginner's Luck; Little Papa; Little Sinners; Our Gang Follies of 1936; Sprucin' Up;* and *Teacher's Beau.*

1936: *Arbor Day; Bored of Education; Divot Diggers; General Spanky; The Lucky Corner; Pay as You Exit; The Pinch Singer; Second Childhood; Spooky Hooky;* and *Two too Young.*

1937: *Fishy Tales; Framing Youth; Glove Taps; Hearts Are Thumps; Mail and Female; Night 'n' Gales; Our Gang Follies of 1938; The Pigskin Palooka; Roamin' Holiday; Rushin' Ballet;* and *Three Smart Boys.*

1938: *Aladdin's Lantern; The Awful Tooth; Bear Facts; Came the Brawn; Canned Fishing; Football Romeo; Hide and Shriek; The Little Ranger; Men in Fright; Party Fever; Practical Jokers;* and *Three Men in a Tub.*

1939: *Alfalfa's Aunt; Auto Antics; Captain Spanky's Show Boat; Clown Princes; Cousin Wilber; Dad for a Day; Dog Daze; Duel Personalities; Joy Scouts;* and *Tiny Troubles.*

1940: *Alfalfa's Double; All About Hash; The Big Premiere; Bubbling Troubles; Goin' Fishin'; Good Bad Boys; The New Pupil;* and *Waldo's Last Stand.*

1941: *Baby Blues; Come Back, Miss Pipps; Fightin' Fools; Helping Hands; 1-2-3 Go; Robot Wrecks; Wedding Worries;* and *Ye Olde Minstrels.*

1942: *Doin' Their Bit; Don't Lie; Going to Press; Melodies Old and New; Mighty Lak a Goat; Rover's Big Chance; Surprised Parties;* and *Unexpected Riches.*

1943: *Benjamin Franklin, Jr.; Calling All Kids; Election Day; Family Troubles; Farm Hands; Little Miss Pinkerton;* and *Three Smart Guys.*

1944: *Dancing Romeo* and *Radio Bugs.*

[6] Thomas Cripps, *Black Film as Genre* (Bloomington: Indiana Univ. Press, 1979), p. 20.

[7] Thomas Cripps, *Slow Fade to Black: The Negro in American Films, 1900-1942* (New York: Oxford Univ. Press, 1977), p. 131.

[8] Cripps' *Slow Fade to Black*, p. 421.

[9] Klotman, p. 324.

[10] Klotman, p. 504.

[11] Klotman, p. 477.

[12] Abby Ann Arthur Johnson and Ronald M. Johnson, "Forgotten Pages: Black Literary Magazines in the 1920s," *Journal of American Studies*, 8 (December 1974), p. 364.

[13] Nelson Manfred Blake, *A History of American Life and Thought* (New York: McGraw-Hill, 1963), p. 579.

Chapter Five

All-Black Afro-American Films: Silents

The most persistent early Afro-American filmmaker, and probably the first, was William Foster. Through the Foster Photoplay Company, he made the three earliest known all-black films, *The Pullman Porter* (1910), with Lottie Grady and Jerry Mills, *The Railroad Porter* (1912), also with Grady and Mills, and *Fall Guy* (1913). Many of his early shorts were comedies similar to the Keystone Cops series of the teens. Among Foster's films of the teens are *Birth Mark* (n.d.), *Brother* (n.d.), *Fool and Fire* (n.d.), *Mother* (n.d.), and *A Woman's Worst Enemy* (n.d.). Also in the teens was a detective film, *Butler*(n.d.), and a melodrama with a screenplay written by Jerry Mills, *The Grafter and the Maid* (n.d.), also titled *The Grafter and the Girl*. Sometime early in the twenties, he did a film for Kalem's studio, *Florida Crackers* (n.d.), which included a controversial portrayal of a lynching. By the late twenties, Foster had joined Hollywood rather than competing with the consolidated studios. He resurfaced in this era as producer of the all-black sound comedies, Pathe's *"Buck and Bubbles" Series* (1929-1930). With Afro-Americans Ford Lee "Buck" Washington and John "Bubbles" Sublette, the series was made to compete with the popular all-black Christie Comedies.

During the generation covered by Foster's career, the potential for Afro-American filmmakers had been explored. For most of these independents the pattern was the same. They began as independent filmmaking companys and then either joined Hollywood or accepted the backing of Anglo-American producers. In the twenties, many Hollywood studios merged and, despite some successful anti-trust suits, these studios remained viable and formed the Central Casting Corporation in 1926 from which to draw most of their actors. Afro-American independents could not effectively duplicate these moves. The introduction of sound further burdened the independents, for it doubled the cost of filmmaking. And by 1929, Hollywood began to seriously compete for the Afro-American audience by producing all-black musicals like *Hearts in Dixie*, *Hallelujah*, and *The St. Louis Blues*. These films brought increased exposure to the talents of many Afro-Americans, and the promise thus held out by Hollywood drew many who might otherwise have stayed with or gravitated to the Afro-American independent filmmakers.

With few exceptions, Oscar Micheaux was one, most of the Afro-American independents from the silent era did not emerge again in the sound era. In the period covered by this study, then, there were two generations of Afro-American independents. Those from the silent era are treated in this chapter while those from the sound era are treated in the following chapter. Throughout both generations, in contrast to Hollywood, the common plight of Afro-American filmmakers was a lack of capital to finance films and a lack of technological know-how. Thus, these independents made films which were for the most part inferior in quality to the Hollywood productions of the same era. Frederick Douglass Film Company's *The Colored American Winning His Suit* (1916) presented the Afro-American success theme, epitomized by the characters' names, Bob Winall versus Mister Hinderus, but it returned its makers no profit. As poorly edited as its predecessor, Douglass' *The Scapegoat* (1917) did fare better in part because it was based on the work of the Afro-American author, Paul Laurence Dunbar. That these filmmakers worked around the handicaps of scarce money and slight skills makes the record they put together over the years all the more remarkable.

There was a diversity of themes in these early independent films as the Douglass productions illustrate. Often the American success story was present, or an attempt to interprete on film the works of a black author, and equally often the films were little different from the topis white filmmakers used. Some even duplicated the negative black images of white filmmakers. An Afro-American critic, for instance, protested the black independent film, *Money Talks in Darktown* (ca. 1916), calling it "humiliating to the race."[1] Many of these short films, which varied in length from a few minutes to half-hour productions, relied on comedy. Among these were the Colored and Indian Film Company's *Love and Undertakers* (1918) and *Clef Club Five Minutes for Train* (n.d.). J. Luther Pollard produced the Ebony Film Corporation's "two-reelers," with the acting troupe of Ebony Players, which included such titles as *Wrong All Around* (1917), *Spying the Spy* (1917), with Sambo Sam hunting down a German spy, and the derivative detective film, *Black Sherlock Holmes* (ca. 1918). Among the long list of Ebony Film Corporation's films from 1918 alone are the following: *Are Working Girls Safe?*, *A Black and Tan Mix Up*, *A Busted Romance*, *Do the Dead Talk?*, *Luck in Old Clothes*, *Milk-Fed Hero*, *The Porters*, *Some Baby*, *Spooks*, *When Cupid Went Wild*, and *When You Hit, Hit Hard*.

Along with the prolific output of the Ebony Film Company during World War One were patriot productions which emphasized the Afro-American contributions on the battlefield, among them Toussaint Motion Picture Company's documentary, *Doing Their Bit* (1918) and Frederick Douglass Film Company's *The Heroic Black Soldiers of the War* (1919). In these years, Democracy Film Company made *A Minister's Temptation* (1919), *Upward Path* (1919), and a film with a romance set in war-torn France, *Loyal Hearts* (1919). The Afro-Americans Sidney Preston Dones and Thais Nehli Kalana are featured in this story of a nurse who finds romance when she goes to help the wounded in France after it is discovered that she is "passing" in America.

In the teens, there were few Afro-American theaters to show the films of these Afro-American filmmakers and most Anglo-American theaters neglected such films. Overcoming the disadvantages of producing an Afro-American film only to find unsurmountable problems with the distribution and showing of the film was another major problem for independents. The film which best illustrates the situation in the late teens is Afro-American Emmett J. Scott's three-hour epic, *Birth of a Race* (1918), originally titled *Lincoln's Dream*. It was the most ambitious film project to come out of the Afro-American community in the silent era.

For three years, during which time he was also a special assistant to the Secretary of War, Scott worked to produce what was intended to be an in-depth rebuttal to *The Birth of a Nation* (1915). Seeking to counteract the impact of Griffith's film, Scott helped form the Birth of a Race Company which initially had the moral and financial support of the NAACP and Universal Pictures. When their financial backing was withdrawn, Scott was left with only an empty bag of encouragement from many civil rights spokespeople. The promotional material announced that the film would be

> the true story of the Negro--his life in Africa, his transportation to America, his enslavement, his freedom, his achievements, together with his past, present, and future relations to his white neighbor and to the world in which both live and labor.[2]

Scott had undertaken too much and the film that emerged was technically faulty, due in large measure to a lack of clear vision as to its purpose by those doing the producing. Mismanagement of its limited capital by the company's professional promoters meant that the story as originally planned was never finished. Changes made to satisfy the interests of the investors caused the final product to be a film about World War One and its antecedents rather than a film about "the birth of a race." It failed to attrack much popular or critical attention. In the end, the venture was a financial fiasco for Scott and his backers, both Afro-American and Anglo-American.

Scott's failure convinced many that propagandistic rebuttals to propaganda were not yet feasible, especially from an Afro-American producer. Indeed, contemporary with Scott's *Birth of a Race*, Democracy Photoplay Corporation produced all-black films which showed Anglo-American aspirations being paraded by Afro-Americans. Produced by Anglo-Americans, *Injustice* (1919) and *Democracy, or A Fight for Right* (1919) were World War one films supporting the American cause. *Democracy, or A Fight for Right* glorified Afro-American war heroes and *Injustice*, a long western directed by Afro-American Sidney P. Dones, misrepresented racial reality in America by portraying an integrated Red Cross. Far from being rebuttals to films like *The Birth of a Nation*, Democracy Photoplay Corporation's films reveal essentially Anglo-American values projected through a wish-fulfillment world of film. Rather than seeking a clearly delineated and separate identity, these all-black films were obviously attempting to find a way to bring Afro-Americans into American culture.

The Herculean effort by Scott was important, nonetheless, for it furthered the development of Afro-American filmmakers. Although his personal efforts were thwarted, his leadership encourged the brothers George P. Johnson and Noble Johnson to form the Lincoln Motion Picture Company which produced *The Realization of a Negro's Ambition* (1917), sometimes titled *The*

Realization of the Negro's Dream. This film, with Clarence Muse and Beulah Hall, was an American success story about an Afro-American college graduate, played by Noble Johnson, which applied the "luck and pluck" Horatio Alger plot to an Afro-American rather than an Anglo-American.

Lincoln's *The Trooper of Troop K* (1917), also variously titled *Trooper K* and *Trooper of Company K*, was a topical film, again with Beulah Hall in it and Noble Johnson as the hero, about border skirmishes with Mexicans. A threat to Anglo-American superiority had been played out by Pancho Villa when he crossed into New Mexico and attacked the town of Columbus in March 1916. Retribution, rhetorically couched in the same jingoism as that directed at the "Yellow Peril" and the "Black Peril," became a matter of national pride. The frantic John J. "Blackjack" Pershing took until June to catch up with the *Villistas* in his military invasion of Mexico. Among those killed in this irresponsible demonstration of Anglo-American superiority, particularly at the Carrizal battle, were ten Afro-American soldiers. *The Trooper of Troop K* was another early example of an attempt to build race pride through film by showing that Afro-Americans were allied militarily with Anglo-Americans.

Most of the Lincoln productions engaged matters of Afro-American pride and dignity, such as in *The Law of Nature* (1917), *A Man's Duty* (1919), and *By Right of Birth* (1921). Clarence Brooks appeared in all three, but *The Law of Nature* was Noble Johnson's last film for Lincoln. Johnson turned over the leadership of Lincoln to Clarence Brooks and went full-time with Universal in Hollywood. *By Right of Birth*, "a Negro romance of laughter and tears," according to promotional bills, presented the theme of "passing" among upper-class Afro-Americans on the West Coast. Lincoln was for several years the most successful all-black independent production company. American cultural values in the years of World War One and just after were upheld in these films. A glance at the most connotative words in the titles--"Ambition," "Trooper," "Law," "Duty," and "Rights"--suggests why the films appealed to Afro-Americans.

Another team of brothers formed the Norman Film Manufacturing Company, an Afro-American venture with productions, mostly westerns with black cowboys, spanning much of the twenties: *The Green-Eyed Monster*

(1921), with Jack Austin and Louise Dunbar, includes an exciting competition with trains and the green-eyed monster, jealousy; *Crimson Skull* (1921), alternately titled *Scarlet Claw*, features Lawrence Chenault and Anita Bush in a mystery western that includes the real Bill Pickett, an Afro-American rodeo champion; *The Bull Doggers* (1923), again with Anita Bush and Bill Pickett and more rodeo crafts by Pickett and others; *A Debtor to the Law* (1924); and *Black Gold* (1928), with Lawrence Corman and Kathryn Boyd. Other Norman films included *Regeneration* (1923), an adventure story with the staples of castaways, romance, and buried treasure, and Kathryn Boyd in *The Flying Ace* (1926), a film that is sometimes titled *The Fighting Ace*.

Among the many all-black westerns of this era was Sidney P. Dones and Bookertee Investment Company's *The $10,000 Trail* (1921), a typical western with an East/West conflict and a love triangle similar to Lincoln's *The Law of Nature* (1917). The film starred Sidney P. Dones himself and the large cast included, among others, Nina Rowland, Dorothy Dumont, Frances Henderson, "Kid" Herman, and Clinton Ross. The Afro-American Wild West Rodeo appeared in *Saddle Daze* (n.d.), Ben Roy Productions put out *The Man from Texas* (1921), and the Black Western Film Company made *Shoot 'Em Up, Sam* (1922). In an early all-black feature-length western, Superior Film Company's *Smiling Hate* (1924), the plot turns a gold mine into a vehicle for treachery and romance.

Boxing pictures, many of them about the former champion, Jack Johnson, were popular among Afro-American filmmakers early in the twenties. Andlauer Production Company's *As the World Rolls On* (1921) has the former heavyweight champion playing himself as he provides leadership to a youthful baseball player. Johnson starred in a family drama which included boxing scenes in Blackburn Velde Productions' *For His Mother's Sake* (1921). Many of the Afro-Americans who appeared in this film were also in other all-black independent productions, among them: Matty Wilkens, Adrian Joyce, Jack Hopkins, Jack Newton, Dick Lee, Hank West, Everett Godfrey, Edward McMowan, and Ruth Walker. During his self-exile in Spain, Johnson and A.A. Millman did yet another boxing picture with Johnson in it, *Black Thunderbolt* (1922).

Another early all-black boxing picture was E.S.L. Colored Feature Productions' *Square Joe* (1921), with Joe Jeanette, John Lester Johnson, Bob Slater, and

Marian Moore. The training of the Afro-American prize fighter, Harry Wills, was the subject of *Harry Wills in Training* (1924) by Acme Film Distributors. Together with Walt Miller, the Afro-American boxer Tiger Flowers, known as "The Fighting Deacon," made a dramatized documentary of his career titled *The Fighting Deacon* (1925). In an Anglo-American film of the era, there is a strange application of a black/white pair. The light-heavyweight boxing champion, Anglo-American Benny Leonard is shown in the ring practicing with a "black shadow," not listed in the credits, in *Flying Fists Series* (1924). Films about black boxers were not confined to American filmmakers, either, for the career of the early black boxer Tom Molyneux is depicted by the British in *When Giants Fought* (England, 1926).

Mystery and detective films, sometimes combined with comedy, were developed as a popular genre in Afro-American independent films in this era. In the comic vein, Acme Film Distributors produced *The Disappearance of Mary Jane* (1921) with the Chicago Bathing Girls and Jimmie Cox as players. Anglo-American Ben Strasser produced *A Shot in the Night* (1922) for North State Film Corporation, a mystery story with Bobby Smart, Walter Holeby, Walter Long, Ruther Freeman, Tom Amos, and the Tolliver Brothers. In the detective genre, Monarch Productions' *The Flaming Crisis* (1924) starred Dorothy Dunbar, Calvin Nicholson, Henry Dixon, and Talford White in a feature film about a man who escapes from jail, where he was wrongly sent, and goes to the Southwest for adventure before the film ends happily. In another detective film with John Burton, Charles Pearson, Anna Kelson, John Lester Johnson, and Frank Colbert, Western Film Productions' *The Flames of Wrath* (1923), it is a female, played by Roxie Mankins, who catches the villains. Dunbar Film Corporation did *Tony's Shirt* (1923) and then, with Afro-American Swan Micheaux as director, *The Midnight Ace* (1928). *The Midnight Ace* was a feature-length detective film in which the woman was forced to choose between two futures, one good and one bad, embodied in the two men in her life. Mabel Kelly, Susie Sutton, A.B. Comathiere, William Edmondson, and Walter Cormick were featured in this film.

Always popular, there were many all-black comedy shorts in the twenties. Lone Star Motion Picture Company made *The Stranger from Way Out Yonder* (1922), *You Can't Keep a Good Man Down* (1922), *Wrong Mr. Johnson* (1922), and *Why Worry?* (1923). *Why Worry?* was a comedy short about two youngsters on their first visit to the big city and it featured Byron Smith, Mae Morris, and Frank Brown. In Seminole Film Company's comedy short, *How High Is Up* (1922), Corrine Smith is featured along with Moss and Fry who attempt to put an airplane in the air. Typical of the stage and film names Afro-Americans took, the team of Butterbeans and Sue, actually Joe and Susie Edwards, appeared in the comedy short by Colored Motion Picture Producers of America, *Nine Lives* (1926).

A relative latecomer was the Colored Players Film Corporation, a company backed in part by Jewish interests. Afro-Americans Lawrence Chenault and Harry Henderson appeared in all of their films which included *A Prince of His Race* (1926), *Ten Nights in a Barroom* (1926), *The Scar of Shame* (1927), and *Children of Fate* (1928). In *A Prince of His Race*, with Shingzie Howard, the hero loses his girl and goes to prison. In this film, family pressure is behind the achievement of status of success in the Afro-American community. *Ten Nights in a Barroom* is best remembered as an all-black temperance tract in the Prohibition Era--and earlier all-black temperance film was Sidney P. Dones' *Reformation* (1919) for Democracy Film Corporation--and for being the only film appearance of the famous Afro-American stage actor, Charles Gilpin. Gilpin had been signed in 1926 for the title role in Universal's new *Uncle Tom's Cabin* (1927) but, perhaps because his interpretation of the role was overly enterprising, his contract was terminated before filming began. In any case, he was freed to do *Ten Nights in a Barroom* with Arline Mickey. The best produced and most polished Colored Players film was *The Scar of Shame*. Along with the ever-present Lawrence Chenault and Harry Henderson, it featured Lucia Lynn Moses in a satiric view of the competititve ups and downs in the color caste system of urban Afro-America. Shingzie Howard appeared again in *Children of Fate* in which gambling leads to a fortune but happiness must await a woman.

By putting Afro-American literary classics on film during the twenties, Anglo-American Robert Levy's Reol Motion Picture Corporation became an important factor in the newborn Harlem Renaissance. Lawrence Chenault also appeared in most of Reol's films, as did Edna Morton; others who appeared regularly were Edward Brown, Inez Clough, and S.H. Dudley. Reol's were among the best independent productions to show that Afro-American life and culture differed little from Anglo-American life and culture. At the same time, the films often focused on problems from an Afro-American viewpoint. Among Reol's many contributions to all-black films was *The Burden of Race* (1921), a dramatic film about an Afro-American college student falling in love with an Anglo-American girl. In Reol's *The Call of His People* (1922), an Afro-American businessman "passes" for an Anglo-American before realizing that egalitarianism should take precedence over race consciousness. *The Schemers* (1922) boasts one of the few portrayals in the era of an Afro-American scientist, a successful chemist who is in conflict with swindlers. *The Sport of the Gods* (1923), a popular film based on the work of Paul Laurence Dunbar, was about wrongful imprisonment and the problems faced by Afro-Americans moving to the North. Additional Reol Motion Picture Corporation titles were *The Simp* (1921), *Ties of Blood* (1921), *Easy Money* (1921), *The Spitfire* (1922), *Secret Sorrow* (ca. 1923), and *The Jazz Hound* (ca. 1923), which may also have been titled *The Jazz Sound*.

Reol was not the first independent to present either race-pride films or films about Afro-American family life. Others have been noted already in passing, but several others stand out. A joint venture by Afro-Americans and Anglo-Americans, Royal Garden Film Company's *In the Depths of Our Hearts* (1920) presented an all-black cast in a film about the problem of racism within the Afro-American community between light-skinned and dark-skinned blacks. Herman De LaValades, Agusta Williams, Irene Conn, and Virgil Williams were featured. North State Film Corporation's *A Giant of His Race* (1921), with Mabel Homes, Walter Holeby, and Ruth Freeman, was another dramatic film which portrayed an Afro-American son of a slave as an achiever who made good as a doctor. All-black colleges were publicized through such films as Monumental Pictures Corporation's *Howard-Lincoln Football Game* (1921) and Crusader's documentary about Tuskegee Institute titled *Tuskegee Finds a Way Out* (1922).

Afro-American family life was featured in such films as the following: J.W. Fife Productions' *A Modern Cain* (1921) with Norman Ward, Vivian Quarles, Theodore Williams, Harriet Harris, and Fred Williams; Trio Productions' *Greatest Sin* (1922) with Mae Evlyn Lewis and Victor Mix; Lone Star Motion Picture Company's feature-film *The Wife Hunters* (1922) with Bob White, Jessie Purty, Edward Townsend, V. Stevens, P. Massey, H.C. Grant, J.T. Walton, and J.G. Selby; Young Producers Filming Company's *Foolish Lives* (1922) with Frank

Chatman, Henry Harris, Frank Carter, Jewell Cox, Marquerite Patterson, and Jonella Patton; Young Producers Filming Company's *The Perfect Dreamer* (1922); and North State Film Corporation's *His Last Chance* (1923) about a country boy who gives show business a try.

Many other all-black films attempted to compete with exotic themes, melodramas, or even ganster films, the latter a genre which would become a major source of film stories in the thirties and forties for all-black films as well as Hollywood productions. Maurice Film Company's *Nobody's Children* (1920) was an early example of such a film which featured kidnapping, murder, and gangland connections; it featured Richard Maurice, Jacque Farmer, Alex Griffin, Joe Green, Vivian Maurice, and Howard Nelson. The melodramas included Progress Picture Association and Afro-American Exhibiters Company's *The Lure of a Woman* (1921) with Regina Cohee, Charles Allen, and Dr. A. Porter Davis, D.W.D. Film Corporation's *A Child in Pawn* (1921), White Film Corporation's *A Fool's Promise* (1921), which may also have been titled *A Fool's Errand*, with William Fountaine and Shingzie Howard, and Superior Art Motion Pictures' *Stepin High* (1924) with William Lee. Superior Art Production's had earlier produced *Hearts of the Woods* (1921), about a married man seeking yet another wife, with Clifford Harris, Lawrence McGuire, Don Pierson, and Anna Lou Allen. Late in the twenties, Richard D. Maurice Productions was back with *Eleven P.M.* (1928), a whimsical combination of reincarnation and ghetto life dreamed up by a writer seeking a new plot. And an unknown producer relied on a voodoo plot in making *The Witching Eyes* (ca. 1928).

There were many other films made in the silent era which were by, with, or about Afro-Americans. Unfortunately, since many of these productions were low-budget and quickly made, copies of them were in existence for only a short time. In fact, oftentimes, only one or two prints were made. Little is known about many of the films included in this chapter or about the following: Quality Amusement Company's *Eyes of Youth* (1920) with Abbie Mitchell; *Home Brew* (1920); Mount Olympus' *Darktown Affair* (1921); Tropical Photoplay Company's *Shuffling Jane* (1921); White Film Company's *Hot Dogs* (1921); Cotton Blossom Film Company's *Undisputed Evidence* (1924); Afro-American William H. Clifford Photoplay Company's *The Black Boomerang* (1925); and Sherman H. Dudley, Jr.'s *Reckless Money* (1926), starring himself and John LaRue.

For every independent company that made more than one film there were a dozen that went under after one production. One of the few successful Afro-American filmmakers was Oscar Micheaux who was born near Metropolis, Illinois, in 1884. His career spanned both generations of Afro-American filmmaking but, for convenience, he will discussed only in this chapter. Micheaux's success, to be sure, was gauged in terms of sustained output rather than in financial gains. As early as 1914, Micheaux produced a series of short films. His career as a novelist, with an output of ten novels like *Masquerade* and *The Case of Mrs. Wingate*, overlapped his filmmaking efforts. Between 1920 and 1948, he produced or had a hand in producing over forty films. He sought Anglo-American backing only occasionally and only late in a career which closely paralleled and reflected the artistic endeavors of the Harlem Renaissance. In fact, many of the films he worked on were made before the Great Depression, during the apex of the Harlem Renaissance. A shrewd businessman and self-promoter, Micheaux managed to stay in filmmaking by booking his films first and then shooting them with the advance monies. He was more than just another independent Afro-American filmmaker, for he was a maverick and, most unusual among independents, a survivor.

As the following paragraphs reveal, Micheaux's talents were far-fetched, if undisciplined, and his films often explored the ironies of Afro-American life. He shied away from few topics and his canon of films, despite his frequent use of stock storylines, is representative of the eclective themes that other filmmakers touched but rarely. He dealt with lynching, "passing," race purity, prostitution, gangland life, and he even made a jungle film. Ironically, like other Afro-American filmmakers, he often employed light-skinned Afro-Americans to portray white characters.

Micheaux's serious film production began with *Homesteader* (1919) which was based on his autobiographical novel of his years in the Dakotas with the same title. *Within Our Gates* (1920) was a dramatic murder story about a real lynching (the Leo Frank case) in the South. *The Brute* (1920) starred the Afro-American boxer Sam Langford in an exciting film with an anti-lynching statement. *The Gunsaulus Mystery* (1921), also titled *The Gonzales Mystery*, reworked *Within Our Gates* into a mystery story. *The Symbol of the Unconquered* (1921) not only opposed "passing" but took an anti-Ku Klux Klan stand at a time when the Klan was becoming as politically powerful as it would ever be. *Deceit* (1921) took on film censorship in America. *The Dungeon* (1922) was a melodrama about a wife-murderer. *The Virgin of the Seminole* (1922) gave a glimpse of the rewards heroism can bring in the Northwest Territories. *Son of Satan* (1922) contained the ghostly theme of a night in a haunted house. *Body and Soul* (1924), about what to do with misguided preachers, was one of Micheaux's most artistic ventures and it was also the film which gave Paul Robeson his first role. *Birthright* (1924) featured discrimination by Afro-Americans and Anglo-Americans alike against a black graduate of Harvard University who returns to the South to found a college.

Marcus Garland (1925) burlesqued the Black Moses, Marcus Garvey, who had made himself president of "The Republic of Africa" before being convicted and sent to jail for mail fraud in 1925. *The Conjure Woman* (1926) and *The House Behind the Cedars* (1927) were efforts to bring the works of the Afro-American writer Charles Waddell Chesnutt, in greatly altered form, to the screen. *The Spider's Web* (1926) was the story of a young Afro-American girl accosted by an Anglo-American planter's son and of obsession with gambling in the ghetto. *The Broken Violin* (1927), based on Micheaux's novel, *House of Mystery*, depicted one of the few early characterizations of a beautiful, talented, and successful Afro-American woman, a violinist. *The Millionaire* (1927) was another success story, based on another of Micheaux's novels, this one seamy and more reflective of American cultural values than Afro-American cultural values in its emphasis on fortune-making. *Thirty Years Later* (1928) included some sound segments and depicted the plight of a man who learns he is a mulatto and is proud of it long after he is married to a white woman. *The Wages of Sin* (1929) looked at the differing reactions of two brothers to urban Afro-American family life. That affliction of the Great Depression, bankruptcy, ended the first stage of Micheaux's career at the time when silent films were being replaced by sound films. His failure was representative of the end of the first generation of independent all-black productions generally which could not survive the competition from Hollywood and the extraordinary costs of the new sound films.

That Micheaux came back when most of the others did not is testimony to his commitment to films as an avenue of Afro-American expression. Already unprecedented and unrivaled in output as an independent Afro-American filmmaker, he continued to break new ground. Arab slavers and a mulatto girl make for adventure in *Daughter of the Congo* (1930) which, like some of his earlier films, included sound but not dialogue. *The Exile* (1931), about a man who finds happiness in the rural West after leaving the corruption of Chicago, was poorly received, but it was the first talking picture to be made by an Afro-American producer. *Ten Minutes to Live* (1932) plummeted to the use of stereotypes of Afro-American entertainers, comics, and coons in their most conventional Anglo-American forms. *The Girl from Chicago* (1932) featured an Afro-American as a federal agent in a remake of Micheaux's silent film, *The Spider's Web* (1926), but it suffered from poor filming and editing. Mistaken identity in love is the theme of *Lem Hawkins' Confession* (1935), also titled *The Brand of Cain*, a film typical of the poor quality productions that plagued Micheaux and other independent filmmakers. *Temptation* (1936), a "sex drama" that ran into censorship problems, resorted to a scantily draped temptress on promotional bills.

Underworld (1937), among the best of Micheaux's films because of its tension between the South's rural values and Chicago's underworld values, was a gangster film starring Oscar Polk and Bee Freeman. *Swing* (1938) was a musical drama. *God's Stepchildren* (1938), alternately titled *All God's Stepchildren*, reverted to the "passing" issue which was used by Marxists to launch a vigorous protest of the film's slanderous view of Afro-Americans in stereotypical roles. In 1939, Micheaux remade *Birthright* (1939) with sound. *Lying Lips* (1939), featuring a battle of the sexes, and *The Notorious Elinor Lee* (1940), a boxing film, were among Micheaux's poorest films, perhaps because two quite different pictures were made from the same footage with Edna Mae Harris, Robert Earl Jones, Carmen Newsom, Amanda Randolph, and Juano Hernandez. *The Betrayal* (1948), "the strangest love story ever told," opened in an Anglo-American theater in New York City but was poorly received and marked the retirement of Micheaux from filmmaking. It was, appropriately enough, a refilming of his first picture, *The Homesteader* (1919), with additions from his novel titled *The Wind from Nowhere*. Micheaux's career yielded few critical or financial successes, though many firsts for Afro-American filmmakers. Only a few prints of his films survive, but from 1920 to 1948 he was the single most consistent contributor to the effort to bring Afro-American themes to the film medium.

Micheaux's additional films included *Jasper Landry's Will* (1923)--also titled *Uncle Jasper's Will--The Devil's Disciple* (1926), *When Men Betray* (1928), *Easy Street* (1930), *Darktown Revue* (1931), *Veiled Aristocrats* (1932), *Black Magic* (1932), *Ten Minutes to Kill* (1933), *Phantom of Kenwood* (1933), *Ghost of Tolston's Manor* (1934), and *Harlem after Midnight* (1934). Micheaux's favorite leads and major supporting players included Evelyn Preer, Shingzie Howard, Ethel Moses, E.G. Tatum, Cleo Desmond, Lawrence Chenault, Lorzenzo Tucker, William E. Fountaine, Andrew S. Bishop, and William (W.B.F.) Crowell. Though not widely recalled as famous names, some of them appeared in other all-black films like Shingzie Howard and Lawrence Chenault, both of whom were in *Ten Nights in a Barroom* (1926) and *Scar of Shame* (1927), William E. Fountaine, who played Hot Shot in *Hallelujah* (1929), Evelyn Preers in Octavious Roy Cohen's *Melancholy Dame* (1929) and Harry Gant's *Georgia Rose* (1930), and Cleo Desmond in *The Spirit of Youth* (1937).

Occasionally, Micheaux featured widely recognized celebrities like the boxer Sam Langford in *The Brute* or the stage actor, Richard B. Harrison, in *Easy Street*, and those who would become well-known like Paul Robeson in *Body and Soul*, Oscar Polk and Bee Freeman in *Underworld*, and Juano Hernandez in *Lying Lips* and *The Notorious Elinor Lee*. Even these professionals were not enough, though, for Micheaux's filmmaking was racked by uneven talents and close budgets that resulted in few sets and much location shooting. He stands, nonetheless, as a symbol of unfulfilled success in America. Suffering as much misfortune as any one person could experience, he attempted to make good in the American fashion. As a result, his career is representative of all but a handful of Afro-Americans who tried mightily but failed to fulfill the American Dream through its most elusive means, motion pictures.

Another Afro-American who was moderately successful was Spencer Williams. Williams had appeared in films in the twenties, but one of the earliest that he directed was Midnight Productions' *Tenderfeet* (1928), a silent feature-length film which featured himself, Mildred Washington, Flora Washington, Spencer Bill, and James Robinson. This same Spencer Williams had already produced, or would shortly produce, *Hot Biscuits* (n.d.). He would survive the silent era to make a name for himself as a second generation independent filmmaker as well as writer, producer, and actor in both independent and Hollywood films. Williams' career, discussed in more detail in the following chapter, lasted into the early television era when he starred with Afro-American Tim Moore in the short-lived *Amos "n" Andy Show* (ca. 1950). Among his many distinctions, Williams co-wrote the script and starred in the first all-black talking film, Anglo-American Octavious Roy Cohen's *Melancholy Dame* (Paramount, 1928). This Christie Comedy--Al Christie was the producer--also starred Evelyn Preer and Eddie Thompson in a burlesque of Birmingham's middle class Afro-Americans. Williams co-wrote and acted, along with Evelyn Preer and Eddie Thompson, in the other Christie Comedies for Paramount, all produced in 1929: *Brown Gravy, The Framing of the Shrew, The Lady Fare, Music Hath Charms, Oft in the Silly Night*, and *The Widow's Bite*. It was at this point that the Afro-American with whom independent all-black films began, William Foster, returned to filmmaking with the *"Buck and Bubbles" Series* (1929-1930) for Pathe. Featuring the Afro-Americans Ford Lee "Buck" Washington and John "Bubbles" Sublette, this two-reeler series effectively competed with the Christie Comedies. The *"Buck and Bubbles" Series* included the titles *Black Narcissus, Darktown Blues, Darktown Follies, Foul Play, High Toned, Honest Crooks*, and *In and Out*.

In the years from William Foster's *The Pullman Porter* (1910), through Norman Film Manufacturing Company's *The Love Bug* (1920), to some of the last films of the silent era, Rosebud Film Corporation's *Absent* and Famous Artists Company's *Hello Bill* (1929), the persistence and dedication of scores of Afro-American independent filmmakers had been demonstrated. A significant number of these filmmakers had made enlightened attempts to capture on film the culture of Afro-Americans. The number of independent Afro-American film companies had increased as the number of theaters run by and for Afro-Americans increased. By the late twenties there were seven hundred Afro-American movie theaters in America, reflecting the impact of the Harlem Renaissance which encouraged the arts generally. Most of these theaters went out of business during the Great Depression, so that by 1937 there were only slightly more than two hundred remaining. With the efforts of the second generation of Afro-American independent filmmakers, the number of Afro-American theaters rose again to over four hundred by the middle of

World War Two. While serious efforts to bring to the screen faithful representations of Afro-American life and culture would continue, many, probably most, of the Afro-American filmmakers moved away from this endeavor in favor of films that mimicked, or at least neutralized, the propaganda messages of Hollywood films. The twenties alone had witnessed the production of well over one hundred Afro-American independent films, by far the greatest output until the latter years of the thirties and into the forties. There were many reasons for the failure of these early films to maintain the consciousness of an Afro-American point of view: the Great Depression eliminated most of the smaller companies, the introduction of sound in films had the drastic consequence of skyrocketing the expense involved in film production, Hollywood forestalled major competition from the Afro-American filmmakers with the production of all-black musicals, and Afro-American films did not attract a significant number of Anglo-Americans to the box office.

There was yet one other important reason for the Afro-American filmmakers not developing a consistent point of view or a clear aesthetics of film and that was that the kind of propaganda used so effectively by D.W. Griffith in films like *The Birth of a Nation* was not available to the Afro-American community. The first generation of Afro-American independents, best represented by the efforts of Emmett J. Scott, the Lincoln Motion Picture Company, the Reol Motion Picture Company, and Oscar Micheaux's productions, had demonstrated that propagandistic rebuttals to propaganda were not yet feasible, especially from the Afro-American community. If their films briefly fostered race pride, they also made it clear that the cultural pluralism which many American historians extoll has singularly excluded the Afro-American community, at times even in their own eyes. Peter Noble, in *The Negro in Films* (ca. 1948), comments that "Thomas Edison once truthfully said: 'Whoever controls the film industry controls the most powerful medium of influence over the public.'"[3] The range of significant viewpoints on racial issues in films was limited to Anglo-American perspectives, for even the efforts of Afro-American filmmakers reached only Afro-American audiences and no "equal time" provisions existed for the film medium. The strongest weapon for combatting propaganda, pluralism, was not yet possible in the American film industry. The exclusion of Afro-American points of view like Scott's *Birth of a Race* from the general American public, combined with the overwhelmingly negative stereotypical portrayals of Afro-Americans in Hollywood productions, meant that film as a communications medium, ironically, failed to help America face its ethnic problems and communicate solutions for them.

Notes

[1] Daniel J. Leab, *From Sambo to Superspade: The Black Experience in Motion Pictures* (Boston: Houghton Mifflin, 1975), p. 13.

[2] Leab, p. 61.

[3] Peter Noble, *The Negro in Films* (London: Skelton Robinson, ca. 1948), p. 9.

Chapter Six

All-Black Afro-American Films: Soundies

Most of the independent Afro-American film companies which made it to the late twenties did not survive the Great Depression, the competition from Hollywood all-black musicals, and the doubling of production costs brought on by the introduction of sound and then color to films. Those filmmakers who did survive often turned to Anglo-Americans for both the money to back their films and for the technological skills which many of the Anglo-Americans brought with them from Hollywood. While these major changes in the film industry were being sorted out, relatively few all-black independent films were made in the first years of the thirties.

The potential for a genre of films devoted to Afro-American culture in a serious manner did not materialize much beyond a few good efforts by Oscar Micheaux and Spencer Williams. Afro-American filmmakers turned instead to entertainments featuring all-black casts that often paralleled the same fads found in Hollywood films. Westerns, gangster films, musical revues, melodramas, and comedies were popular. Now and again, a Spencer Williams would produce a significant film portraying some unique aspect of Afro-American religious life, for instance, that neither Hollywood nor other independents would seriously venture into. No firm stance on politics, cinema aesthetics, or social aims for Afro-Americans developed, despite the possibilities inherent in the political, social, and economic climate. That Herbert Hoover and the Republican Party had rejected Afro-Americans in 1928 and 1932, that Jim Crow remained in force both legally and socially, and that the Great Depression had greatly altered the outlook of the Afro-American community did not result in an exploration by Afro-American filmmakers of how the Afro-American community was affected by or dealing with these problems.

There were many reasons for this lack of involvement in important issues by independent Afro-American filmmakers, among them that control of the independent companies making films with all-black casts was held primarily by Anglo-Americans; that there was little demand by the Afro-American community for films that might be controversial; that there may well have been the feeling that a public debate might ensue on the merits of such films, a debate that might have done more harm than good for the Afro-American community; and that the audience for these films was essentially Afro-American, and any messages in the films would not have reached Anglo-Americans directly.

In the early thirties, some all-black independent films were still being made as silents while Hollywood had already converted to sound. With Anglo-American producer Charles Allman White, Paragon Pictures made such all-black silents as *Hell's Alley* (1931), *The Dusky Virgin* (1932), which was also titled *The Dusky Village*, *The Crimson Fog* (1932), and *Dixie Love* (1933). Thomas Moseley appeared in all of these films and Inez Clouth, Lawrence Chenault, Vera Temple, Alvin Childress, and Fay Miller appeared in several of them. The screenplay for *Hell's Alley* was done by the Afro-Americans Hattie Watkins and Jean Webb. The silent films were no longer competitive, however, and few more would be made by indepednets. Feature-length musicals were more competitive, and Lincoln Productions made *Harlem Is Heaven* (1932), or *Harlem Rhapsody*. Among the entertainers were Putney Dandridge, James Baskett, Eubie Blake and His Orchestra, John Mason, and Bill Robinson. Robinson, soon to make a career in Hollywood films as well, had already appeared in an independent film from the late twenties, *Hello Bill* (1929).

The musical would become a mainstay for independent filmmakers. Negro spirituals were featured in the dramatic short, Organlogue's *Rhapsody in Black* (1933). The well-known Afro-American evangelist, Elder Solomon Lightfoot Micheaux, was one of the first to use the medium of film to promote religious works. He produced a film about himself, *We've Got the Devil on the Run* (1934), and Jack Goldberg did two documentaries for Micheaux. Goldberg's *The Negro Marches On* (n.d.) was on Micheaux himself and in *We've Come a Long, Long Way* (1945), Micheaux narrated the highlights of Afro-American achievements. The most interesting depictions of Afro-American religious life were to come from an Afro-American who had been involved in films and filmmaking since the twenties, Spencer Williams.

In the thirties, Williams first appeared in Aristo Films' *Georgia Rose* (1930), directed by Anglo-American Harry A. Gant. An early independent feature-length comedy with sound, this film also featured actors who would become prominent through numerous appearances in all-black independent films: Evelyn Preer, Edward Thompson, and Clarence Brooks. Williams and Brooks also appeared together in Gateway Productions' *Bad Boy* (1937). By the early forties, Williams was again involved as a director. He directed and starred in both United Films' *The Girl in Room 20* (ca. 1940's) with July Jones and Geraldine Brock and Sack Attractions' *Of One Blood* (ca. 1940's) with Geraldine Maynard. Anglo-American Alfred R. Sack produced many independent films in this era, including one of the films for the "Colored Americans on Parade" series, a short documentary titled *Life in Harlem* (1940). In the forties, Spencer Williams would direct many of the Sack productions (variously named as Sack Amusement, Sack Attraction, and Sack Amusement Enterprises).

With the backing of Sack, Afro-American religious life was treated in three films directed by and starring Spencer Williams: *The Blood of Jesus* (1941), *Brother Martin* (ca. 1942), and *Go Down Death* (1944). Amegro Films, a splicing of "American Negro" formed the name, also had a part in the production of *The Blood of Jesus* which was one of the more popular independent films of the era. It presented an allegorical religious theme and starred Williams as Ras Jackson and Cathyrn Caviness as Sister Jackson.[1] The religious theme and title of *Go Down Death* were premised on a famous poem by the Afro-American author, James Weldon Johnson.

Among his other appearances in the forties, Williams was featured along with the Four Toppers in Hollywood Productions' musical short, *Toppers Take a Bow* (1941), directed by Anglo-American Richard C. Kahn. Williams then directed *Marching On* (ca. 1943) during World War Two, a combination documentary and adventure story. Like many of the war-time all-black documentaries, it built race pride through showing Afro-American participation in the war effort and by taking an anti-segregation stand. After the war, Bert Goldberg produced and Williams directed and acted in, along with July Jones, both *Beagle Street Mama* (1946) and *Dirty Girty from Harlem, U.S.A.* (1946). Williams also directed and starred in Harlemwood and Sack Attractions' *Juke Joint* (1947) with July Jones and Mantan Moreland.

Other Afro-Americans had worked on the production side of independent filmmaking as well as on the performance side. Not always recalled because of his many roles in Hollywood films, Clarence Muse had many talents beyond the ability to play the domestic and the coon which were rarely taken advantage of during his Hollywood career. In one of the earliest all-black films, for instance, he was assistant producer of *Custard Nine* (Pathe, 1911), a film about a black baseball team's antics. In mid-career, Muse starred as a concert violinist, Arthur Williams, in a script he wrote himself for the Goldberg Brothers' *Broken Strings* (1940). The story revolves around an accident to the violinist's hands and the successful operation that allows him to play again. The surgeon was played by Jesse Lee Brooks and Matthew Beard, Stymie in the early years of the *Our Gang Series*, played the wild teenager. It was one of Muse's finest performances and the film was one of the best indendent productions of the era.

Afro-American Frank Wilson wrote the stories for and acted in two other Goldberg Productions' films, *Paradise in Harlem* (1939) and *Sunday Sinners* (1941). Jazz music and a ganster plot provided the opportunity for Mamie Smith, Edna Mae Harris, and Alec Lovejoy to perform in *Paradise in Harlem*. They also appeared in *Sunday Sinners* with music by Afro-American Donald Heywood. Frank Wilson did the story and Donald Heywood did the music for a musical drama with a gangster and rackets storyline, *Moon over Harlem* (Meteor Productions, 1939), which featured Slim Thompson, Alec Lovejoy, Bud Harris, Cora Green, Izinetta Wilcois and others. *Moon Over Harlem* caught the ambience of Harlem and its social ills, as did another film with a screenplay by Frank Wilson, *Murder on Lenox Avenue* (1941). With a cast that included Mamie Smith, Alec Lovejoy, Edna Mae Harris, Sidney Easton, and Wilson himself, *Murder on Lenox Avenue* rivalled Hollywood in the quality of its production while at the same time establishing itself in the best of the independent filmmaking tradition because of its social message directed at unity rather than class distinctions in Harlem.

The gangster genre hit its peak in the years 1937 to 1941. The Afro-Americans George Randol and Ralph Cooper produced Million Dollar Pictures' slickly photographed *Dark Manhattan* (1937), which featured Afro-American gangsters in a modern setting. Along with Clarence Brooks, Sam McDaniel, Jesse Lee Brooks, and Cleo Herndon, Ralph Cooper played in the film as well.

Cooper was Curly Thorpe, who makes it to the top of the numbers racket in Harlem. In the same era, Million Dollar Pictures produced *Bargain with Bullets* (1937), also titled *Gangsters on the Loose, Gang Smashers* (1938), also titled *Gun Moll, Gang War* (1939), and *Straight to Heaven* (1939). Ralph Cooper wrote the screenplay for both *Bargain with Bullets* and *Gang Smashers*. He starred as Mugsy in the underworld tale of *Bargain with Bullets* which also featured Francis Turnham as Kay and Teresa Harris as Grace; Lawrence Criner, Clarence Brooks, Edward Thompson, Sam McDaniel, and Reginald Fenderson appeared as well. *Gang Smashers*, about the rackets in Harlem and the woman who rules them, featured Nina Mae McKinney, Lawrence Crimer, Monte Hawley, Edward Thompson, Mantan Moreland, and Reginald Fenderson. Jesse Lee Brooks appeared in *Gang War*, a film which starred Ralph Cooper and Lawrence Criner as the leaders of rival gangs in conflict over whether to work for or against the established authority in Harlem. In the last of these, the gangsters are at odds with the detectives in *Straight to Heaven* with Nina Mae McKinney, James Baskett, Percy Verwagen, Jackie Ward, and Lionel Monogas.

Two similar films were Jack and Bert Goldberg's *Double Deal* (1939) and Supreme Pictures' *Am I Guilty?* (1940), or *Racket Doctor*. Afro-American Flounoy E. Miller wrote the screenplay and appeared in *Double Deal*, another tale of rival gangsters and double-dealings. Edward Thompson, Maceo Sheffied, and Freddie Jackson were the gangsters and Jeni LeGon played Freddie's girlfriend. *Am I Guilty?* was yet another gangster film with an all-star all-black cast. Ralph Cooper played Dr. Dunbar, Lawrence Criner was "Trigger" Bennett, and Clarence Brooks appeared as the police lieutenant, along with Dewey "Pigmeat" Markham, Reginald Fenderson, Cleo Desmond, Jesse Lee Brooks, Eddie Thompson and others. While several of these gangster films, most notably *Moon over Harlem* and *Murder on Lenox Avenue*, seemed to be developing the potential for social statements through film, the genre as a whole only flirted with that potential.

It would be the same with other independent films. In Million Dollar Pictures' *Life Goes On* (1938), also titled *His Harlem Wife*, Louise Beavers plays a widowed mother of two quite different sons. One son, played by Edward Thompson, is an attorney; the other son, played by Reginald Fenderson, is accused of murder. The possibilities for social comment existed, but the film fell short of developing the potential inherent in the plot. Jesse Lee Brooks, Lawrence Criner, Monte Hawley, Hope Bennett, and Lillian Randolph were featured along with Beavers, who would also have a major role in Million Dollar Pictures' *Reform School* (1939). Million Dollar Pictures' *One Dark Night* (1939), produced by the Afro-American team of George Randol and Ralph Cooper and directed by Anglo-American Leo C. Popkin, revealed the potential of Mantan Moreland's acting abilities when he appeared in a commanding noncomedic role. Familiar names appeared, among them Lawrence Criner, Monte Hawley, Bettie Treadville, and Josephine Pearson, but again the drama was not as powerful as it could have been given Moreland as a man making a success of himself in the interests of his family. Again with Mantan Moreland, Leo C. Popkin directed Million Dollar Pictures' *While Thousands Cheer* (1940), also titled *Crooked Money* and *Gridiron Graft*. The All-American football star Kenny Washington was featured in this film about corruption in sports, and he was backed up by the usual crew of Jeni LeGon, Lawrence Criner, Monte Hawley, Edward Thompson, Joel Fluellen, Ida Belle, and Gladys Snyder.

In the forties, Jack Goldberg directed *Othello* (ca. 1940's) and produced *The Unknown Soldier* (ca. 1940's), a documentary on Afro-Americans in America's wars. After World War Two, the company the Goldberg Brothers established, Million Dollar Pictures, did *Four Shall Die* (1946), also titled *Condemned Men*, a typical murder mystery with Mantan Moreland as the detective and Dorothy Dandridge as an heiress involved in a love triangle. Jack Goldberg and Herald Pictures did yet another murder mystery, *Miracle in Harlem* (1948) with Stepin Fetchit and Lawrence Criner.

In the musical genre, Million Dollar Pictures worked with Toddy Pictures to produce *The Duke Is Tops* (1938), also titled *Blonde Venus*. One of the better all-black films of the era, Ralph Cooper starred and Lena Horne made her first film appearance. A musical about show business, the film also featured Lawrence Criner, Monte Hawley, and Everett Brown. Despite being used by the NAACP for charity fund-raising, *The Duke Is Tops* was not widely circulated. That same year, the Goldberg Brothers produced *Mystery in Swing* with Flournoy E. Miller and Monte Hawley. Together again with Toddy Pictures, Million Dollar Pictures made *Night Club Girl* (1942) with Mantan Moreland; originally titled *One Dark Night* by Toddy, that title was dropped since

Million Dollar Pictures had just used it. The Goldberg Brothers featured Lena Horne in *Harlem on Parade* (ca. 1944) and *Boogie Woogie Dream* (1944). *Boogie Woogie Dream* also featured Teddy Wilson, Albert Ammons, and Pete Johnson. Through various companies like Herald Pictures, Jack Goldberg continued to produce all-black musicals such as *Boy! What a Girl!* (1946), with Billy Daniels, and *Sepia Cinderella* (1947). Both films were unusual in that they included "guest appearances" by Anglo-Americans Gene Krupa in the first and Freddie Bartholomew in the second.

The achievements of Million Dollar Pictures and the Goldberg Brothers were many, among them providing a format in which Mantan Moreland and Louise Beavers could on occasion break free of their Hollywood stereotypes, presenting films of solid, sustained quality that could rival the production expertise of Hollywood, and including on occasion Anglo-Americans in all-black casts. The technical accomplishments were due in large measure to the fact that Million Dollar Pictures uniquely combined Hollywood expertise with the talents of Afro-Americans. The company was among the first major independent enterprises within Hollywood to allow a substantial amount of control over production, primarily through Ralph Cooper and George Randol, to Afro-Americans.

One of the few companies to be founded and run by an Afro-American in the second generation of independent filmmaking was William Alexander's Alexander Productions. Alexander Productions made *Flicker Up* (1946) with Billy Eckstine and May Lou Harris, and then a combination boxing and juvenile delinquency film, *The Fight Never Ends* (1947), with Joe Louis as himself--"The Brown Bomber"--Ruby Dee, the Mills Brothers, William Greaves and Emmett "Babe" Wallace. Alexander's musical, *Jivin in Be Bop* (1947), was co-directed by Spencer Williams and the Anglo-American Leonard Anderson. It featured Dizzy Gillespie and many other Afro-American performers like Freddie Carter, Helen Humes, Dan Durley, and Daisy Richardson. In his last production, *Souls of Sin* (1949), Alexander presented many new faces along with a few old ones: Savannah Churchill, William Greaves, Jimmy Wright, Billie Allen, Louise Jackson, Powell Lindsay, Charlie Mae Rae, Bill Chase, Jessie Walter, and Harris and Scott.

By the time Joe Louis appeared in Alexander Productions' *The Fight Never Ends*, ten years after he became the heavyweight boxing champion of the world, he had been in many films. The independent all-black genre had produced several films with real Afro-American heroes. One was the story of Joe Louis' life, Grand National Pictures' *Spirit of Youth* (1937). Louis starred and was backed up by three staples, Clarence Muse, Mantan Moreland, and Clarence Brooks. This boxing picture appeared the same year that Louis became the champion. Louis also appeared in Toddy Pictures' documentary, *Sergeant Joe Louis on Tour* (1943), the patriotic Hollywood production for the troops, *This Is the Army* (Warners, 1943), and Harry M. Popkin's production for Million Dollar Pictures and Sack Amusement, *The Brown Bomber* (ca. 1940's), another film on Louis' life as a boxer. Henry Armstrong, another Afro-American boxing champion, was the subject of Alfred Sack's *Keep Punching* (1939). Featuring Canada Lee and Dooley Wilson, the film portrayed Armstrong's rugged rise to success and his subsequent moral rejuvination.

Other filmmakers than Toddy had done all-black documentaries during World War Two. Beginning just prior to the war, All American News produced *Colored America on Parade* (1940), the first of a series on Afro-American life and culture that would be continued throughout the war years. After the war, Anglo-American Bud Pollard directed *It Happened in Harlem* (1945) and the musical short, *Romance on the Beat* (1945), for All American News. Dotty Rhodes appeared in both and a variety of other Afro-Americans played in one or the other, among them Phil Gomex, Lionel Monagas, Juanita Pitts, Hughie Walker, George Wiltshire, Ida James, Tiny Dickerson, and Milton Woods. George Wiltshire also appeared in All American News' *Midnight Menace* (ca. 1946), with Sybil Lewis, James Dunsmore, Harold Coke, Leon Poke, Amust Austin, Jimmy Walker, and the Black Diamond Dollies. With Astor Pictures and the directing of Bud Pollard, All American News made *Big Times* (ca. 1946) with Moms Mabley, Stepin Fetchit, Dotts Johnson, Milton Woods, and Francine Everett.

Anglo-American Josh Binney directed at least four of the All American News films: *Chicago after Dark* (1946), a musical short, *The Joint Is Jumping* (1948), which included one Anglo-American, Charles Ray, *Boarding House Blues* (1948), and *Killer Diller* (1948). *Boarding House Blues* was typical of these productions. Moms Mabley is being evicted from a boarding house that caters to entertainers and in the romp that follows the talent is displayed by Dusty Fletcher, Lucky Millinder and his band, and a host of others. Moms Mabley, actually Jackie "Moms" Mabley, also appeared in *Killer Diller* along with Dusty Fletcher, Butterfly McQueen, George Wiltshire, the King Cole Trio and others. All American News also did the comedy short, *Lucky Gamblers* (1946) with Lollypop Jones, Edith Graves, Augustus Smith, and Anglo-American Frederick Johnson, and the musical shorts with Hadda Brooks, *Queen of the Boogie* (1947) and *Boogie Woogie Blues* (1948).

Bud Pollard, who directed several films for All American News, was one of the major figures as both director and producer in Astor Pictures Corporation. Beginning just after World War Two, Astor primarily made musicals. Their first was *Caldonia* (1945), a short musical comedy with Louis Jordan, Nicki O'Daniel, Roxie Joynes, Richard Huey, George Wiltshire, and Milton Woods. In Astors many feature-length musicals, Louis Jordan, Lorenzo Tucker, Milton Woods, Frank Wilson, Mantan Moreland, Monte Hawley, Dotts Johnson, Edna Mae Harris, Ruby Dee, Henri Woods, and many others would put in appearances. Typical of these musicals was the Golden Slipper night club setting in *Tall, Tan and Terrific* (1946), with Francine Everett as "tall, tan and terrific." The other Astor musicals were *Look Out, Sister* (1946), *Beware* (1946), *Woman's a Fool* (ca. 1947), *Love in Syncopation* (1947), *Ovoutie O'Rooney* (1947), and *Reet, Petite, and Gone* (1947). The last Astor production was *The Dreamer* (1948) with Mantan Moreland, June Richmond, Mabel Lee, and Pat Rainey.

Anglo-American Ted Toddy produced diverse all-black films, primarily in the forties. His company, Toddy Pictures, on occasion teamed up with Lucky Star Productions or Million Dollar Pictures to make a film. An early Toddy Pictures' film was *Mr. Creeps* (1938) with Mantan Moreland and Flournoy E. Miller. With Lucky Star Productions, Toddy Pictures made *Mantan Runs for Mayor* (ca. 1940's), also with Mantan Moreland and Flournoy E. Miller. Moreland then appeared in Toddy Pictures' *What a Guy* (1947), with Ruby Dee and Anna Lucasta, and in *Mantan Messes Up* (ca. 1940's) with Monte Hawley and Lena Horne. Along with the films *Crime Street* (ca. 1940's), a feature about juvenile delinquency, *Eddie Green's Laugh Jamboree* (ca. 1940's), and *Rufus Green in Harlem* (ca. 1940's), Toddy Pictures did a series of documentaries during World War Two: *Who's Who in Colored America* (ca. 1940's), *Colored Americans in the Nation's Capital* (ca. 1940's), and

Colored Men in White (ca. 1940's). Toddy Pictures did the feature mystery-comedy, *The Corpse Accuses* (1946), as well as *Super Sleuths* (ca. 1940's), *A Night with the Devil* (ca. 1945), and *Voodoo Devil Drums* (ca. 1940's). This last film was reminiscent of the earlier *Drums O'Voodoo* (1933), also titled *Voodoo Drums* and *Louisiana*, produced by International Stage Play Pictures. It was a cliched picture based on a play by Afro-American J. Augustus Smith. Smith starred in it along with Laura Bowman, Chick McKinney, Lionel Monagas, A.B. Comathiere, Alberta Perkins, and Paul Johnson. Having already had numerous titles attached to it, this may be the same film that was re-released in 1940 as *She Devil*.

Ted Toddy, along with the Anglo-Americans James Frederick and Jed Buell, formed Dixie National Pictures to produce comedies and detectives with such personalities as Mantan Moreland, Flournoy E. Miller, Eddie Anderson, Clarence Brooks, Lawrence Criner, and Zack Williams. Among these films were *Mr. Washington Goes to Town* (1940), *Lucky Ghost* (1941), *Professor Creeps* (1941), and *Up Jumped the Devil* (1941). Those like *Mr. Washington Goes to Town* were demeaning comedies similar to Hollywood productions with Moreland doing his coon act. These films were not well-received by the Afro-American press for this reason, but they did achieve a measure of success at the box office. While Moreland's career in Hollywood came to an end in the forties, he would continue to appear in independent films in the fifties such as Austin Productions and Fritz Pollard Associates' *Rockin' the Blues* (ca. 1950's) with Flournoy E. Miller.

Another Afro-American who produced some of his own films was Dewey "Pigmeat" Markham. With a screenplay by Afro-American Ralph Cooper, Markham produced and acted in *Mr. Smith Goes Ghost* (1940) along with Monte Hawley, Lawrence Criner, and Millie Monroe. Markham also produced *One Big Mistake* (1940) and, after World War Two, he starred in many of the Toddy Pictures' comedies, including *Fight That Ghost* (1946), a mystery comedy that also featured John "Rastus" Murray and Sidney Easton; *House Rent Party* (1946), with John Murray and Macbeth's Calypso Band; *Shut My Big Mouth* (ca. 1946), also with John Murray; *Hell Cats* (ca. 1946); and *Pigmeat Markham's Laugh Hepcats* (ca. 1946). Among his other films, Markham appeared, again with John Murray, in *The Wrong Mr. Right* (ca. 1940's), and in *Swanee Showboat* (ca. 1940's) with Nina Mae McKinney, Mabel Lee, Helen Barys, The Lindy Hoppers, and others.

Afro-American George Randol produced and directed *Midnight Shadow* (1939) and directed both *Darktown Strutters Ball* (ca. 1938), and *Rhythm Rodeo* (1938). *Midnight Shadow* featured Frances Redd, Buck Woods, Richard Bates, Ollie Ann Robinson, Clinton Rosemond, and Ruby Dandridge. Randol's *Rhythm Rodeo* was a musical western with Troy Brown, the Jackson Brothers, Rosalie Lincoln, and Jim Davis. Like the all-black westerns put out during the first generation of Afro-American independent filmmaking by the Norman Film Manufacturing Company, Jed Buell's Hollywood Productions and Associated Pictures made carbon copies of Anglo-American westerns. *Bronze Buckeroo* (1938), *Harlem on the Prairie* (1939), *Harlem Rides the Range* (1939), and *Two Gun Man from Harlem* (1939) were horse operas similar to those of Tom Mix and Gene Autry. Afro-American Herb Jeffries was the singing cowboy and Flournoy E. Miller was his partner. In *Bronze Buckeroo*, light-skinned hero Jeffries as Bob Blake was contrasted with the dark-skinned Afro-Americans Lucius Brooks and Spencer Williams as the comic and the villain respectively while Flournoy E. Miller was Dusky, Blake's sidekick. The same characters appeared in *Harlem on the Prairie*, which had a plot revolving around stolen gold. *Harlem Rides the Range* was a musical western written by Spencer Williams and Flournoy E. Miller. Among the other actors who appeared in several of these westerns were Arti Young and Clarence Brooks. Like the Anglo-American westerns, until the symbolic reversal that occurred in *High Noon* (1952), Afro-American westerns fell into the archetypal trap of identifying light skin with heroic people and dark skin with sinister people. Toddy Pictures did a follow-up of these westerns with *Prairie Comes to Harlem* (ca. 1940's) and late in forties such westerns were still being made by Goldmax Productions. Goldmax had done *She's too Mean to Me* (1948) with Mantan Moreland, Johnny Lee, and Flournoy E. Miller, and then used Moreland and Lee, along with Mauryne Brent, in *Come on Cowboy* (1948).

The record for all-black films in the second generation was in many ways a disappointment. The first generation's efforts, like Afro-American Leigh Whipperis production of *Come Back* (1922), were rarely built upon by the second generation. An aesthetics of black film did not develop and most of the films from the thirties onward were copies of Hollywood films intended for Afro-American audiences in Afro-American theaters. With some exceptions like Million Dollar Pictures, the quality of the independents' film production was not up to Hollywood standards. The films did parade Afro-American talent across the silver screen. Instead of a host of serious films, however, the independents relied primarily on musicals similar to those of Hollywood. Among those not previously mentioned are Harlem Productions' *Cavalcade of Harlem* (1937); Century Productions' *Murder with Music* (1941) with Bob Howard, Noble Sissle and His Orchestra, and Milton Williams; Creative Cinema's four musicals which included entertainers like James Baskett, Ethel Moses, Count Basie, and Nina Mae McKinney, *Harlemania* (1938), *St. Louis Gal* (1938), *Gone Harlem* (1939), and *Sugar Hill Baby* (ca. 1940); *Rhythm on the Run* (1942) with Lucky Millinder and Edna Mae Harris; the three musicals by Associated Producers of Negro Motion Pictures with performers like Ruby Dee, Billy Ekstine, Hazel Tillman, and Emett "Babe" Wallace, *That Man of Mine* (1947), *Rhythm in a Riff* (1947), and *Sweethearts of Rhythm* (1947); Herald Pictures' *Harlem Follies* (1950) with everyone from Stepin Fetchit to the Slam Stewart Trio; and well into the fifties, and after the *Brown* decision of 1954, Studio Films' *Rhythm and Blues Revue* (1955), *Rock "n" Roll Revue* (1955), and *Basin Street Revue* (1955).

Just as it had done in Hollywood films, the entertainer mode overshadowed all others in the films of the independents. Comedies were far behind, though they too were numerous. Entire series were made, including the comedy shorts by Sepia Productions with James Baskett, Amanda Randolph, Lorenzo Tucker, and Gene Ware: *What Goes Up* (1939), *Dress Rehearsal* (1939), *Comes Midnight* (1940), *One Round Jones* (1946), and *Mr. Adam's Bomb* (1949). The achievement of the all-black films was in quantity rather than quality. For every *Take My Life* (Goldseal, 1941), also titled *Murder Trap*, in which there was at least an attempt to be relevant by showing a Harlem youth getting out of trouble by going into the Army, there were a dozen films like Norwanda Pictures' *No Time for Romance* (1948) and *Sun Tan Ranch* (1948). The record was certainly no worse than that of Hollywood, but independent all-black films had a potentially viable medium with which to fight the Anglo-American portrayal of the Afro-American image, and the majority of these filmmakers failed to make an enlightened attempt to correct these images. The rut into which the black stereotypes in Hollywood films had fallen was made deeper by independent filmmakers. The problems involved in projecting a suitable Afro-American image through film apparently went far deeper than just the color of the writer's or actor's skin or the source of the capital used to produce the films. Possibly, the psyche of the Afro-American community was so conditioned to the prevalent images emanating from Hollywood that it could not rebel or demand something better from its own producers. Certainly it could not demand any better of the Anglo-American producers who made most of the all-black films during the second generation.

Only in the late sixties, far beyond the 1896 to 1954 scope of this study, did a third generation of Afro-American independent filmmaking get underway. It developed concomitantly with the most sustained, and most effective, civil rights activities in American history. The one or two hundred post-1968 films made for Afro-American audiences, most of which were again produced by Anglo-Americans, managed to maintain the ingredients of Anglo-American cinema while substituting Afro-American for Anglo-American victories on film. With some outstanding exceptions of films oriented toward consciousness-raising as well as toward Afro-American audiences--most notably such films as *The Learning Tree* (1969), *The Great White Hope* (1970), *Lady Sings the Blues* (1972), *The Autobiography of Miss Jane Pittman* (1973), and *Malcolm X*--little had apparently been learned from the two earlier generations of all-black films. And overall, the independent Afro-American films of the first two generations had lost the opportunity to write an even more significant chapter in the history of film culture and the black image in films.

Notes

[1] Thomas Cripps treats *The Blood of Jesus* in great detail in his *Black Film as Genre* (Bloomington: Indiana Univ. Press, 1979), pp. 86-99.

Chapter Seven

The Great Depression and the Ku Klux Klan

As women's skirt lengths descended during the Great Depression, so did the morale of the American public. The influx of Afro-Americans into the urbanized northern cities also declined with the Great Depression. Economic survival had become a more desperate concern for nearly everyone in America. The acute economic struggle did not reflect a large increase in overt racism, except through the influence of the German Nazis and the home-grown Ku Klux Klan, two rabidly racist groups always capable of exploiting hard times. No one, it seemed, was getting jobs in America. Although Jim Crow continued to be the entrenched social system, and Hollywood continued to make segregated films, "for the first time in history the great majority of both races in the South joined the same political party," notes historian C. Vann Woodward in *The Strange Career of Jim Crow*.[1] Only a united effort on the part of both Afro-Americans and Anglo-Americans, the logic of political unity suggested, could reverse the conditions of world-wide depression which the South had already been feeling for nearly a generation.

The dynamism of Eleanor and Franklin Roosevelt attracted the support of the majority of Afro-Americans. Solidarity behind the Democratic Party in the Afro-American community reflected an increased political optimism on the part of many Afro-Americans. Little progressive action was forthcoming as a reward for this consolidation of their hard-won political input. The first Afro-American federal judge, William H. Hastie, was appointed in 1937. As late as 1939, however, the year of the monument to the South, *Gone with the Wind*, a "Back to Africa" bill was introduced in the United States Senate by a Southerner. Hastie was also appointed an aide to the Secretary of War, but he resigned early in World War Two because no effort was made to change the policies of segregation in the miitary. The Secretary of War was suitably embarrassed by this breach in the united front America was fostering, but Hastie's resignation led to few beneficial changes in official policy toward Afro-Americans in the military.

In the long run, the Afro-American community perhaps lost an opportunity to influence the major parties by making the Democratic Party their bastion. By entrenching themselves on one side of the political spectrum they gave up what little political leverage they had with either the Democrats or Republicans. The civil rights groups recognized this dilemma, but they were still too weak to correct it during the depression years. The potential was lost for implementing a balance of power through political clout which might have occurred if the civil rights groups had been stronger, or at least more unified in their strategies. Historically, of course, the Afro-American community had no realistic choice, for the Republican Party had rejected Afro-Americans out of hand in 1928 and won, and they tried again to do the same in 1932 but lost.

It was left to the new class of intellectuals, both Anglo-American and Afro-American, to move beyond this political dilemma. Unlike the civil rights groups, outspoken critics of capitalism rejected both Hoover and Roosevelt in 1932 and allied themselves with a radical third party, the Communists. America's progressive paradigm fell apart with the depression and many too the opportunity to look outside of America for a new one. Afro-American writers like Langston Hughes and Richard Wright, as well as many Anglo-American writers, rejected reform in favor of Marxian revolution during the thirties. In the midst of the conflict between domestic-oriented Communists who were pro-America, and foreign-oriented Communists who were pro-Soviet Union, most Afro-Americans who turned briefly to Communism in the thirties remained pro-America. They did not desire direction from Moscow, but they did feel that Communist precepts could be successfully implemented in an America that was obviously suffering from a failing capitalistic economy.

The influence of the Soviet Union was present in several films of the thirties. These films were intended to appeal particularly to the Afro-American community by inducing race pride and showing that Afro-Americans would be tolerated on an equal basis with other people under a Communist order. For instance, the early life of the part-black Russian poet, Alexander Pushkin, was given straightforward treatment with no attempt to involve the race issue in Arady Narodistky's *Young Pushkin* (Russia, 1935), which was distributed with English subtitles. In G.V. Alexandrov's feature for Mosfilm, *The Circus* (Russia, 1937), a white woman leaves America because she has a mulatto child and is accepted in the Communist state. Another natural topic for the Soviet Union was the relationship between Huckleberry Finn and the black slave, Jim.

Of the seven filmings of Mark Twain's *The Adventures of Huckleberry Finn* (1884), three were produced in the thirties. The decade opened with Norman Taurog's *Huckleberry Finn* (Paramount, 1931). Clarence Muse played Jim to Jackie Coogan's Huck. Jim was presented as intelligent but burdened with an awkward dialect and a faithful servant role. The core of Huck's being, his conscience, was not featured in this film so that there was simply an acceptance of rather than a commentary on race. The decade closed with Richard Thorpe's *The Adventures of Huckleberry Finn* (MGM, 1939), with Rex Ingram as Jim and Mickey Rooney as Huck. Jim was presented more favorably in this film as an archetypal teacher helping Huck through the rituals of entering manhood. Slavery is incidently condemned in that the theme of a flight to freedom for Jim as well as Huck is present. Between these two American versions came the Soviet Union's *Huckleberry Finn* (Russia, 1937), directed by Weyland Rudd. Like the others, it too was a celebration of the primitive but with a measure of equality in the relationship between Huck and Jim. In the thirties, the appeal of the Huck and Jim relationship was that they were both outsiders seeking the freedom of the mighty Mississippi River rather than the hostile shore life. The economic collapse in America made the easy going life of Huck and Jim an idealistic alternative.

The first American filming of the Huck and Jim relationship was in William D. Taylor's silent *Huckleberry Finn* (1920). Afro-American George Reed played Jim to Gordon Griffith's Huck. Griffith was already well-known for his parts in Tarzan films of the era, and Reed had been one of the few Afro-Americans to appear in *The Birth of a Nation*. This first film, unfortunately, concentrated on the story of budding love between Huck and Mary Wilks rather than on the story of Huck and Jim. After the three filmings in the thirties, no version was appear for a generation. Michael Curtiz' *The Adventures of Huckleberry Finn* (MGM, 1960) used the light-heavyweight boxing champion Archie Moore as a servile Jim in his first film appearance, and Eddie Hodges as Huck. Encyclopedia Britannica produced *Huckleberry Finn* (1965) and Paul Winfield played Jim to Jeff East's Huck in J. Lee Thompson's *Huckleberry Finn* (1974). The latter film added one new dimension by presenting Jim's wife, played by Odessa Cleveland, but the essence of the Huck and Jim relationship which revolves around Huck's conscience was explored only in passing, just as it was in the first thirties filming, *Huckleberry Finn* (1931). Most of these films failed to develop the theme of societal rejection inherent in Mark Twain's book. They fail also to come up to the dignity and awareness which Twain intended, relying instead on a Robinson Crusoe/Friday relationship in which Friday is a servant or, worse, the object of Crusoe's missionarying. With the one exception of the late thirties *The Adventures of Huckleberry Finn* (1939), with Rex Ingram as Jim, the Huck and Jim relationship has been presented as the superior white boy and the inferior and ignorant, or, if intelligent, tomming black man.

Beginning in the thirties, the New Deal era both altered and crystalized the views of many Americans on a broad spectrum of social and ethnic issues. The New did incidently provide jobs and relief for some Afro-Americans, as the Work Projects Administration (WPA) propagandistically pointed out in its newsreel highlighting Afro-American participation in the WPA, *We Work Again* (1936). But segregation similar to that portrayed through the film versions of the Huck and Jim relationship was reinforced through the New Deal economic programs and employment, even within the federal governments burgeoning bureaucracy, was segregated. Afro-Americans in reality were still relegated economically to the very situations reflected in the films of this era as holders of menial, unskilled, token jobs or, worse, as incompetent comics either in these positions or with no employment at all.

In his first film, Willie Best acquired his nomenclature, "Sleep 'n' Eat," for that is what he did in *Up Pops the Devil* (Paramount, 1931). Louise Beavers established her film personality as a maid in movie after movie in the early thirties: *Annabelle's Affairs* (Fox, 1931), *Girls About Town* (1931)--also titled *Girls Around Town*--*Young America* (Fox, 1932), *Divorce in the Family* (MGM, 1932), and *What Price Hollywood* (RKO, 1932). The latter film also included Eddie Anderson as James, the servant. Clarence Muse was the comic valet in *A Royal Romance* (Columbia, 1930) and *Washington*

Merry-Go-Round (Columbia, 1933), and an elevator operator in *From Heaven to Hell* (Paramount, 1933). Lois Gardella was Aunt Jemima and Stepin Fetchit was the comic impersonation of George Bernard Shaw in the Shirley Temple pep rally which included its own new deal addition to the bureaucracy, a Secretary of Amusement, in *Stand Up and Cheer* (Warners, 1934). The real New Deal programs, like the fictional Secretary of Amusement, presented Afro-Americans with the same cards they had always been dealt by Washington.

Many films of the thirties, again like the Huck and Jim relationship, bear out the view that the Angl-American man was predominant in both the Anglo-American and Afro-American communities. The Afro-American man, on the other hand, was "next to nothing" in either community. Most films of the thirties, excepting those which were set prior to the Civil War, presented the Afro-American as a free man without his approaching equality with the Anglo-American man, as in Stepin Fetchit as the comic bartender in *Marie Galante* (Fox, 1934), Afro-American Sam Baker as yet another Mose in *Public Hero Number One* (MGM, 1935), or the resort to the Our Gang type of film where a measure of equality is possible because the relationships are among youths like that which included Afro-American Philip Hurlic in one of the Penrod Series, *Penrod and Sam* (Warners, 1937). Similarly, Afro-American Fred Toones is named in the film credits only as "Snowflake" for his portrayals of a domestic in *Lady by Choice* (Columbia, 1934)) and a porter in *20th Century* (Columbia, 1934), and no film credit is given to the black shoe shine boy in *Smart Money* (Warners, 1931). According to the images in these films, the value emphasis in American culture was on the ideal of liberty rather than the ideal of equality. In actuality, however, neither ideal by itself was of value to Afro-American culture.

The problems of the era led to a consistent trampling of the individual. The depression inspired new attitudes toward collective economics as an alternative to Marxism as the concept of a work ethic came to be questioned. These attitudes prospered in the American culture as a whole as well as in the Afro-American community. A self-financed effort by a multitude of labor activists and Anglo-American King Vidor, who had directed the all-black *Hallelujah* (1929), resulted in a powerful cultural statement recorded on film titled *Our Daily Bread* (1934). In addition, Anglo-Americans and Afro-Americans alike had been part of the "Hooverville" bonus army which in 1932 camped in Washington, D.C., as part of its demonstration for better veteran's benefits. On film, it was white Al Jolson and black Edgar Connor in a take-off on the "Hooverville" demonstration, Lewis Milestone's *Hallelujah, I'm a Bum* (United Artists, 1933), or *Heart of New York*. Connor, a dwarf, is Acorn, Jolson's ally in the hobo haven of New York's Central Park. Whether to work, and what to do with the money if they do work, is the essential conflict. The film attempts to show equality between blacks and whites, but obviously showing equality on the part of whites was only possible with black dwarves and cooperative effort was only possible in the lowest possible economic stratum, that of the hoboes.

Even the conservative American Legion, however, had taken up the collective effort. Unwittingly perhaps, the Legion's applications on behalf of veterans, a large number of whom were Afro-Americans, to institute a G.I. Bill of Rights, contributed more to the creation of an American sense of social responsibility for those in need than most of its political arch-enemies had done in politicking for socialism. Some unions were in the forefront of change as well. "With its avowed philosophy of non-discrimination," the Congress of Industrial Organization (CIO), formed in the thirties, "made the notion of an alliance of black and white workers something more than a visionary dream."[2] No Hollywood films of the era represented a black as a member of a union, however. Prior to this time only the quasi-union known as the International Workers of the World (WW), whose members were called "Wobblies," accepted Afro-Americans as equals. This is why Paul Robeson could put so much feeling into his singing of "Joe Hill," a modern folksong which immortalizes the Wobbly who was framed and executed by the state of Utah. Only in the seventies would a film, *Boxcar Bertha* (1972), dramatize the ideals of racial brotherhood advocated and practiced by the IWW. These ideals were among the reasons why the IWW was considered radical and, therefore, undesirable, by the Anglo-American establishment. With the exception of the new CIO and waning IWW, the benefits of these worker's movements to the Afro-American community reached only the talented who could rise on the economic scale and the middle class who were already relatively secure. Labor alliances which allowed the inclusion of Afro-Americans were new and well-intended, at least in the beginning, but the number of Afro-Americans who actually held unionized jobs remained small. Further, many Anglo-

Americans were willing and even anxious to find a conspiracy of color, more black villains, by focusing on Marxism within the Afro-American community. Thus, when charges of Communist infiltration into the CIO were made public, the injuries to the Afro-American community went deep.

Optimism was present in other quarters, nevertheless: "The South had begun to pull out of its seventy-five year stalemate of an underprivileged and colonial economy," Woodward points out, and "in the process the South had begun to realize that it is easier to share prosperity than poverty with the minority race."[3] This potentially bounteous development in the economic realm was not reflected in films, despite the obsession in Hollywood with southern-oriented pictures throughout the thirties. In a panoramic view of feature films up to the late forties, Peter Noble, in *The Negro in Films* (ca. 1948), outlines these vehicles of bias in this manner:

> From the early days of D.W. Griffith's *The Battle*, *A Child's Strategem*, *American Aristocracy* and others, through the period of Buster Keaton's *The General*, J. Walter Ruben's *Secret Service*, Henry King's *The House of Connelly*, King Vidor's *So Red the Rose*, David Butler's *The Littlest Rebel* and Victor Fleming's *Gone with the Wind*, and up to the more modern era of Leslie Fenton's *Arouse and Beware*, Raoul Walsh's *The Dark Command*, Michael Curtiz's *Santa Fe Trail* and Frank Borzage's *The Vanishing Virginian* American film-makers have concentrated on whitewashing the South and dealing with those phases of American history which give sympathy to the Confederate Army and the southern cause generally, while portraying the northern "nigger lovers" as "the villainous destroyers of the Old South and its glorious traditions." It is not suggested that this was done with any consciously sinister motive, but the facts support this contention.[4]

The catering to southern tastes reflected the North's almost complete and uncritical adherence to long-standing southern attitudes toward Afro-Americans and it led to an abundance of films about the Ku Klux Klan in the thirties. In addition, the cultivated southern bias which insisted upon setting the Afro-American firmly in a pastoral and feudal tradition, rather than in a modern tradition, was prevalent in Hollywood films before, during, and after the thirties. These glossified and nostolgic films about the Old South were to decline only after World War Two when the studio system all but disintegrated.

Throughout the thirties, there were films like *Only the Brave* (Paramount, 1930), *Secret Service* (RKO, 1931), and *Young Mr. Lincoln* (Twentieth Century-Fox, 1939), which used a Civil War setting, presented a southern point of view, and used Afro-Americans only for establishing atmosphere in the film. Other films about the pre-Civil War South represented Afro-Americans as domestics, slaves, or coons. Among these films were those in which Stepin Fetchit appeared: Fetchit as a coon in New Orleans in *Cameo Kirey* (1933), in a bit role in film about a North/South conflict, *The House of Connelly* (Fox, 1934), as domestic and farm hand named Scipio in another North/South romance, *Carolina* (Fox, 1934), and as Zero, along with Hattie McDaniel as Dahlia and numerous "pickaninnies" in the comedy, *Zenobia* (Universal, 1939). The images were not far removed from those of an early D.W. Griffith film, *The Feud and the Turkey* (1908) with black servants named Aunt Dinah and Uncle Daniel. Similarly, Clarence Muse was "Old Joe" in another version of Stephen Foster's career, *Harmony Lane* (Mascot Productions, 1935), and Brutas in the New Orleans setting for *The Toy Wife* (MGM, 1938). Still in the pre-Civil War South genre, Louisiana is the setting for *Jezebel* (Warners, 1938), a film which included numerous roles for slaves and servants played by, among others, Eddie Anderson, Matthew Beard, Theresa Anderson, and Lew Payton. And at the end of the decade, Clinton Rosemond appeared as the slave, Enoch, in *Stand Up and Fight* (MGM, 1939).

Other films of the thirties used the South, but not necessarily with a Civil War setting. Mississippi River life is the background for Madame Sul-te-Wan to appear as Voodoo Sue in *Heaven on Earth* (Universal, 1931). Libby Taylor is Jasmine, maid to Mae West, in old New Orleans in *Belle of the Nineties* (Paramount, 1934), which also included music and an appearance by Duke Ellington. It was Libby Taylor again as Lavinia in *Mississippi* (Paramount, 1935), the film in which W.C. Fields delivered his oft-repeated line to a black man: "Get along, you Senegambian." And then Jerome Kerr made revisions for a remake of the 1929 version of *Show Boat*, James Whale's *Show Boat* (Universal, 1936). The setting was also riverboat life on the Mississippi. An unmistakably black Paul Robeson played Captain Joe and sang "Old Man River" in contrast with an unmistakably white Julie as the mulatto, played by Anglo-American Helen Morgan. Many famous Afro-American actors of the period appeared: Hattie McDaniel as Queenie, Clarence Muse as Sam the Doorman, George Reed as the Old Negro, and Eddie Anderson as the Young Negro.

Another indicator of the emphasis on the South during the thirties was the number of films about Kentucky alone. Kentucky was revived as an idealized version of the South in these films. Four of many were Willie Best in the comedy, *Kentucky Kernals* (RKO, 1934), for which he was listed in the credits as "Sleep 'n' Eat." Typical was the horse racing film with Eddie Anderson, Madame Sul-te-Wan as Lily, and George Reed as Ben in David Butler's *Kentucky* (Twentieth Century-Fox, 1938). *In Old Kentucky* (1927) was remade with Stepin Fetchit and Will Rogers. The new version of *In Old Kentucky* (Twentieth Century-Fox, 1935) was Will Rogers' last film and it included Bill Robinson as a tap dancer and Nina Mae McKinney and Wash Jackson as servants. And Clarence Muse was the leader of the Hall Johnson Choir in one of many musicals set in Kentucky, *Follow Your Heart* (Republic, 1936).

Among the worst of these films about the South was *So Red the Rose* (Paramount, 1935), directed by the eclectic King Vidor. *So Red the Rose* shows slaves as being pro-South at the beginning of the Civil War and as being excessively wild when freedom is granted them. Strong acting is brought out in the conflict between Afro-American Daniel Hayne's loyal butler, William Veal, and Clarence Muse's rebellious brute, Cato. Scores of Afro-Americans appeared in this film, including George Reed. The message of the film was reactionary, for the rebellious blacks are made to justify the South's interpretation of the Civil War and Reconstruction. A similar message comes across in Kurt Newmann's *Rainbow on the River* (RKO, 1936). Clarence Muse and the Hall Johnson Choir appeared, and Lillian Yarbo played Seline, Matthew Beard played "Lilybell," and Louise Beavers was the mammy named Toinette who looked after an Anglo-American boy during and after the Civil War. Beavers, as Toinette, is made to declare very convincingly that she does not desire freedom. Hollywood was back in the teens with such films as *The Old Oak's Secret* (n.d.) in which Old Mose cannot bear the thought of freedom so he hides the freedom documents in the old oak, or Metro's *Marse Covington* (1915) which presented a slave who also did not want to be freed after the Civil War. The images would continue strong in the thirties. The irresponsible Afro-American drunk in the Reconstruction Era in *The Texans* (Paramount, 1938), the presentation of John Brown as an irresponsible fanatic in *Sante Fe Trail* (Warners, 1940), and, of course, David O. Selznick and Victor Fleming's ambivalent *Gone with the Wind* (MGM, 1939), at the close of the decade.

Based on Margaret Mitchell's best-selling romance, *Gone with the Wind* was firmly rooted in the tradition best represented by a similar monumental film, *The Birth of a Nation*. Comparisons between the two films were frequent in both artistic and financial terms, as well as in the degree of racism they perpetuated. In *Gone with the Wind*, the Afro-American characterizations were considerably less volatile. As it finally appeared on the screen, in fact, *Gone with the Wind* was not entirely unrepresentative of Afro-Americans in the antebellum South. But in 1939, it incited numerous accusations of ethnic slander from an increasingly sensitive and outspoken Afro-American community. Oscar Polk, Ben Carter, and Eddie Anderson appeared in familiar roles, and Butterfly McQueen was the frantic overgrown pickaninny. While the film may have been regressive in the context of the social commitment films made during the thirties, Hattie McDaniel's Academy Award for her performance as Scarlett's mammy, the first Oscar ever for an Afro-American, represented a certain measure of progress for Afro-Americans in the Hollywood scheme of things. Hers was an opinionated, humorous mammy and confidante to Scarlett O'Hara and the O'Hara family. Little of the inferiority associated with the mammy image was present, and McDaniel was sensitive as well as maternalistic. While the NAACP did not protest the film, it did work prior to the film's release for changes in the portrayals of Afro-Americans. The National Negro Congress and the American Communist Party did protest the film.

It was in this milieu of the thirties that the Ku Klux Klan, the group at the political extreme farthest from the Communist Party, went through yet another resurgence. The Klan had held its first national conventional in 1867 and, despite the so-called Ku Klux Klan Acts of 1870 and 1871 by the federal government under President Grant, the Klan remained a threat to Afro-Americans. After the end of Reconstruction the Klan quietely faded away until it was revived again in 1915 at the same time as D.W. Griffith's *The Birth of a Nation*. The Klan became a potent political force in the twenties when new restrictions were placed on immigration favoring Anglos and when "scientific racism" was the fad with such books as Lothrop Stoddard's *The Rising Tide of Color* making the rounds. In the thirties, the Klan was still advocating that Afro-Americans be sent back to Africa. For their supremacist anti-black stands, the Ku Klux Klan's publications cited such authorities as Abraham Lincoln in the years just before he became president:

> Negro Equality! Fudge!! How long, in the government of a God, great enough to make and maintain this universe, shall there continue knaves to vend, and fools to gulp, so low a piece of demagogism as this.[5]

Concern with the waxing and waning fortunes of the Ku Klux Klan often took the spotlight in the film medium of the thirties. The two most pro-Klan films of the thirties were *Legion of Terror* (Columbia, 1937), and *A Nation Aflame* (Halperin, 1938). C.C. Coleman's *Legion of Terror* was about a secret society, obviously the Ku Klux Klan, operating in the thirties. Victor Halperin's *A Nation Aflame*, another film about a secret society and the attempt to infiltrate it, was based on the work of Thomas Dixon, the author who wrote *The Clansman* and *The Leopard's Spots* on which *The Birth of a Nation* was based. Hollywood films like *Fury* (1936), *They Won't Forget* (1937), and *The Black Legion* (1937), had presented counter-attacks to such propaganda, but no rebuttal specifically aimed at these two films appeared.

Interest in the activities of the Klan continued, but after the thirties the films were negative portrayals of the Klan. After World War Two, Walter Colmes' *The Burning Cross* (Somerset-Screen Guild, 1947), presented Afro-American Joel Fluellen in the role of a Klan murder victim. Afro-American Maidie Norman appeared as well in this film which emphasized the violence the Klan has traditionally perpetrated. Well into the sixties and seventies, the Klan remained active. Charles Kuralt's documentary, *Ku Klux Klan--The Invisible Empire* (CBS, 1965), was an unfavorable view of the Klan's bigotry. Lola Falana and O.J. Simpson appeared in yet another anti-Klan film, *The Klansman* (Paramount, 1974).

Back in the twenties, the *Our Gang Series* had parodied the Klan with its creation of the Cluck Cluck Klams in *Lodge Night* (1923). Another kind of clan, modeled on the secret society but toned down for young boys, was suggested by Edgar Rice Burroughs in the thirties. He first proposed in 1933 what later became the *Official Guide of the Tarzan Clans of America*. In 1935, Burroughs suggested using the still unwritten guide as a theater handout to promote *The New Adventures of Tarzan*, a Tarzan film then in the making. After it was finally written and published in 1939, Burroughs again suggested that it be used in promoting Tarzan, specifically Metro-Goldwyn-Meyer's *Tarzan Finds a Son* (1939). This film's theme made it a natural for launching the Clans, since the hope of being the adopted son of Tarzan of the Apes was appealing to youngsters interested in the Tarzan Clans of America. The Clans were designed as para-military outfits similar to the Boy Scouts of America. The most popular film Tarzan, Johnny Weissmuller, fittingly was named Chief of Chiefs of the Tarzan Clans of America in 1939. The Ku Klux Klan and its invisible empire continued beyond the Second World War, but the war effectively stunted the growth of the Tarzan Clans of America. The war did not end the making of Tarzan jungle films like *Tarzan's New York Adventure* (1942), however. This film did not do well at the box office, for it used the concrete jungle of New York City more than the African jungle. Mantan Moreland appeared in this film which also brought back Elmo Lincoln, the original Tarzan, in a minor role.

A welcome alternative to these images of blacks in the jungle genre, images which paralleled those which Hollywood used in its films about the South, was initiated in 1935 by the federal government. An integral part of the WPA, the Federal Theater of America helped sustain the Harlem Renaissance by spawning the American Negro Theater which prospered primarily between the years 1935 and 1939. Even prior to this development, the stage had been relatively receptive to Afro-American performers, certainly far more so than the American cinema industry. The American Negro Theater gave Afro-American performers, writers, and producers their first large-scale exposure to the American stage. In so doing it contributed immensely to the development of Afro-American talents which should have been transferable to the silver screen. There was, unfortunately, little transfer of these ripening talents; Sidney Poitier is the major exception and even he failed his initial audition with the American Negro Theater because of his West Indian accent. Despite their ability to gather together the talents of hundreds of Afro-Americans, these federally subsidized programs put only a tiny dent in the employment problems faced by both the Afro-American and Anglo-American artistic communities.

Nearly all filmmakers during the thirties, Afro-American independents included, seem to have been disposed to ignore serious ethnic issues in favor of demeaning portrayals of Afro-Americans or even inflamatory versions of racial conflicts. Rather than challenge the cultural biases, or at least expose them, the films of this era overwhelmingly accepted the biases in their film content; likewise, in their blatant lack of filmic content of relevance and their general silence on issues of subsequence, they reinforced the cultural biases. Like most Americans in the employ of others, regardless of ethnic background, the director of *So Red the Rose*, King Vidor, was constantly caught in the dilemma of keeping his ideals intact in the face of the necessity to earn a livelihood. With such films representing the output of the thirties, a regular cinema-goer might wonder if the South actually won the Civil War. Such free publicity for the aims of the Ku Klux Klan, no longer the political power it was in the twenties, kept alive its American feudalism.

In the films of the thirties, Afro-Americans were still relegated to the lowest echelons of the American social and economic orders. Figures of authority in these films were almost exclusively Anglo-Americans. Hattie McDaniel, for instance, had a small role in John Ford's *The Prisoner of Shark Island* (Twentieth Century-Fox, 1936), and Ernest Whitman appeared as Buck, the faithful servant to Samuel Mudd, the imprisoned doctor who had treated Abraham Lincoln's assassin, John Wilkes Booth. The film was a good portrayal of the milieu of the Civil War era, but in the face of an armed and threatening mob of Afro-Americans, an Anglo-American's demand is complied with when he orders, "Put that gun down, Nigrah!" The expressed superiority of Anglo-Americans was precisely waht the Ku Klux Klan was implementing in America by force. In *Slave Ship* (Twentieth Century-Fox, 1937), the slaves on the ship are the Hall Johnson Choir. In the sort of act for which the Klan might actually praise blacks, they commit mass suicide chained together with the anchor for weight.

The contrast between Afro-American and Anglo-American social and economic standings created a pregnant conflict between the blacks and whites in Hollywood films, whether the tone of the conflict was covertly subdued or overtly vicious. Hollywood's Motion Picture Code of Production, issued in 1933, sought to prohibit ethnic insults. All comments or acts which might tend to "incite bigotry or hatred among peoples of differing races, religions, or national origins" were supposed to be eliminated from American films made in conjunction with the Hollywood movie industry. The Code, like the earlier Hays Office guidelines, was simply not enforced. Like many idealistic pronouncements, it was not backed with any teeth. There was virtually no qualitative change to be found in the Afro-American images that appeared in films after the Code was adopted, though quantitatively there were slightly fewer Afro-Americans appearing in some genres like the jungle films.

Films were thought of principally as a money-making entertainment medium and not as a vehicle for changing old ideas or projecting new ideals. In fact, the first serious treatise on the topic of blacks in American films came only in the late forties when a British writer, Peter Noble, published *The Negro in Films* in London. No American writer had bothered. The notion of a stock of stereotypes that dramatically and influentially misrepresented Afro-Americans, when recognized, was not seen as important enough to correct. Originally an all-black film, *The St. Louis Blues* (Paramount, 1939), was remade from the 1929 version. Afro-American Maxine Sullivan was featured, but the remainder of the cast was Anglo-American. This alteration of an Afro-American film was indicative of the thirties' desire to either remove the Afro-American image from the screen or keep it within traditional boundaries. Only in the fifties version of *The St. Louis Blues* (Paramount, 1958), would the film be remade with an all-black cast.

The thirties was also an era when radical cultural ideas were cultivated, particularly in the social, economic, and political realms. The traumatic condition of American culture was conducive to the injection of assorted ideological panaceas. America was undergoing a belated recognition, for instance, that it no longer had an economy based on an idealistic southern agrarianism, and that it was in the throes of an impersonal and unnatural northern industrialism. Each of the panaceas, ranging from those espoused by the Nazis and the Ku Klux Klan to those espoused by the Communists and the young Black Muslins, received a sympathetic hearing from at least some Americans. In fact, one of the principals behind the creation of the Provincetown Theater group which launched the "Little Theater" movement and the playwright Eugene O'Neill in the teens, two precursors to the American Negro Theater in the thirties, was John Reed. Reed died in 1920. In the thirties, Reed, after whom the Communist-front John Reed Clubs were named, was martyred by the Soviet Union.

As in films, the panaceas were effectively disseminated by the new and complementary medium of radio. It was no coincidence that the first radio station went on the air in the mid-twenties and that the first talkie film arrived shortly thereafter. Technical developments such as radio and sound movies for the first time in history allowed nearly simultaneous presentation of the same message to millions of people. There were extraordinary benefits as well as extraordinary perils to be faced. Roosevelt used "fireside chats" over the radio to strenghten his presidency, but demagoguery was a less savory use of radio as a propaganda tool. There were Father Divines and Sister Goists but, beginning in the early thirties, Father Charles E. Coughlin wrung the most one could get out of the radio medium. A demagogue, Father Coughlin attracted the largest regular listening audience in the history of humankind. Between thirty and forty million Americans were listening to his powerful rhetoric which in 1932 condemned the idealistic Americans who were turning to communism for a solution to the failure of capitalism which the Great Depression represented.

As a radio evangelist, the demagogue Father Coughlin initially had plenty of contributions coming in to support his activities. His fascistic tendencies ultimately alienated so many Americans that by 1934 his programs all but disappeared. As America deliberated over the plight of Spain, Italy, and Germany in 1938, Couglin was back on the air as an ardent sympathizer and propagandist for the German Nazis. His passion for scapegoating led to the creation of stormtrooper gangs called Social Justice Clubs which utilized the Ku Klux Klan's terror-tactics in spreading anti-Semitism and anti-Afro-Americanism. America's anti-Nazi sentiments again drove Father Couglin from the airwaves in 1940, this time forever. In the early fifties another new communications medium, television, was to suffer a similar fate at the hands of another fascist, Senator Joe McCarthy.

Emerging during the thirties in revolt against the fascism of demagogues like Father Coughlin was a new breed of inspired and socially conscious writers. In addition to the Afro-Americans already mentioned, these writers included Anglo-Americans like Clifford Odets, James T. Farrell, Erskine Caldwell, John Dos Passos, and John Steinbeck who produced humane classics about the proletariat for American literature. Most potent during the same period was the outstanding Afro-American writer, Richard Wright, who penned artistically crude but realist versions of America's peculiar savageries in *Uncle Tom's Children* (1938) and *Native Son* (1940).

At the close of the thirties, there was one film made about the South that attempted to counteract some of the images of films like *So Red the Rose* and *Gone with the Wind*. The screenplay was written by the Afro-Americans Langston Hughes and Clarence Muse. Muse also helped Anglo-American Bernard Vorhaus in the directing of *Way Down South* (RKO, 1939), a film which included the Afro-Americans Muse, Steffi Duna, Sally Blane, Matthew Beard, Lillian Yarbo, Jack Carr, Marguerite Whitten, and the Hall Johnson Choir. It was one of the better portrayals of the antebellum South. In this film, the entire trend of the thirties films is reversed when the mean oversear is gotten rid of by the young white master and the black slaves. It was a small victory, however, and the slavery which Hollywood imposed on the images of blacks in films was not to be overcome so easily.

Notes

[1] C. Vann Woodward, *The Strange Career of Jim Crow*, 2nd. rev. ed. (New York: Oxford Univ. Press, 1966), p. 118.

[2] *Report of the National Advisory Commission on Civil Disorders* [*The Kerner Report*], (New York: Bantam, 1968), p. 222.

[3] Woodward, p. 130.

[4] Peter Noble, *The Negro in Films* (London: Skelton Robinson, ca. 1948), p. 193.

[5] Roy P. Basler, *The Collected Works of Abraham Lincoln*, vol. 3 (New Brunswick, NJ: Rutgers Univ. Press, 1953), cited as an unused fragment for a speech.

Chapter Eight

America, The Dark Continent

American filmgoers and filmmakers have been obsessed with Africa as the Dark Continent. Africa is where Afro-Americans came from and, apparently, "once a slave, always a slave," to recast a line from *Imitation of Life* (1934). If not as slaves, literally, then as servants, as bearers, as background props, as exotics, erotics, and black menaces. Twentieth-century conceptions of black magic and voodoo originate from this Africa, and superstition and savagery are yet today most frequently associated with this Africa. The people there generally speak a language of mishmash with a few clearly enunciated "ooga boogas" and "bwanas" tossed in. It is the place where white goddesses exist in the midst of blackness, literal and symbolic, just as in film culture's vision of the Old South glorified by D.W. Griffith and transferred to Africa by Edgar Rice Burroughs. In the films of the Old South, the white women face a sexual menace from blacks, but on the Dark Continent film helped create the sexual menaces for white women are not only blacks but apes, gorillas, and orangutans. The distinctions between black people and the lower orders have thus been blurred by the perspectives of America's film culture.

It is the contention of this chapter that it is America that deserves the label "The Dark Continent," rather than Africa. The Africa which appears in films was the creation of Anglo-American or European minds and, with few exceptions, that Africa is a falsity based on outlandish representations of West Africa as the "heart of Africa" or the Congo, of East Africa as the domain of Mau Maus, and of South Africa as the seat of savagery because of the Zulus. The essential nature of the resulting genre of jungle films was racist and sexist. Africa was used to construct a fantasy world in which film audiences could adventurously play out formulaic rituals and tensions over and over again to to reaffirm the Anglo superiority complex. The assumed need by Anglos to either rule the natives with Tarzans and Sanderses, or raise these "inferiors" to "civilized" standards with hordes of white missionaries and scientists with "white magic," rarely resulted in the latter option, even after several generations of jungle films. In addition, the settings were primarily the jungles of Africa (or equally exotic locations like India, Samoa, Laos, and Suva), rather than the cities of Africa. If present at all, the cities are inhabited still by out-of-place natives and represented as bordello-infested dark alleyways. Cities are troublesome spots because whites invariably find misfortune there. Or the cities may be those fantastic vine-covered lost cities with sacrificial temples as the main attraction, generally built centuries before by lost races of whites for the convenience of modern day white explorers having something to discover in Africa besides real Africans, which they rarely found because Hollywood rarely put them there.

The prevailing image in these films of blacks as savage natives was originally based on the bloody revolt of the Zulus in 1906-1907 against the British colonizers. Even during the revolt, Zulus appeared in films. The British fought the war and they produced its first representation on film in *How a British Bulldog Saved the Union Jack* (1906). D.W. Griffith's *The Zulu's Heart* (1908), in which the Anglo-American version of the loyal servant stereotype was imposed on the blackface Zulu chief who turns traitor on his fellows in defense of a white family, was the first American film to use Zulus. *Rastus in Zululand* (1910), also titled *Rastus Dreams of Zululand*, played Griffith's film for comedy and thus established the popular use of Africa as a backdrop for comedy. Another early comedy was *The Zulu King* (1913) in which a white man becomes king of the Zulus out of self-defense against his wife. In *Queen for a Day* (n.d.), "the black maid of a missionary and his daughter saves their lives by taking over the Zulu throne and helping them escape."[1] Even the French managed a play on Zulu in Marc Allegret's film, *Zou Zou* (1935), with Afro-American Josephine Baker as an exotic native. The British-made *Rhodes of Africa* (Gaumont, 1935), released in America the following year, depicted the savagery of the Zulu war using Africans, including an African in the role of a chief. Many other films using Zulus and Zululand followed, but it was not until the British, with whom it all began in film culture, put out *Zulu* (1964), directed by Cy Endfield, that a film at all accurate about the Zulu war with the British was made. Prior to that film, Zulus and other "natives" of a similar ilk, appeared as loyal to whites, as fierce savages or exotic natives, as fantasy symbols for sex couched in comedy, and as a haven in which whites could become dominant when on the run from Anglo society.

By the time *The Birth of a Nation* (1915) codified the Afro-American image in films, interest was high in Africa as an alternative to the Old South as a setting for superiority fantasies. As Thomas Cripps has pointed out, early documentaries like *Tauregs in Their Country* (1909) and *Life in Senegal* (1910) fed this interest. Fictional versions quickly followed. Films like *Missionaries in Darkest Africa* (1912) raised the threat of miscegenation; *Voodoo Vengeance* (1913) featured Mau Mau-like savages; *Sultan's Dagger* (ca. 1913) pictured slave hunting in Java; *A Night in the Jungle* (1915) revealed the viciousness of Africa with its watch-leopard, which kills a native, instead of a watch-dog to protect whites from blacks; *The Lad and the Lion* (1916) became the first film based on the works of Edgar Rice Burroughs, author of the Tarzan series which began appearing on film with *Tarzan of the Apes* (1918); Peter P. Jones Film Company's *The Slaver* (1917) presents a white woman being sold by a white slaver to a black chief, but a young black gives his life to save the white woman; Fox's *The Jungle Trail* (1919) used the Tarzan theme of a white man lording it over a black tribe; D.W. Griffith's *The Love Flower* (1920), or *Black Beach*, used "'Blacks' as natives" in the South Seas; and Griffith's *The Idol Dancer* (First National, 1920) used blackface islanders in the South Seas again to suggest a threat to white women. The two people most responsible for these images of blacks were the contemporaries, D.W. Griffith and Edgar Rice Burroughs, both born in 1875; Griffith died in 1948, two years before Burroughs' death. Primarily through their efforts, the image of Africa as the Dark Continent, and of jungle islands as extensions of the Dark Continent, were well-established by the end of the teens.

By the early twenties, in response to Walter White and the NAACP, the Hays Office had issued a "directive to all studios to cease casting the Negro in an unfavorable light."[2] Like earlier NAACP responses to the black image in films, the approach was negative rather than positive. No guidelines followed concerning how to positively present Afro-Americans in films. In essence, blacks often became invisible as "blacks" and appeared instead as a host of mongrelized species. As a successful roll of film needs careful developing to produce a positive image from the negatives, so the production of Afro-American images from negatives to positives required careful developing. Hollywood became adept at developing films, but it failed to develop the content of films in regard to Afro-Americans. Instead, in the twenties a trend was established which paradoxically both inhibited the portrayal of blacks as exotic natives and encouraged it at the same time. The inhibition came from the Hays Office directives which banned black/white miscegenation and darkskinned villains.[3] For instance, in Willis O'Brien's *The Lost World* (First National, 1925), based on a Professor Challenger story by Conan Doyle set in South America, the black member of the white exploring party, led by Wallace Beery, is loyal while the villains are mulattoes. Another Wallace Beery picture, which included a small role for Clarence Muse, was William K. Howard's *Volcano* (Paramount, 1926). In this film, set in Martinique, the miscegenation ban is sidestepped by presenting only the "possibility" that a white woman has some black blood; at the same time, however, the ban was adhered to because the villain was not a full-blooded black but a quadroon.

For black men, then, the result of the ban was that they appeared in negative contexts not as Africans or Afro-Americans but as all manner of substitutes. For black women, the result was that white actresses were established in the role of exotic goddesses who were usually represented as mulattoes. At about the same time as the Hays pronouncements, the Broadway production of *White Cargo* (1923) fostered the popularity of jungle settings for films. The mulatto character, Tondeleyo in *White Cargo*, would be represented in these films by white actresses. Popular films in which white goddesses were set in primitive surroundings included *The Queen of Sheba* (n.d.) with Betty Blyth, *A Daughter of the Gods* (n.d.) with Annette Kellerman, and both *Aloma of the South Seas* (1925), in which Noble Johnson appeared as well, and *The Devil Dancer* (1927) with Gilda Gray. As a result of these films,

> Racial taboos became ironclad because the whites, as surrogates for exotics, simultaneously evaded prohibitions against miscegenation, disarmed racist criticism of interracial roles, and denied the roles to Negroes.[4]

Even British films like *The Jungle Woman* (England, 1926) adopted the Tondeleyo model found in *White Cargo*, a trend that would continue also in American films based on this Broadway play. Anglo-American Gypsy Rhouma played the mulatto Tondeleyo in the 1930 film version of *White Cargo* and, in the more famous remake with Walter Pigeon and Heddy Lamarr, *White Cargo* (MGM, 1942), it was Lamarr who played this mulatto African vamp. In the latter version, Afro-Americans Oscar Polk appeared as Umeela, Leigh Whipper as Jim Fish, and Darby Jones as a houseboy.

Other films of the twenties used the jungles of India rather than Africa, as in *The Tiger's Coat* (1920) and *The Tiger's Claw* (1923). Afro-Americans appeared as exotic natives far from Africa in such films as *South of Suva* (1922) with Benny Ayers. The ambiguity of racial identities was furthered by the use of Haitians rather than Afro-Americans to portray racial antagonisms in films like *Billy and the Big Stick* (n.d.), a throwback to the Teddy Roosevelt world view of speaking softly but carrying a big stick. Noble Johnson appeared in *Cannibal Island* (1924), and other exotic locales in which Johnson was placed include Raoul Welsh's film about a sultan's intrigues, *Lady of the Harem* (1926), John Griffith Way's film using the jungles of Bolivia, *Gateway of the Moon* (Fox, 1926), and Howard Higgins' film of the Far East, *Sal of Singapore* (1928).

In the comedy short, *Mummy Love* (F.B.O., 1926), a villainous but love-struck sheik has a white girl locked in a mummy's tomb until a black porter cheats the guards, also blacks, at craps to free the girl. Similar locales were used in the Lon Chaney films of the twenties. In *The Road to Mandalay* (1926), hundreds of Afro-Americans, including Sam Baker and Clarence Muse in small roles, were used as background to diversify Singapore's population. Other late twenties Lon Chaney films used Afro-Americans as Siamese natives, as in *East Is East* (n.d.), in addition to hundreds of Afro-Americans as African miners at the Kimberly diamond works in *Diamond Handcuffs* (n.d.) and as natives in the jungle scenes for *West of Zanzibar* (1929). Some films used Afro-Americans in stereotypical but uncontroversial roles as Africans. Sam Baker, for instance, was there is Darryl Zanuck's *The Missing Link* (1927), a topical film set in Africa and spurred by the Scopes trial in 1925 concerning the teaching of evolution.

There were exceptions to the strictures set down by the Hays Office concerning black villains and black/white miscegenation. Noble Johnson appeared as an African king in Paramount's *Drums of Fate* (1923), for instance, in which a white man is captured by the obvious villains, black natives. In a film starring Noal Beery, *Passion Song* (1928), it fell to Afro-American Edgar "Blue" Washington to go further and, as Ulamba, kill a South African Boer. Miscegenation appears in the jungle film, *The Lion's Mate* (1924), in the same era. Other films tried to circumvent the Hays Office by producing quasi-documentaries about Africa, such as *Untamed Africa* (n.d.), or films posing as real representations of Africa, such as Columbia's *Africa Speaks* (1930), which may also have been titled *When Africa Speaks*. But like the others, these films relied on stock stereotypes of blacks as non-survivors in their own jungles. In typical films like *Baboona* (n.d.), *Congorilla* (n.d.), and *Jango* (1930), blacks are no more than African savages in jungle settings.

As with *She* (England, 1925), many films of the twenties spliced in footage of Africa to produce, as Thomas Cripps points out,

> poorly edited glimpses of animals interrupted by bits of pygmies and staged dances: *Gorilla Hunt* (1926), *Through Darkest Africa: In Search of the White Rhinoceros* (1927), *Simba* (1927), and *The Bushman* (1927) . . . . The era closed with the preposterous fake, *Ingagi* [1930], a legendary gorilla who allegedly kidnapped a white woman.[5]

If one era of jungle films had closed, another would soon begin, for *Trader Horn* (1931), *Tarzan the Ape Man* (1932), and *King Kong* (1933) were still to come and, a generation later, *Simba* (1955) was revived in the format of a British semi-documentary about Mau Maus which included the black actors Orlando Martins, Ben Johnson, and Joseph Tomelty.

The twenties had bred numerous offsprings from the dark fantasies of Africa despite the landmarks in film realism produced by Robert J. Flaherty. His humane anthropological films, primarily *Nanook of the North* (1922), about Eskimo culture, and *Moana* (1926), about Samoan culture, contributed to the interest in foreign peoples and thus to foreign settings for films. Rather than his realism, which would have tempered the worst aspects of the developing black stereotypes, filmmakers instead turned to exotic fantasies more in line with the Broadway play *White Cargo*. Flaherty himself moved in this direction when he and F.W. Murnau did *Tabu* (1930), shot in Tahiti and Bora Bora, which focused on lovers breaking taboos.

By then, however, Hollywood had already begun its own Flaherty tradition with Paramount's *Chang* (1927), shot in Laos by Merian C. Cooper and Ernest B. Schoedsack. These two men then went to the Sudan and, along with Lothar Mendes, produced a British film titled *Four Feathers* (England, 1929). In addition to the filming in the Sudan, there were scenes with hundreds of Afro-Americans standing in as natives which were done in Hollywood rather than in an English studio. The Afro-Americans Noble Johnson and Zack Williams were among the aggressive "Fuzzy Wuzzies" against whom the British were shouldering the "White Man's Burden." The British remake, Zolton Korda's *Four Feathers* (England, 1939), was somewhat better than the original, for both the negative image of blacks and the theme of white superiority were somewhat tempered by the beginnings of World War Two. Korda's version of the film was popular enough to warrant yet another remake, again filmed in the Sudan by Zoltan Korda, titled *Storm over the Nile* (England, 1956).

After *Chang* and their original version of *Four Feathers*, which provided the experience from which they developed their ideas for later films, Merian C. Cooper and Ernest B. Schoedsack went to RKO to do *The Most Dangerous Game* (1932), also titled *The Hounds of Zaroff*. Schoedsack and Irving Pichel directed and Cooper and David Selznick produced this film based on Richard Connell's suspenseful story of a diabolical great white hunter, played by Joel McCrea, who tracks down human visitors to his jungle island. Fay Wray was in it, Afro-American Leslie Banks had a part, and Noble Johnson served as the Tartar attendant and bodyguard. The same studio set and many of the same people then appeared in and worked on RKO's *King Kong* (1933) and *Son of Kong* (1933).

Cooper and Schoedsack produced and Cooper and Edgar Wallace did the story for the Fay Wray as white goddess version of *King Kong* (RKO, 1933). This "beauty and the beast" film was an obvious parallel to the Afro-American experience. Like the African slaves, Kong is brought in bondage by ship to America. His hugeness and blackness tittered the imagination when he was coupled with frail white Fay Wray. Rex Ingram was depicted as a crew member on the voyage to Kong's island and Noble Johnson ruled as the black chief of the superstitious primitives who spent much of their time, as they were to do in the late seventies remake of *King Kong*, dancing and dabbling in the black arts. Fay Wray was absent from Schoedsack's sequel, *Son of Kong* (RKO, 1933), but Noble Johnson appeared again. Usurping the role of blacks in most jungle films, it is Kong's son who leads the white intruders to a treasure and rescues the white hero from an earthquake. Continuing his work in this vein, Cooper produced RKO's *She* (1935), directed by Irving Pichel and Lansing G. Holden. Randolph Scott and Helen Gahagan starred in this remake of the British version of *She* (1925) with adventuresome whites searching for a lost kingdom in Africa ruled by She. Noble Johnson was again present in the 1935 version, this time as the Amahaggar chief.

The threat of miscegenation between black and white which *King Kong* had altered to mean miscegenation between big black ape and tiny white woman, was an exaggerated version of the motif found in *Tarzan of the Apes* (1918) when Tarzan fights the black kidnapper of Jane (which in the book version by Burroughs was a huge ape), and in Congo Picture Company's *Ingagi* (1930), filmed in California. The gorilla (read "black man") involved with a white woman in *Ingagi* is Ingagi of the Congo, who is given sacrifices by the natives to inhibit further kidnappings of women. The suggestions of sex between a white woman and a gorilla were exploited in *Ingagi* as they were in Burroughs' adventure stories and in *King Kong*. In fact, even the latest Tarzan film, *Tarzan the Ape Man* (1981), with Michael O'Keeffe and Bo Derek, includes scenes, particularly in the romp at the end of the film, in which there is the suggestion of sexual foreplay between Jane (Bo) and an orangutang.

A take-off on *Ingagi* was Richard C. Kohn's *Son of Ingagi* (1940), an all-black adventure story by Harly Wood Productions and Sack Amusement Enterprises. Afro-American Spencer Williams did the screenplay and appeared in the film as a detective. Jungle films with all-black casts were somewhat of a novelty. The year prior to *Son of Ingagi* Goldberg Productions' *The Devil Daughter* (1939), with Nina Mae McKinney, Jack Carter, Ida James, and Hamtree Harrington, used a voodoo theme in a Jamaican plantation setting. In the same era, Toddy Pictures made *Voodoo Devil Drums* (n.d.) with a standard storyline based on black magic and the raising of zombies. Earlier, in the transitional years between silents and soundies, Oscar Micheaux had produced the all-black *Daughter of the Congo* (1930), a silent film to which some sound and music was later added. The story in Micheaux's film revolved around a valiant cavalier saving a mulatto from Arab slave traders and included among the cast members Kathleen Noisette, Lorenzo Tucker, Clarence Reed, and Percy Verwayen. Micheaux in 1930 was trying to do for Afro-American audiences what films like *White Shadows in the South Seas* had done for Anglo-American audiences two years before.

In *White Shadows in the South Seas* (1928), MGM's first sound film, W.S. Van Dyke attempted to return to the Flaherty tradition by shooting a film about the exploitation of South Sea islanders in the Marquesas Islands. Van Dyke and MGM went on to do the two big jungle film hits of the new sound era, *Trader Horn* (1931) and *Tarzan the Ape Man* (1932). With footage from East Africa, the Sudan, and the Congo--parts of which were later used in the Tarzan film--*Trader Horn* was Hollywood's best effort at using an African jungle as well as a studio lot for the setting. Rex Ingram had a role and the African actor, Mutia Omooloo, came off well as the gun-bearer for the white hunter, Trader Horn (Harry Carey). Despite the elaborate efforts, the depiction of Africa was not accurate. *Trader Horn* contributed to the misleading image of black Africans as primitive savages exuding an aura of mystery which was then exploited in Johnny Weissmuller version of *Tarzan the Ape Man* and lesser jungle films. The Rod Taylor and Anne Heywood remake of *Trader Horn* (n.d.) added nothing to the posture of black Africans and it was unsuccessful at the box office.

Trader Horn and *Tarzan the Ape Man* were the spearheads for the thirties' jungle films of much worse quality. Black natives in the Congo were used in a poor attempt to copy these two films in William Cowan's *Kongo* (1932), also for MGM, and Paramount created a Tarzan derivative, *King of the Jungle* (1933), whose only attribute was that Afro-American Sam Baker appeared in it as the native, Gwana, and Olympic swimming standout Buster Crabbe showed some of the style that made him a champion. Buster Crabbe, "king of the jungle," had the same year portrayed Tarzan, the "lord of the jungle," in *Tarzan the Fearless* (1933). Other Afro-Americans or foreign blacks who, like Sam Baker, frequently appeared in jungle films also played in the Tarzan series. Among the many through the years are the following: Bessie Tomer as Esmeralds (an exception, actually, for this is her only known film role), and possibly Rex Ingram as a native in *Tarzan of the Apes* (1918); Nathan Curry as a native in *Tarzan and His Mate* (1934); Dorothy Dandridge as an exotic jungle girl in *Tarzan's Perils* (1951); Orlando Martins as Chief Ogonooro in *Tarzan and the Lost Safari* (1957); Woody Strode as Knan/Tarim and Earl Cameron as Mang in *Tarzan's Three Challenges* (1963); Rafer Johnson as Barcuna in *Tarzan and the Great River* (1967); Rafer Johnson as Nagambi and Edward Johnson as Bhara in *Tarzan and the Jungle Boy* (1968); and Kenny Washington appeared along with Woody Strode as Marstak and Robert DoQui as Metusa in *Tarzan's Deadly Silence* (1970).

The Tarzan films spawned many imitators. Afro-Americans Darby Jones and Theron Jackson played the natives Keega and Bayla in *Zamba* (Eagle-Lion, 1949), a film about a young boy forced to parachute from an airplane over Africa (essentially the storyline of *Tarzan Finds a Son*), who is taken under the paw of a gorilla named Zamba (essentially the storyline of the original Tarzan film). In her early days in films, Shirley Temple too was involved in a take-off on Tarzan, the comedy short titled *Kid 'n' Africa* (1933), which took up major themes used in the jungle genre of films:

> Shirley Temple on a child-sized African missionary safari is captured by "mini-cannibals" (real black children). She is rescued from the cooking pot by a junior Tarzan (Diaperzan) and his friendly elephant.[6]

The comedy tradition using Africa as the setting continued in thirties' films like *Laughing with Medbury in Ethiopia* (n.d.). Frank Buck made *Darkest Africa* (1933) and Wheeler and Woolsey made both *So This Is Africa* (1933) and *Africa Speaks English* (1933), the latter featuring the ventriloquist Edgar Bergen.

There was little difference in the jungle films of the thirties from those of the twenties except that sound had been added to films and miscegenation creeped back into films. In Tay Garnett's *Prestige* (RKO, 1932), set in the jungles of French Indochina, Clarence Muse as Nahum served loyally a French Legionnaire fighting for the colonizers. Muse also appeared as the native

Malango in *Fury of the Jungle* (1934). Mulattoes played by Afro-Americans resurfaced in films like *Drums in the Night* (1933), with Fredi Washington as a mean mulatto islander, and Fredi Washington again as a mulatto in Paramount's *Drums of the Jungle* (1935), which was also titled *Ouanga*. Miscegenation in the jungle then reappeared in Paramount's *Jungle Princess* (1936) and Paramount's *Her Jungle Love* (1938). Love on a safari filmed in Hollywood was the topic of *White Hunter* (Twentieth Century-Fox, 1936), with Ernest Whitman as Ahdi and Ralph Cooper as Ali. Other familiar themes were present, too, like Africans intermixed with the Indians of Brazil being inferior to the pure Portuguese race in *Glimpses of Northern Brazil* (1937). Henry King's *Stanley and Livingston* (Twentieth Century-Fox, 1939) cast Spencer Tracy as Stanley in search of Livingston on the Dark Continent populated by many Afro-American stand-ins for Africans.

Familiar to audiences through both independently produced all-black films and through Hollywood films, Noble Johnson had been cast in bit roles as an exotic of various hues in numerous jungle films beginning in the twenties. In the thirties, he appeared in many more, some of which have already been mentioned and some of which will be mentioned further along. But among those in the first half of the decade in which Johnson appeared are *Kismet* (First National, 1930), an early sound feature set in the orient and based on the fear of a white man's daughter being placed in a harem. After this small role, Johnson was featured in George Melford's film, set in the jungles of Borneo, *East of Borneo* (Universal, 1932). As Ram Singh, fighting in Bengal province in Northeast India, Johnson appeared with Gary Cooper in Henry Hathaway's *The Lives of a Bengal Lancer* (1935). In *Escape from Devil's Island* (Columbia, 1935), Noble Johnson as Bisco and Daniel Haynes as Dkikki are the exotics escaping from the Devil's Island prison fortress. One of the films of this era in which Johnson appeared had a plot typical of American-made jungle films. Johnson is the head boatman and Everett Brown is Noger in Ernest Frank's *Nagana* (Universal, 1933), a film in which a white woman is saved from a native African sacrifice. Africa is presented as an unhealthy place to live, for the plot forms around the sleeping sickness carried by the tsetse fly. Ironically, the white scientist summoned to cure the epidemic is played by Anglo-American Mylvyn Douglas while Afro-American Dr. Billie McClain plays the native king. In another black-as-guide role,

Johnson as Queochie led Anglo-American Nigel Bruce through the swamps of Trinidad in the detective film, *Murder in Trinidad* (Fox, 1934).

Afro-Americans like Noble Johnson and Rex Ingram played in similar projections of the exotic based on the Arabian Nights tales of the Orient. Johnson, for instance, was the Indian prince, and Afro-American Sam Baker appeared as well, in Raoul Welsh's *The Thief of Bagdad* (United Artists, 1924), a satirical and entertaining silent film, starring Douglas Fairbanks, which included a stock of black eunuchs. The British made the next version, Alexander Korda's *The Thief of Bagdad* (England, 1940), with roles for Afro-Americans Adelaide Hall and Rex Ingram. In this fantasy, Ingram as the reprieved genie, Djinni, cries "Free! I'm free at last!" In the remake of Korda's *The Thief of Bagdad*, Alfred Green's *A Thousand and One Nights* (Columbia, 1948), Ingram appears again but this time as the giant rather than the genie. Ingram continued to appear in such exotic fantasies as well as jungle films at least into the fifties when he played Gorman in *Congo Crossing* (1956) and Umbopa in a remake of *King Solomon's Mines* (1937), Kurt Newmann's *Watusi* (MGM, 1959).

The motifs of voodoo and zombies had been present in early films, as when a black woman uses voodoo for the benefit of whites in *The Voice of Conscience* (Metro, 1917). Clarence Muse appeared in two such films in the early thirties, the first being Victor Halperin's *White Zombie* (United Artists, 1932), a Bela Lagosi horror film in which the dead are put to work as field hands in Haiti. The West Indies was again the setting for voodoo in a plot by blacks to kill the white islanders in Columbia's *Black Moon* (1934); Fay Wray, riding a wave of popularity after *King Kong* (1933), starred while Clarence Muse and Madame Sul-te-Wan were present to emphasize the contrast between blacks and whites, evil and good.

Historically, the legends about zombies had originated in West Africa and it was in the West Indies, a way station for slave ships voyaging to America, that voodoo developed its greatest following. The motifs were revived for yet another cycle of these films in the early forties to keep alive the African flavor in films and to emphasize the primitiveness of people who believe in black magic and witchcraft. Noble Johnson was involved with zombies and voodoo in the Bob Hope and Paulette Goddard comedy set in Cuba, George

Marshall's *The Ghost Breakers* (Paramount, 1940). Willie Best was in typical coon form as Hope's valet. You are "a blackout in a blackout," Hope tells Best as they look for buried treasure and wander through a haunted castle. In H.C. Potter's *Congo Maisie* (MGM, 1940), it is Maisie's magic that keeps order among the natives of the Congo in a film that includes Afro-Americans Ernest Whitman as Varnoi, Martin Wilkins as Zia, and Nathan Curry as Laemba. The same emphasis is present when an African expedition, with Clarence Muse as the native, Bino, searches for a skull with which to subdue the superstitious natives in Harold Schuster's *Zanzibar* (Universal, 1940).

The superstitiousness of blacks and their use of witchcraft was the primary message of other zombie movies of the early forties. This cycle of films was not confined to Hollywood productions, however, as indicated by the previously noted film with an all-black cast, Toddy Pictures' *Voodoo Devil Drums* (n.d.). Afro-American Leigh Whipper appeared in *King of the Zombies* (Monogram, 1941), a film which co-starred Afro-American Mantan Moreland and Anglo-American Dick Purcell. Moreland and Purcell appeared together again in both *Revenge of the Zombies* (Monogram, 1943) and *The Phantom Killer* (1943). These films, degenerate representations of blacks to begin with, further degenerated in *I Walked with a Zombie* (RKO, 1943), which included the song and dance routines of Afro-Americans Teresa Harris and Jeni LeGon as well as black zombies, probably played by Darby Jones and Sir Lancelot.

The fine but often under-utilized Afro-American actor Ernest Whitman appeared in many of the jungle genre films. As King Malaba, Whitman was in Universal's *Drums of the Congo* (1942), another film flavored with the African motif, this time with secret agents added; Afro-Americans Jules Bledsoe played Kalu, Jesse Lee Brooks played Chief Majeduka, and Dorothy Dandridge played Malimi. The light-skinned Dandridge also had a bit part as an islander, Thalia, as did Leigh Whipper as Morales, in Edward H. Briffith's *Bahama Passage* (Paramount, 1942). Dandridge appeared again in exotic settings in films like *Jungle Queen* (1946) and *Tarzan's Peril* (1951). Like Josephine Baker in the thirties, Dandridge fled overseas in an attempt to find better film roles. But in the British film, *Tamango* (England, 1959), she was still playing the exotic islander. As the character Aicher she is involved in an interracial love affair on a slave ship. The miscegenation theme, even in the late fifties, kept American distributors away except for Hal Roach.

Africa as the locale for comedy remained popular in such films as the Hope, Crosby, and Lamour comedy, Victor Schertzinger's *Road to Zanzibar* (1945) and the Abbott and Costello comedy with its choir of comic coons, Huntington Hartford's *Africa Screams* (1949). Among the nonsensical representations of Africa which America's film culture created, there were a few bright spots both from Hollywood and independents in America, and from foreign filmmakers. Universal's *Dark Rapture* (1937) was a competent film about Africa, though its authenticity remains questionable because of the focus on such stereotypes as ritualistic African dances little different from those found in more grotesque fashion in jungle films. Jean Cocteau and Francois Villiers recorded the cultural arts of French Equatorial Africa (Chad) in *L'Amitie Noire* (France, 1944) and, later, a short documentary on Chad called *Rhythm of Africa* (1947) featured Afro-American Kenneth Spencer and included a screenplay written by Afro-American Langston Hughes. Andre Haguet's *Il Est Minuit, Docteur Schweitzer* (France, 1952), dramatized the experiences of Dr. Albert Schweitzer in Gabon. These films were exceptions, though, and not intended for the same large audiences that viewed the typical jungle-film version of Africa. For some conscientious Afro-Americans, the alternative to appearing in the typical American films was to go overseas. In the thirties, Josephine Baker went to France and Paul Robeson went to England.

The French jungle film tradition developed similarly to the American. The French, however, rarely reached the extremes of racism commonly found in American films and, indeed, blacks are found in nearly any role, within the realms of probability, that whites could be found in. The French films appealed to same desire to exoticism Americans demanded, but often with more eroticism than Americans allowed. As with the work of the American Robert J. Flaherty in the twenties, French filmmakers started with a documentary format that quickly spawned fictional films. Marc Allegret and Andre Gide, for instance, produced a film about courtship in Africa titled *Voyage au Congo* (1927), or *The Courting of Djinta*. The documentary content was present also in Leon Poirier's late-twenties film, *L'homme du Niger* (n.d.), and in Poirier's *Caïn* (1932). In *Caïn*, the fictional content took precedence over the documentary, for the Robinson Crusoe story is given a twist that would have been impossible in America: "miscegenation" takes place between the white castaway Cäin and the black islander Zou Zou, played by black actress Rama-Take, in what is supposed to be Madagascar. A similar fictional derivative of the French documentary tradition appeared in Pathé's *Croix du Sud* (1932), filmed in Africa with a typical French story--so contradictory to American fantasies--in which a black man rejects a white woman in favor of a black woman. The fictional treatments of exotic settings was thus in full swing in French films by the time Afro-American Josephine Baker appeared in them.

Baker, who became famous as a singer and dancer in Paris prior to appearing in foreign films, was cast as an exotic native in the French films *Zou Zou* (1935); *The Siren of the Tropics* (1937), titled in French as *La Sirene des Tropiques*; and *Princess Tam Tam* (1938). None of the films was praiseworthy, although the last two were more widely distributed in the United States than any of the earlier French films, including the documentaries and semi-documentaries. Typical of Baker's roles and the plots of these films was *The Siren of the Tropics* in which she plays the native mulatoo, Papitou, who is in love with a white Frenchman. The belief, fostered by the migration of artists to Europe in the twenties, that resorting to foreign films would allow better roles for Afro-Americans was, in essence, a myth.

Paul Robeson was also an on-again off-again expatriate during the thirties--between such American-made films as *The Emperor Jones* (1933), *Show Boat* (1936), and *Tales of Manhattan* (1943)--who turned to the British rather than the French for a better airing of racial issues. His first foreign film was *Borderline* (Switzerland, 1930), discussed earlier, which was a fine art film made in conjunction with British producers in Switzerland. But his better known British films properly belong in the jungle genre of films despite his efforts to have them appear otherwise.

Robeson's second foreign film was Zoltan Korda's *Sanders of the River* (England, 1935), drawn from an Edgar Wallace story. Sanders is a Tarzanian ruler of his African domain and the film makes British colonialism look prim and proper. There were strong performances by Robeson as Bosambo the chief and Nina Mae McKinney as his wife, Lilongo, but, while Robeson does appear majestic with blacks, the film presents him as subservient to whites. In *Jericho* (England, 1937), also titled *Dark Sands*, Robeson plays an American deserter on the run from France after being convicted of a crime he did not commit. Robeson's wife, Eslanda Goode Robeson, appeared in this film along with the actor, Orlando Martins, and the African actress Princess Kouka. In this film, Robeson becomes chief of a Tuareg tribe in the Sahara before being caught up with. The storyline differs little from those films in which it is a white self-exile who first seeks refuge, and then becomes ruler of an African tribe.

In *Song of Freedom* (England, 1937), Robeson plays Zinga, an expatriate African who attempts to return to his ancestral people after learning of their needs. Elizabeth Welch, Orlando Martins, and Robert Adams appeared too in *Song of Freedom*. Welch, Martins, and Adams were black actors whose roles were almost entirely in British films. Indeed, both of Welch's other films were British, *Big Fella* (England, 1938), also with Paul Robeson, and *Dead of Night* (England, 1945). Martins appeared in some American films, but his career was primarily in British films like *Java Head* (England, 1935), *Murder in Soho* (England, 1939), and *The End of the River* (England, 1947). Similarly, the Guyanese Adams appeared mostly in British films like *Midshipman Easy* (England, 1935), in which he was the cabin boy who saved the life of Midshipman Easy, and *It Happened One Sunday* (England, 1945).

The popular overseas' film in which Robeson appeared was based on one of the jungle stories of H. Rider Haggard's epic cannon on Africa, *King Solomon's Mines* (England, 1937). Robert Adams is Twala and Makubalo Hlubi is Kapsie in this restatement of the thesis that Africa is the Dark Continent. Robeson is Umbopa, the Mashona chief who leads the whites to the elusive mines. As in his other films, Robeson's performance is dignified and it effuses the strong presence always felt in his films. But these films on the whole were no better than the American jungle films and, unfortunately, Robeson was always portrayed as being in the service of the whites. That he sings with his powerful voice in these films does nothing to counter the feeling that his is an unfulfilled heroism that no film of the era, American or British, could have brought out.

Nor was the British tradition of jungle films on the whole any better than the American. In addition to the films already discussed, *Palavar: A Romance of Northern Nigeria* (England, 1926), filmed in Nigeria during the era when documentary content was the fashion, portrays whites as superior to the Nigerians; the jungle film, *Black Waters* (England, 1929), included Noble Johnson as a native in what was probably his first sound film; *Tiger Bay* (England, 1933), with Orlando Martins, used Lascars as the backdrop for adventure; *Timbuctoo* (England, 1934), presented a white woman who goes to Africa "to marry a black man to spite her Uncle George";[7] *Old Bones of the River* (England, 1939), burlesqued *Sanders of the River* (England, 1937) and British colonialism with Robert Adams as Bosambo; and Robert Adams in George Pearson's *An African in London* (England, 1943) and Two Cities' *Man of Two Worlds* (England, 1946). In his better roles, as in these last two films, Adams showed that he was a fine actor. In *Man of Two Worlds*, Adams is the hero, Kisenga, a musician who returns to Tanganyika where he and the witch doctor, played by Orlando Martins, fight for control of the tribe. Because of the assertive black presence, *Man of Two Worlds* was banned in the United States until 1952 when it was released under various titles such as *Witch Doctor* and *Kisenga, Man of Africa*.

Other British films capitalized on Africa in ways similar to the early fifties American films, *The African Queen* (1952) and *Mogambo* (1953). Harry Watt's *Ivory Hunters* (England, 1952) and its sequel, *West of Zanzibar* (England, 1955), both featured white actor Anthony Steel in stories about the creation and protection of the Kenyan game preserves. Orland Martins, Jafeth Ananda, and Johanna Kitou appeared as Kenyans in *Ivory Hunters*, and Martins, Edric Connor, Peter Illing, and Juma appeared in *West of Zanzibar*, a film which included footage from Mombasa, Kenya, and from Zanzibar.

In America, the jungle films of the fifties began with Compton Bennett and Andrew Marton's version of *King Solomon's Mines* (MGM, 1950), a vehicle for Stewart Granger and Deborah Kerr which gave roles to the African actors Kimursi and Siriaque. Henry King's *The Snows of Kilimanjaro* (Twentieth Century-Fox, 1952) was made from the works of a real great white hunter, Ernest Hemingway. Starring Gregory Peck and Susan Hayward in a look at the thoughts of a white hunter near death, the film also had roles for Afro-Americans Paul Thompson, Everett Smith, and the jazz musician Benny Carter.

John Huston's *The African Queen* (United Artists, 1952), attempted to return to where *Trader Horn* (1931) left off by using Africa, East Africa in this case, as background. Filmed in Zaire, *The African Queen* used many blacks as scenery for the Bogart/Heburn conflict based on C.S. Forrester's novel and James Agee's script. The answer to *The African Queen* by MGM was John Ford's *Mogambo* (1953) with Clark Gable, Ava Gardner, and Grace Kelly. A remake of *Red Dust* (1932) set in Kenya, *Mogambo* was not much more than another Dark Continent safari with blacks as bearers. The Mau Mau uprisings in the fifties accounted in large part for the Kenya settings in jungle films of the era. Another film set in Kenya was Edward H. Griffith's *Safari* (1956), a new version of Griffith's earlier filming of *Safari* (Paramount, 1940). The earlier version used an African safari as the vehicle for a love story, and the Afro-Americans Clinton Rosemond and Ben Carter had roles in it. In the 1956 version, Afro-Americans Earl Cameron and Cy Grant appeared along with Kenyans Lionel Ngakane and Juma. In the latter, it was Victor Mature in a typical western plot transferred to Kenya: Indians (Mau Maus) kill his family and he seeks revenge.

With *Bwana Devil* (United Artists, 1953), Hollywood turned to "3-D" for a more vivid look at Africa. Black actors Kalu K. Sankur and Miles Clark, Jr., appeared in this film about African lions disrupting the work of railroad builders. Other films also returned to location shooting, like Henry Hathaway's *White Witch Doctor* (Twentieth Century-Fox, 1953), which was filmed in the Congo. The storyline was familiar with its white missionaries and white hunters, but many black actors had parts, including Joseph C. Narcisse and Elzie Emanuel, Mashood Ajala as Jacques the gun-bearer, Everett Brown as the Babuka king, and Otis Green as the Babuka boy. More in the old mode of African jungle films was Andre de Toth's *Tanganyika* (1954). Filmed in the Universal-International studios, this picture used a plethora of black natives but only one was listed in the credits, Joe Comadore as Andolo. The irony that the jungle films epitomized was still present the year the NAACP won the *Brown versus Topeka Board of Education* case: blacks were visible in American culture and in American film culture, but invisible in these cultures when it came to acknowledging or crediting them.

The most obvious lesson of the jungle films is that they projected domestic American attitudes toward Afro-Americans onto what, it was assumed, were equally primitive peoples in the colonies of Africa and dozens of other lesser developed areas of the globe. The prevailing attitude found in jungle films is not that these people were oppressed or inhibited from developing their own cultures, but that they, like Afro-Americans, were simply in their place. Africans like Mutia Omooloo, who played in *Trader Horn* (1931), were shocked when visiting America at the treatment they received because of the color of their skin. Implicit in the jungle films is the "Why don't they go back where they came from" idea expressed in anger so much more frequently when it comes to blacks than whites who are dissatisfied with their lot in America. Africa and its surrogates in films are where colored people come from, where they belong, and where they should return to. Marcus Garvey and the Ku Klux Klan had jungle films as allies in support of their programs.

That Garvey and the Klan supported such ideas speaks for itself, but the fact that these jungle films spread their propaganda for them through the most influential communications medium of the era does not speak for itself. Something more was involved. One difference was that Garvey and the Klan were jingoistic while the jungle films were chauvinistic. Rather than sudden heated feelings flaring into rhetoric or momentary violence, the jungle films were a sustained expression of ingrained attitudes and, as such, they show just how accepting Americans have been of reactionary concepts, emanating from the nineteenth century, that most Americans would deny they believe in. Few Americans would have stated that they went to see these films for their exploitations of racism and sexism. Filmviewers went, after all, for entertainment. What is most damning about that attitude is the ease with which the racism and sexism was accepted without question by most filmviewers.

For the fact remains that the jungle film genre has been a disastrous reflection of America's attitudes toward colored people, whether Americans or foreigners. They have served as a form of self-flattery, a tolerated, even enouraged, form of publicity for attitudes that should never have been possible on such a wide scale in a country that lays claim to the platitudes that America is the land of the free, home of the brave, and so on. And so on. Opponents in America's wars--Germans, Japanese, Italians--have never been subjected to such a sustained derogatory portrayal of their character or culture as has been the lot of fellow Americans with black skins who helped fight these foreigners when America thought it necessary.

The black/white relationship in the jungle films rarely approached the better portrayals of the Jim and Huck relationship; they were always on par with or below the standards of the Friday and Crusoe relationship. Nearly always it was the black/white equals evil/good form of symbolism through which the blatant racism was presented. There were good and evil whites in the jungle films, to be sure, but rarely a really good black unless he or she was a "Tonto" figure or an above-average black who had seen the light and abdicated in favor of the great white way. Africa was at one time a land of promise, an exotic continent about which any fantasy was possible. The fantasies that were developed did not approach the implied potential of the original promise; they fell far short, indeed, with stock images of slave trading, romantic but danger-filled safaries, white goddesses, missionary gods, great white hunters or guardians, menacing or superstitious natives, and white magic to counteract black magic. Left out of these films were the motivations behind the actions of black people and such images, squaring more with reality, as Zulus as prosperous people, Mau Maus as justly reclaiming self-rule for Kenya, or the Congolese as building universities and developing their country. Instead, the image was of whites surviving the meeting of blacks in the most primitive areas on earth. For American audiences, this form of entertainment brought the thrill of conquest and the tingle of suspense: Will the white man prevail against the dark forces of Africa? The black presence, like that of the Indian in most westerns, was simply as an obstacle to be reformed or, failing that, to be rolled over with the might that made it right. There were few meaningful human-to-human relationships, for it was the fantasized *machismo* of Anglo-American males at its worst.

Sadly, the writer who looks back in twenty years with a well-deserved full-length critical study of these films will find that the same attitudes toward Africa and the same images of blacks remain powerful in the film culture of the eighties, for two of its most popular films rely almost exclusively on them: *Raiders of the Lost Ark* (1981) and *Tarzan the Ape Man* (1981).

Notes

[1] Phyllis Rauch Klotman, *Frame by Frame: A Black Filmography* (Bloomington: Indiana Univ. Press, 1979), p. 420.

[2] William Thomas Smith, "Hollywood Report," in *Black Films and Film-Makers: A Comprehensive Anthology from Stereotype to Superhero*, ed. by Lindsay Patterson (New York: Dodd and Mead, 1975), p. 137.

[3] Thomas Cripps, *Slow Fade to Black: The Negro in American Films, 1900-1942* (New York: Oxford Univ. Press, 1977), p. 127. For a more detailed yet fascinating discussion of these developments and many of the films cited here, see particularly Cripps' chapter on "The Silent Hollywood Negro."

[4] Cripps, p. 153.

[5] Cripps, p. 133.

[6] Klotman, p. 284.

[7] Klotman, p. 534.

Chapter Nine

The Tarzan Formula for Racial Stereotyping

A modern reincarnation of the archetypal superman is Tarzan of the Apes. The domain of this particular super-Anglo is the Dark Continent (a popular term when Edgar Rice Burroughs' Tarzan tales were most popular), an outstanding locale for presentation of the extremes of white superiority and black inferiority, of the "white ape myth" and the "black ape myth." Starting with the popular silent film, *Tarzan of the Apes* (1918), Tarzan has been represented as the fictional overseer of the world's largest plantation. His appeal has been "to a self-satisfied racial cockiness rather than hyperaggressive racism," states Thomas Cripps,[1] and, in this role, Tarzan has shouldered the "white man's burden."

Racial myths were reinforced and recreated in the silent film version of *Tarzan of the Apes*. Of the many derogatory images of blacks in this film, the two which exemplify the worst extremes of the black peril are the male black brute and the female black coon. The black brute is a burly African male who is not just any African, but a chief, decked out in necklace, plumed headpiece, and painted face. He is first seen mischievously poking innocent chicks in a nest. Before long his mischievousness turns to maliciousness as his arrow kills Kala the Ape, Tarzan's foster mother. This savagery catered to preconditioned audience attitudes toward blacks and the "black ape myth," and the incident created a foil for Tarzan to bring into play the "white ape myth." Tarzan and his foster mother are innocents wantonly harmed by a savage. There must be vengeance, a horrible exemplary vengeance in this case in the form of death by strangulation. Thus the African character is associated with malignant aggression. Purposeless destructiveness is stereotypically perpetuated by a dark-skinned native of the Dark Continent. As the forces of the wilderness are turned against such evils by the western hero in cowboy movies, so the forces of the wilderness are channeled through the singular justice of a superior white man-ape, Tarzan.

In the transformation to film of the book by Edgar Rice Burroughs, *Tarzan of the Apes* (1912 serial/ 1914 book), a subtle and revealing shift takes place in the characterization of Jane's kidnapper. In the book, the kidnapper is Terkoz, successor to Tarzan as leader of the ape tribe. Terkoz is an inept leader who is ostracized by the tribe before long. Still raging, he is described as a "horrible, man-like beast" who confronts Jane: "she saw the awful face and the snarling, hideous mouth thrust within a foot of her."[2] Instead of killing Jane, Terkoz decides to keep this "hairless white ape" for his mate.

The filmic translation of this scene replaces the ape with a huge, black, bald-headed, paint-faced, diabolically grinning African buck who kidnaps Jane. Like Terkoz in the book--and like the chief who murders Kala--this black "beast" is destroyed by Tarzan (Elmo Lincoln in this film). To have an ape kidnap Jane in the reader's imagination is one thing, but on the screen the emotional encounter is far more volatile when it is a black man, or "black ape," carrying off the white and virtuous Jane. To have a black man kidnap a white woman for a mate raises the specter of miscegenation for American audiences. Not even the ape Terkoz makes the impression on the minds of Anglo-Americans that is made in having a giant black man kidnap a dainty white woman. Audiences caught the intent, for miscegenation has always been a critical problem in American race relations. If there is no mixing of bloodlines--if the black African or Afro-American remains a "pure" Negro--there is less likelihood of problems arising, particularly, racists point out, when it is the mulattoes like Frederick Douglass, Booker T. Washington, and W.E.B. DuBois who become the leaders of the Afro-American community.

Such portrayals as Jane's capture by the African native fed racial antagonisms. By 1919, the year of the worst outbreak of racial rioting in American history prior to the mid-sixties, *Tarzan of the Apes* had become one of the six biggest money-making films. Many of these riots were produced by the dislocation coming about through the influx from South to North of both Afro-Americans and Anglo-Americans with prejudices already firmly embedded. For the Anglo-Americans, these prejudices were abetted by Jim

Crowism and included a proclivity toward the resurgent Ku Klux Klan; both Jim Crow and the Klan existed in the North as well as the South, particularly in the urban centers. In Indianapolis in the twenties, Klan fever was rampant; it was there that the One Hundred Per Cent Americans made a record on which was the song, "Daddy Swiped Our Last Clean Sheet and Joined the Ku Klux Klan."[3]

The racial overtones of *Tarzan of the Apes* are similar to those in D.W. Griffith's *The Birth of a Nation* (1915) in which the apishness of Gus is considerably de-emphasized from Thomas Dixon's "gleaming apelike" creation in *The Clansman: An Historical Romance of the Ku Klux Klan* (1905); in the film, *The Birth of a Nation*, Gus' blackness and dementedness are emphasized instead. The rebirth of the Ku Klux Klan and the appearance of major popular films like *The Birth of a Nation* and *Tarzan of the Apes* are evidence of the psychological appeal of the values projected by the Ku Klux Klan and Tarzan of the Apes. This was especially so for the joiners and superpatriots among Anglo-Americans in the era beginning just before World War One. Racist values in the twenties went far beyond the Klan. The reason the Klan was frequently singled out for attack was not because of its values, but because of the ruthless methods of violent coercion it used in imposing these values on Afro-Americans. The portrayal of violence between whites and blacks in Tarzan films helped reinforce propensities toward hostility in American culture such as the Klan represented. The period of the Klan's greatest political impact, when it organized as a political party and elected many officials across America, came between 1921 and 1926. Ironically, this is the period in the twenties when no new Tarzan films were made, though five silent Tarzan films were made between 1918 and 1921, and three more silents were made between 1926 and 1932.

The Birth of a Nation and *Tarzan of the Apes* engender prevailing national sentiments in the years 1915 and 1918, sentiments which remained strong well into the twenties. It would take less than a decade for the sentiments of the Afro-American community to move from "up from slavery," as in Booker T. Washington's 1901 book title, to "the souls of black folk," as W.E.B. DuBois expressed it in 1903. Washington's emphasis upon the physical struggle to uplift Afro-Americans from dehumanizing slavery to minimal standards of living and education shifted to DuBois' emphasis upon mental and emotional nourishment needed for the long struggle still ahead to gain Afro-Americans their rightful place in America. The factors necessary for this shift in ideology were present already, for an Afro-American consciousness flowered within a decade through the Harlem Renaissance. The Harlem Renaissance represents the grestest Afro-American cultural resurgence since Reconstruction (see the earlier chapter on "Civil Rights Groups and the Harlem Renaissance"). These early films, whether set in a glorified Old South or a newly exploited Dark Continent, preserve the myths which the cultural milieu of early twentieth-century America absorbed like a sponge. Only one of many such myths revolved around the image of the black man as brute.

The second outstanding derogatory image is that of the female black coon. Jane Porter's Afro-American nanny, Esmeralda in *Tarzan of the Apes*, book and film, is a plump Negress who accompanies Jane to Africa where the black African women are naked from the waist up; Esmeralda is adorned with a black-and-white maid uniform and apron which are set off by the handkerchief on her head. One might ask why Terkoz the Ape in the book, and the huge and diabolical African in the film, choose to kidnap Jane and not Esmeralda who is at the time standing next to Jane. Esmeralda's larger size and darker complexion offer no inducement, it seems, for Jane is chosen. It is the Anglo-American concept of beauty, desirability and, above all, purity of white skin left over from the cult of virginity in the antebellum South apparently. This development also assures a plot in which Tarzan of the Apes can throw himself into the rescue operation wholeheartedly.

Jane perhaps endures the kidnapping with more finesse than Esmeralda would have. When Jane is in the arms of her kidnapper, it is Esmeralda who swoons while Jane remains conscious. Esmeralda is one of two Afro-Americans brought to Africa by the Anglo-Americans. The other is the "burly Negro" who, in the book, murders the captain of the *Fuwalda* during the mutiny by splitting his head with an ax. While never primitive like an African, Esmeralda is ignorant. She is the docile and dependent domestic who is the first to show fright and the only one to laugh in a serious situation. Her handkerchiefed head tops a heavyset frame which is always in the uniform of a domestic, a uniform that brands her as more of an outsider than anyone else on the screen. Aside from the vaudevillian humor which only she engages in, her function apparently is to grin and cling to Jane to emphasize the "white" qualities which Jane possesses.

Esmeralda belongs to the mammy tradition in films. The mammy figure is close to the comic coon image, according to Donald Bogle in *Toms, Coons, Mulattoes, Mammies, and Bucks* (1973), but she is "distinguished by her sex and her fierce independence. She is usually big, fat and cantankerous."[4] Her stereotypical offspring in the thirties would include Hattie McDaniel and Louise Beavers in Aunt Jemima roles, and the thin, young version of the mammy, Butterfly McQueen, immortalized as the handkerchief head in her role as Prissy in *Gone with the Wind* (1939). Earlier, in *Rastus in Zululand* (1910), produced by Sigmund Lubin who made both the original Rastus and Sambo series between 1910 and 1911, a lazy Rastus dreams of being shipwrecked in Zululand, in Africa. The storyline is a repeat of the Pocahontas/Captain Smith myth. In this case, however, there is a comic twist in that the princess is obese. An earlier variation on the Pocahontas plot is in *The King of the Cannibal Islands* (1908). This short silent film also presents the comic complication of a rescue by a very fat black queen. These obese princesses and queens from locales as exotic as Burroughs' Africa are pre-mammy figures, with the first fully developed mammy image coming in the blackface film version of Aristophanes' *Lysistrata* (1914).

The image of the black woman in *Tarzan of the Apes* is that of the comic mammy coon; the image of the black man is that of the brutish black ape, the interloper, whose sole purpose is to create trouble for the white ape, Tarzan. All of the black characters are in keeping with the expectations of the audience, for there were in 1918 no expectations for blacks to appear in roles other than those prescribed by traditions of prejudice. Concerning jungle films like *Tarzan of the Apes*, Thomas Cripps contends in *Slow Fade to Black* (1977) that efforts of Hollywood's Hays Office to diminish dark-skinned villainy in films resulted in the drift away from Africans as the antagonists to Africans as "casual objects." As examples, he cites the following films:

In Louise Glaum's vehicle, *The Leopard Woman*

(1920), she impetuously orders her love killed, remorsefully wishes him alive, and when a Negro dies in his stead, "Madame is overjoyed that Culbertson escaped." Fox's *The Jungle Trail* (1919) offers a white "god" who rules a tribe after "his great strength wins him their worship," a gimmick topped by *A White Barbarian* (1923), a British picture featuring the "Songora tribe, who possess a white royal family."[5]

Once their stereotypical image is embedded in a tradition like that of the jungle films, however, the mere presence of blacks in a jungle film will raise expectations in the audience as to what they will witness on the screen. The Hay's Office pronouncements, ironically, may have been responsible for many jungle films in the thirties and forties using whites where African blacks were expected but, even earlier, Boris Karloff appeared in blackface as a Waziri chieftain in a Tarzan film. The appearance of whites in this context was upsetting, if not shocking, because it violated all normal expectations on the part of the audience as to what natives in Africa look like. By 1918, film audiences clearly expected that Tarzan the white must lord it over the apes and the blacks and the beasts; the fact that Tarzan is indeed an English Lord by birth, Lord Greystoke, helps embed the contrast in black and white images.

Because he is the son of an Anglo aristocrat, Tarzan of the Apes is culturally superior, though he chafes at the restrictions which accompany leadership roles. Of all the jungle's inhabitants, Tarzan alone is blessed with possession of the humanizing tool, the knife. He is capable of learning without a teacher how to read and write (according to the book version), a feat which the apes and blacks (and probably all human beings) are incapable of doing. He is a triumph of whiteness in the darkness of Africa, a composite darkness spread across a continent and contributed to by the apes, the blacks, the beasts, and the dense verdure of the jungle.

Feature-length films like *The Birth of a Nation* and *Tarzan of the Apes*, unfortunately, were the beginning of a long era of films derogatory to Afro-Americans. In *From Sambo to Superspade* (1975), Daniel J. Leab summarizes the point in this manner:

> As far as blacks were concerned, the

> patterns set in these early motion pictures would remain unbroken not for years but for decades. The movie industry, as the black author John Oliver Killens has charged, may well have become "the most anti-Negro influence in this nation." Killens has also called the first real film masterpiece, D.W. Griffith's *The Birth of a Nation*, "Hollywood's first big gun in its war against the black American." The castings for that gun were forged in the movies made between the mid-1890s and 1915.[6]

Tarzan of the Apes in 1918 did not deviate from the established mode of warfare. But contrary to the images of the African continent which *Tarzan of the Apes* provided, it was really the American continent that was at its darkest in 1918. Among other reasons, lynchings of Afro-Americans in the uniform of the United States Army were common. The climate of the times is further illustrated by the neglect which greeted Emmett J. Scott's *The Birth of a Race*, the venture which began as a rebuttal film to D.W. Griffith's *The Birth of a Nation*.

Aside from being accessible and acceptable, images such as those projected in popular Hollywood films like *Tarzan of the Apes* were attractive.[7] The Anglo-American audiences identified with the "natural superiority" of the Anglo over the Afro-American or black African. But "we cheered, too," laments Afro-American Francis Ward, "when Tarzan beat up or killed the Afrikan [sic] 'savages.'"[8] Such is the power of the filmic story that Afro-Americans in the audience often mentally transposed their roles and identified with the Anglo-Americans instead of the Afro-Americans or black Africans in the films.

Early audiences viewing Afro-American and black African images reacted intuitively. The communicated messages were irretrievable, and the sustained derogatory imagery was what created the negativism and propaganda inherent in most early Afro-American and black African film images. There was no time for an audience to consider an impression from the screen and the repeated barrages of images simply seeped in and saturated the subconsciousness of the viewers. The stereotypes were further exaggerated in silent movies.[9] Stereotypes such as the male black brute and the female black coon, may even be called archetypes since they are so consistent in equating black with inhumanity and soullessness.

What is excluded in film culture also reflects general cultural attitudes. Excluding positive images of Afro-Americans or black Africans tends to reinforce cultural attitudes by limiting models to choose from. The most extreme Anglo-American attitudes are reflected in exclusion by not bringing into the picture any positive reflection whatsoever of the Afro-American or black African. What are preserved in films and what are remembered by audiences are the outstanding images. These images can be traced through history as genres of stereotypes and archetypes in every major medium; the most impressive work to date in this regard is Thomas Cripps' recent *Black Film as Genre* (1979).

Afro-Americans and black Africans have appeared in seven or eight thousand films in the twentieth century. That which audiences fail to remember about Afro-Americans and black Africans in these films also represents a stereotype of sorts. This stereotype of the faceless black image bombards film investigators with the continual reinforcement that Afro-Americans and black Africans exist, but that their existence is not worthy of a deeper probe that might put human faces in place of a scantily perceived image. Afro-Americans and black Africans in American culture are outsiders. In the Tarzan films of the thirties, for example, Afro-Americans as African natives were replaced by light brown-skinned actors or, in some of these films, the natives were left out almost entirely. The Afro-American and black African images are thus given in part, not in whole, and certainly they are rarely humanly full in their characterizations. Those black faces which are recognized as stereotypes, then, are exceptions to the one overwhelming stereotype of facelessness. Despite their being exceptions, they have been, haplessly, the most studied of the Afro-American and black African images. Few significant Afro-American or black African episodes ever reach the screen either and, when they do, there is rarely an attempt to be accurate historically or in any other way.

The image in mass media, Gabriel Marcel has pointed out, is one step away from reality. It may be argued that popular films are not reflective of the culture which produces them because they are intentional distortions of reality. The Afro-American image may not reflect reality in cultural contexts, but perhaps it reflects a pseudo-reality, a reality implanted in and existing in the minds of whites and blacks alike and which goes beyond stereotypical concepts. A pseudo-reality, perhaps, which fights reality by instituting either a harmony (singing, dancing, good-time Negroes) or, if presenting the Afro-American as brute, by ensuring that the brute is crushed and harmony restored; a pseudo-reality in which both Afro-Americans and Anglo-Americans perceive good as equated with light and bad as equated with dark.

The identification of some of the symbols supporting Tarzan's "white ape myth," juxtapositioned as it is with American culture's "black ape myth," hopefully point to aspects of a theory of popular film in which the concept of a film culture may be more thoroughly developed. Many of the filmic symbols identifiable in *Tarzan of the Apes* no longer work. The audience reaction to the film in 1918 was much different than it is today--if undergraduate literature and film students viewing it for the first time are any indication--both because of artistic and technical advances in the film arts and because of the dated form in which its precepts are presented. The polarity of black and white images in film culture, nonetheless, is perhaps best illustrated by the dozens of Tarzan films made in Hollywood, whether by major studios like Metro-Goldwyn-Meyer or independents like Burroughs-Tarzan Enterprise. Like Hollywood films generally, the Tarzan films were based on irresponsible but popular images of darkness on the Dark Continent of Africa. These images were transferred to Afro-Americans who were there in the role of black Africans as "atmosphere furniture."

The Tarzan films are the most important representatives of the jungle film genre, for no other series has been so popular or led to so many imitators. The positive attributes of the "white ape myth" and the negative attributes of the "black ape myth" in a film like the original *Tarzan of the Apes* represent an interpretation and an ordering of experience in American culture. This film is a creative example of the mythic Golden Age as well, even to the extreme of recreating the timeless Adam and Eve in Eden through Tarzan and Jane in the jungle of the Dark Continent. This Golden Age theme is present in various manifestations in all eras, but it is strongly associated with

America's dreams of lost lands and lost races, whether called up through pulp literature like the Tarzan stories, through the rhetoric of secret organizations like the Ku Klux Klan and the empire-advocating Knights of the Golden Circle, through films like *The Birth of a Nation* which venerate a nineteenth and early twentieth century lost southland and lost southern race of whites, or in the reality of America's conquests under the bloody banner of the "white man's burden." Afro-Americans had little influence on this course of action since, as their film images between 1896 and 1954 reveal, they were America's outsiders. The Tarzan series of books and films helped keep them out of American culture by presenting them as the black peril.

Notes

1 Thomas Cripps, *Slow Fade to Black: The Negro in American Films, 1900-1942* (New York: Oxford Univ. Press, 1977), p. 125.

2 Edgar Rice Burroughs, *Tarzan of the Apes* (New York: Ballantine, 1975), p. 153.

3 "Daddy Swiped Our Last Clean Sheet and Joined the Ku Klux Klan," 100% Americans with orchestra accompaniment (Indianapolis: Ku Klux Klan Label, n.d.).

4 Donald Bogle, *Toms, Coons, Mulattoes, Mammies, and Bucks: An Interpretive History of Blacks in American Films* (New York: Viking, 1973), p. 98.

5 Cripps, p. 127.

6 Daniel J. Leab, *From Sambo to Superspade: The Black Experience in Motion Pictures* (Boston: Houghton Mifflin, 1975), p. 22.

7 Randall Adams, "*The Exorcist* as Popular Culture Artifact," paper presented at the Western Regional Popular Culture Association Meeting, California State Polytechnic Institute (1 February 1975). The termin-

ology is adapted from p. 2 of a copy of Randall's paper.

[8] Francis Ward, "Black Male Images in Film," *Freedomways*, 14 (1974), 223.

[9] Silent films are sometimes thought to have been more universal because language barriers did not exist in them. This is nonsense. Placards, storefront signs, advertisements, and street signs are part of the setting in many films and if the language they are in, say Arabic, is not understood, then certain cultural barriers have been erected to inhibit universality. Communication, in addition, is far more than language, whether spoken or written. The English commands, "Stop!" and "Run!," may be mouthed in a silent film, but if the filmviewer does not know English the effect may be lessened or lost. Gestures and body movements are communicative signals as well which vary from culture to culture, again suggesting that silent films are not necessarily any more universal than sound films.

Chapter Ten

The Invisible Genre: Tarzan Jungle Films

What the images in Tarzan books have in common with the images in Tarzan films is their cultivation of the black, whether Afro-American or black African, as outsider. The black as outsider is a powerful theme in the hands of both Anglo-American and Afro-American writers. Afro-American writers have expressed it over and over again in such books as James Weldon Johnson's *The Autobiography of an Ex-Coloured Man*--published the same year, 1912, that *Tarzan of the Apes* by Edgar Rice Burroughs was first serialized--Ralph Ellison's *The Invisible Man* (1952), Richard Wright's *The Outsider* (1953), and John A. Williams' *The Man Who Cried I Am* (1967). This theme of black as outsider is reinforced by a survey of the present state of the study of black images in films.

Prior to such a survey, it is worth tabulating the number of films based upon the Tarzan stories by Edgar Rice Burroughs. There are over forty American-made Tarzan films, twenty-nine of which were produced between World War One and the Korean War. While the number of foreign-made Tarzan films is unknown, the number of Tarzan films produced in India alone may run into the dozens. In America, the pre-sound era Tarzans and Tarzan films include Elmo Lincoln as Tarzan in *Tarzan of the Apes* (1918) and its sequel, *The Romance of Tarzan* (1918), as well as in *The Adventures of Tarzan* (1920 serial/1928 feature). Gene Pollar is Tarzan in *The Return of Tarzan* (1920), later retitled *The Revenge of Tarzan*. P. Dempsey Tabler is Tarzan and Kamuela C. Searle is Korak in *The Son of Tarzan* (1920 serial), James H. Pierce is Tarzan in *Tarzan and the Golden Lion* (1927), and Frank Merrill is Tarzan in both *Tarzan the Mighty* (1928 serial) and *Tarzan the Tiger* (1929 serial; included some sound segments). Gordon Griffith plays the young Tarzan in *Tarzan of the Apes* (1918) and the young Korak in *The Son of Tarzan* (1920).

Johnny Weissmuller is the star of the first all-sound Tarzan film, *Tarzan the Ape Man* (1932). For a generation Johnny Weissmuller was dominant as the ape man of films, starring in twelve Tarzan films before moving on to the role of Jungle Jim. During this era there was competition from other Tarzans, including Buster Crabbe in *Tarzan the Fearless* (1933), Herman Brix in *The New Adventures of Tarzan* (1935) and *Tarzan and the Green Goddess* (1938), and Glenn Morris in *Tarzan's Revenge* (1938). Weissmuller's last appearance as Tarzan was in *Tarzan and the Mermaids* in 1948; it was Lex Barker who appeared as Tarzan in five more films from this era, ranging from *Tarzan's Magic Fountain* (1949) to *Tarzan and the She-Devil* (1953). Starting in 1955, there have been a dozen more Tarzan films with such actors as Gordon Scott in five, beginning with *Tarzan's Hidden Jungle* (1955), through *Tarzan and the Lost Safari* (1957), the first Tarzan film shot in color, and ending with *Tarzan the Magnificent* (1960). Jock Mahony came next with *Tarzan Goes to India* (1962) and *Tarzan's Three Challenges* (1963), and he was followed by Mike Henry in *Tarzan and the Valley of Gold* (1966), *Tarzan and the Great River* (1967), and *Tarzan and the Jungle Boy* (1968). Dennis Miller was Tarzan in the first remake of *Tarzan the Ape Man* (1959) and, most recently, Miles O'Keeffe played Tarzan in the latest remake of *Tarzan the Ape Man* (1981). On television, Ron Ely played in a popular Tarzan serial for many years that lured such celebrities as the Supremes and James Earl Jones to the cast for guest appearances. Two feature films based on Ely's series were released as *Tarzan's Jungle Rebellion* (1970) and *Tarzan's Deadly Silence* (1970). In the Tarzan films, it is not just Afro-Americans who are treated as objects rather than as human beings, for black Africans are consistently portrayed in a derogatory manner as well. Despite this lack of humanism, these films are the most prolific, most formulaic, and most enduring of the jungle films featuring Africa as a setting.

Incredible as it may seem, since they obviously represent one of the most popular film series ever made, Tarzan films have been generally excluded from discussion in books on film as not being serious material. The two books which deal specifically with Tarzan films, Ray Lee and Vernell Coriell's *A Pictorial History of the Tarzan Movies* (1966) and Gabe Essoe's *Tarzan of the Movies: A Pictorial History of More than Fifty Years of Edgar Rice Burroughs'*

Legendary Hero (1968), concentrate on personalities and production. Neither discuss the historical and cultural context nor the reasons for the popularity of the Tarzan genre of jungle films. An exploration of these significant aspects of film studies will be forwarded by an overview of the sparse materials available at present concerning the invisible genre of films, the Tarzan jungle films.

The American-made Tarzan films often employ Afro-Americans to represent Africans, beginning with the unfortunate chieftain who slays Tarzan's foster mother, Kala the Ape, and is stalked and then choked to death by Tarzan. Books dealing with Afro-Americans in film, however, usually neglect the meanings of these images of Africa and Africans. The Marxist approach by V.P. Jerome in *The Negro in Hollywood Films* (1950), for example, passes over the Tarzan films entirely. Beyond the books by Essoe and by Lee and Coriell, the exceptions to total neglect of this genre of jungle films arises only when an author must address a Tarzan film because it contains a particularly striking incident or because a well-known actor under discussion has appeared in a Tarzan film. Such is the case with the following works, each of which purports to be on the Afro-American image in films. In *The Negro in Films* (ca. 1948), Peter Noble notes without elaboration that Rex Ingram played in "an early version of *Tarzan of the Apes*, produced in 1920."[1] The only documented appearance of Rex Ingram in a Tarzan film is in *Tarzan's Hidden Jungle* (1955), although it is quite probable that he appeared in one of the early Tarzan films. In *Blacks in American Films* (1972), Edward Mapp mentions an incident which illustrates the racism in Tarzan films: an Anglo Bwana's response when an African porter plunges over a cliff to his death is, "What was in that pack!"[2] Afro-American Donald Bogle, in *Toms, Coons, Mulattoes, Mammies, and Bucks* (1973), refers to James Edwards and Woody Strode in *Tarzan's Fight for Life* (1958) and to the vivacity of Dorothy Dandridge's spread and tied legs in *Tarzan's Perils* (1951).[3]

Other books on films are scarcely better, for they too lack revelation concerning the Tarzan genre of jungle films. In *To Find an Image* (1973), also a book on Afro-Americans in film written by an Afro-American, James P. Murray offers the same reference to James Edwards and Woody Strode in *Tarzan's Fight for Life* as does Bogle.[4] Neither Murray nor Bogle note that Woody Strode also appeared in *Tarzan's Three Challenges* (1963) and *Tarzan's Deadly Silence* (1970). Elsewhere, Murray notes simply that Afro-Americans were hired for several films by "Woody" Van Dyke of Metro-Goldwyn-Meyer, "beginning with *Tarzan the Ape Man* in 1932, the first of many African films shot in studio jungles--with studio 'Africans.'"[5] Eileen Landay, in *Black Film Stars* (1973), reprints a photograph from a film she incorrectly titles *Tarzan* (1920). Elmo Lincoln is identified as the Tarzan in the still which means that, if Landay's date is accurate, the title of the film is *The Adventures of Tarzan*. Also in the photograph is a Jane and a "young savage" black, both of whom are left unidentified. In the text itself, Landay offers no discussion of Tarzan or Tarzan films.[6]

A similar lack of attention is accorded the Tarzan jungle films in Jim Pines' *Blacks in Films: A Survey of Racial Themes and Images in American Film* (1974). Pine does use Tarzan in a mulched adjective when he notes that with the rise of the southern plantation genre, "it was really left to Trader Horn-Tarzan-Zombie type movies to carry-on [sic] the black image as a savage type."[7] The only other mention of Tarzan by Pines is not in the text, but in the filmography. The filmography includes a statement that Rex Ingram appeared in *Tarzan of the Apes* (1918).[8]

Because an anthology serves a different function, it cannot be judged in the same manner as works which purport to offer systematic coverage of the black image in films. It can be pointed out, nonetheless, that of the twenty-seven articles compiled by Richard A. Maynard for *The Black Man on Film: Racial Stereotyping* (1974), none deal with or so much as mention Tarzan films; there is not even a Tarzan film listed in Maynard's filmography for featured stereotypes from the thirties to the fifties when Johnny Weissmuller was appearing regularly in such films as *Tarzan and His Mate* (1934), *Tarzan Finds a Son* (1939), *Tarzan Triumphs* (1943), and *Tarzan and the Leopard Woman* (1946). With the twenty-nine essays in *Black Films and Film-Makers* (1975), compiled by Lindsay Patterson, the situation is the same, though Patterson's filmography does, inexplicably, list *Tarzan's Perils* (1951) with Dorothy Dandridge of all the Tarzan films.

While he spends some time on jungle films in *From Sambo to Superspade* (1975), Daniel J. Leab neglects the importance of the immensely popular Tarzan films. Skipping over the era between World War One and the Korean conflict, during which time three-quarters of the Tarzan jungle films were produced, Leab gives them a passing notice only in the context of the fifties. In the exotic locales of the Tarzan films, he states, "blacks were once again cast as ignorant and superstitious savages who could not stand up to whites."[9] This is short shrift for the Tarzan films, but not less than what previous writers on the black image in films had allotted.

The most recent work on the black image in films is also the one in which, for the first time, Tarzan films are taken seriously. Both scholarly and readable, Thomas Cripps' *Slow Fade to Black: The Negro in American Films, 1900-1942* (1977) places Tarzan in the context of other films about Africa and in the context of what was going on in the civil rights arena. While emphasizing the film Tarzans, Cripps does not neglect the importance of the Tarzan series of romances by Edgar Rice Burroughs which, he writes,

> rested on a firm base of nineteenth-century exploration and curiosity about the new anthropology and remote peoples, leavened by the safaris and hunts of Theodore Roosevelt and other public figures, and recent booms in conservationism and in western camping.[10]

Thus Cripps' incisive work is the first to break with the tradition of books that deal with "popular" films about Afro-Americans but fail to condescend to include the Tarzan films. Cripps, of all these writers, recognizes that the Tarzan films and books are perhaps the epitomy of American popular culture. While not focusing on Tarzan films, Cripps' latest work in the field, *Black Film as Genre* (1979), represents yet another step forward in the investigation of black images in films.

In addition to the context of film images in American popular culture, an analysis of characterizations of the Afro-American and black African necessitates tapping the tradition of racism. *Tarzan of the Apes* (1918) was produced at that point in history when America was on the verge of completing its Manifest Destiny by showing its superiority over Europe in World War One. This film is not, certainly, an adequate representation of Afro-Americans and black Africans; partially for this reason, the preceding chapter on "The Tarzan Formula for Racial Stereotyping" took up in more detail aspects of this film and its genre. What is represented in *Tarzan of the Apes* and the more than forty more American-made Tarzan films, has unfortunately too often been interchangeably identified with information about Afro-Americans and black Africans, about Afro-American and black African themes and problems, and about Afro-American and black African cultures. Outlandish Tarzan films with titles like *Tarzan and the Amazons* (1945), *Tarzan and the Huntress* (1947), *Tarzan and the Slave Girl* (1950), and *Tarzan's Fight for Life* (1958) contributed to the misrepresentations of Afro-Americans and black Africans in the post-World War Two era.

As part of the recent attempt to explore these problems in more detail, two articles by Derral Cheatwood, "The Tarzan Sound Film Series" and "Race and Sex in the Tarzan Films," will appear soon in the *Journal of Popular Culture*.[11] In their landmark treatment of the subject in "Ooga Booga: The African Image in American Films," Alfred E. Opubur and Adebayo Ogunbi go to the root of the issue when they remark that it is

> interesting to speculate on what would have happened to the African image as projected in American films and popular culture if Burroughs had never been born. Although the Tarzan films made from his novels constitute only a small proportion of American motion pictures on Africa, their point of view and image of Africa have had an almost preemptive impact on American film making about Africa. Besides they have become the most widely distributed and most frequently repeated American-produced films on Africa.[12]

Tarzan is a mythic, larger-than-life creation nearly as pervasive in American culture as the myth of Anglo superiority itself. There are, despite the Teddy Roosevelts and Elmo Lincolns, no literal or even viable corresponding realities to this filmic vision of race, this symbolic and mythic misrepresentation of the realities of Afro-American and black African life and culture.

In Tarzan, the myth of Anglo superiority is condensed and molded into the myth of the "White Ape."

The Tarzan films themselves have been geared for understanding by a popular audience, Afro-American as well as Anglo-American. The audiences for whom the Tarzan films were made, unfortunately, continued to identify with the magical images on the screen, regardless of their accuracy. Cripps notes that "a survey of Negro audiences confirmed that Tarzan pictures were favorites along with Lena Horne, [Eddie] Anderson, Hattie McDaniel, and six white stars."[13] The stature of Tarzan as the adventuresome white purveyor of Africa, the Dark Continent, is of epic proportions in such films as *Tarzan Escapes* (1936), *Tarzan's Secret Treasure* (1941), *Tarzan's Desert Mystery* (1943), and *Tarzan's Greatest Adventure* (1959). The Tarzan films are thus an incredible twentieth-century collection of the dominant images of Anglo-American superiority and Afro-American and black African inferiority.

It is even more incredible that only in the late seventies has the significance of these cultural experiences on film seeped from the subconsciousness to the consciousness of writers documenting the black image in films. For over sixty years the images of blacks in the Tarzan genre of jungle films have been among the most pervasive images in American popular culture. But only with this recent consciousness have the Tarzan films become visible in the literature on American films.

Notes

[1] Peter Noble, *The Negro in Films* (London: Skelton Robinson, ca. 1948), p. 148.

[2] Edward Mapp, *Blacks in American Films: Today and Yesterday* (Metuchen, NJ: Scarecrow, 1972), p. 252.

[3] Donald Bogle, *Toms, Coons, Mulattoes, Mammies, and Bucks: An Interpretive History of Blacks in American Films* (New York: Viking, 1973), pp. 147, 185.

[4] James P. Murray, *To Find an Image: Black Films from Uncle Tom to Super Fly* (Indianapolis: Bobbs-Merrill, 1973), pp. 25 and 44.

[5] Murray, p. 17.

[6] Eileen Landay, *Black Film Stars* (New York: Drake, 1973), p. 29.

[7] Jim Pines, *Blacks in Films: A Survey of Racial Themes and Images in the American Film* (London: Studio Vista, 1974), p. 77.

[8] Pines, p. 131.

[9] Daniel J. Leab, *From Sambo to Superspade: The Black Experience in Motion Pictures* (Boston: Houghton Mifflin, 1975), p. 136.

[10] Thomas Cripps, *Slow Fade to Black: The Negro in American Films, 1900-1942* (New York: Oxford Univ. Press, 1977), p. 124.

[11] Articles by the author of the present book with discussions of Tarzan and Tarzan films in a cultural context, both in America and abroad, are the following: "Tarzan and Cultural Imperialism in Arabia," *Journal of Popular Culture* [to appear in vol. 15 (1982)]; "The Tenuous Vine of *Tarzan of the Apes*," *Journal of Popular Culture*, 13 (Spring 1980), 483-487; "Tarzan of Arabia: American Popular Culture Permeates Yemen," *Journal of Yemeni Studies*, vol. 3 (Summer 1980); and "Tarzan and the Ku Klux Klan: Anglo-Americanism in the Twenties," *Journal of English*, 6 (September 1979), 79-109.

[12] Alfred E. Opubur and Adebayo Ogunbi, "Ooga Booga: The African Image in American Films," *Other Voices, Other Views: An International Collection of Essays from the Bicentennial*, ed. by Robin W. Winks (Westport, CT: Greenwood, 1978), p. 344.

[13] Cripps, p. 352.

Chapter Eleven

All-Black Hollywood Films

In the 1830's, the song and dance minstrelsy of blackface Dan Rice introduced "Jump Jim Crow." Rice thus popularized the term "Jim Crow," now meaning the systematic practice of segregating and suppressing Afro-Americans, which has become the most apt description of the segregated conditions for Afro-Americans from 1896 to 1954. Blackfacing in film shorts were discussed in detail earlier, a tradition that was well-developed with films like *Mammy's Ghost* (n.d.), a Civil War story with a blackface mammy protecting a Confederate soldier, and Mack Swain's *By Stork Delivery* (1916) in which blackface parents search for their kidnapped child.

The blackface tradition declined in the thirties after Hollywood made a cycle of all-black feature-length musicals which led to hundreds of all-black musical shorts and, over the years, even more feature-length all-black musicals. But the blackface tradition did not go away entirely. In *Whoopee* (MGM, 1930), Eddie Cantor hides in an oven and comes out to do a blackface routine. A similar excuse was used even after World War Two when Alan Carney is singed black from an accident in the Bela Lugosi comedy, *Genious at Work* (RKO, 1946). In *Check and Doublecheck* (RKO, 1930), the Anglo *Amos "n" Andy* radio team of Charles Correll and Beeman Gosden are blackfaced, as is Russell Powell. George M. Cohen is put under blackface for a minstrel act in *The Phantom President* (Paramount, 1932), and Pat Padget and Pick Malone continued the minstrelsy tradition of blackfacing as "Molasses and January" in *Captain Henry's Radio Show* (Paramount, 1933). The British also contributed to the tradition with *Kentucky Minstrels* (England, 1934), titled on its release in America as *Life Is Real*. The film included Afro-American Nina Mae McKinney and background blacks, but it was about the blackface team of Englishmen, Scott and Whaley. Afro-Americans George Reed and the Hall Johnson Choir were in *Swanee River* (Twentieth Century-

Fox, 1940), which included numerous blackface scenes in the minstrel tradition. There were many blackface acts in *Dixie* (Paramount, 1943), and in *Saratoga Trunk* (Warners, 1946), Anglo-American Flora Robson plays the major role in blackface. After this, blackfacing still occurred on occasion, usually as a spoof or parody of blackfacing itself.

One early production company, Biograph, had attempted to star Afro-American Bert Williams, the renowned vaudevillian, in several film shorts, including *Dark Town Jubilee* (1914), *Fish* (1916), and *A Natural Born Gambler* (1916). The first caused a minor riot when it was shown in Brooklyn and after that theaters would not accept films featuring an Afro-American. This was in spite of the fact that Williams played in these films in blackface, what James Weldon Johnson called "a caricature of a caricature." Only with the inevitable evolution of sound films in the late twenties would it become more practical for Hollywood to achieve at least superficial realism by featuring Afro-Americans as the performers in roles intended for Afro-Americans. There were other reasons for the original 1929 cycle of all-black Hollywood musicals which emerged just one century after Dan Rice's "Jump Jim Crow." One was fledgling competition from Afro-American independent filmmakers, and another was the increased interest in and popularity of all types of music disseminated via the other new sound medium of the twenties, radio. Yet another reason was the debate that ensued when sound was introducted as to whose voices recorded best. The central concern was not whether female voices recorded better than male voices, or whether adults recorded better than children, but whether or not race was the key. Caught up in the Afro-American as perfect entertainer stereotype, many people at first thought that the Afro-American's voice recorded better than the Anglo-American's voice. Thus, the cycle of all-black musicals was in part an attempt to capture the apparently better quality of voice by Afro-Americans on films and use this advantage to cash in at the box office. With this mistaken notion firmly in mind, the major Hollywood studios presented two all-black musical features and two all-black musical shorts in 1929: the features *Hearts in Dixie* and *Hallelujah*, and the shorts *The St. Louis Blues* and *Black and Tan*.

Paul Sloane's *Hearts in Dixie* (Fox, 1929), is set on a farm in the South. The music reflects the setting with songs like "Go Ring Dem Bells." Stepin Fetchit plays the worthless Gummy, married to Chloe and the father of two children. Chloe dies, even though a voodoo woman attempts to treat her, and it is left to Chloe's father Nappus, played by Clarence Muse, to see to it that his grandchildren have an opportunity in life that the lazy Gummy is not interested in providing. Nappus' sacrifices allow Gummy's son, played by Eugene Jackson, to go away to school. The storyline was weak, but there was an attempt to render dialect accurately. As a musical comedy, however, it drew upon the favorite Anglo-American stereotypes of Afro-Americans like the emerging coon personality of Stepin Fetchit. One Anglo-American appears as a doctor in the midst of the poor and backward blacks played by Vivian Smith, Zack Williams, Gertrude Howard, and many others.

King Vidor's *Hallelujah* (MGM, 1929), came next. Vidor had written the story and wanted originally to do the film as a silent. Financial backing for the project only came about when the potential for sound in films was beginning to be realized. *Hallelujah* was the first film to portray more than a glimpse of Afro-American family life in the South; it thus constituted, inacurrate as it was, the first exposure for many Anglo-Americans to this aspect of Afro-American life. Daniel Haynes plays Zeke, who accidently kills his brother and as repentance becomes an evangelist. In the midst of the film's mythic behavioral patterns, Ninna McKinney as Chick, the seductress, is pitted against Victoria Spivey as Missy Rose, the good woman. Womanizing, crap shooting, brawling, backsliding are all staples around which the music was scored. William Fountaine, Harry Gray and Fannie Belle were among the many other Afro-Americans to appear in this film.

The St. Louis Blues (RKO, 1929), was one of the best all-black films of the twenties. Like most other all-black films, the director was an Anglo-American, Dudley Murphy. Based loosely on the life and work of W.C. Handy, who did the score along with J. Rosamond Johnson, it boasted an honor roll cast: W.C. Handy , J. Rosamond Johnson, Jimmy Mordecai, Edgar Connor, Jimmy Johnson, Alec Lovejoy, Isabel Washington and, in her only appearance on film, the blues singer Bessie Smith. Though there were still craps being played in the film and Afro-Americans being featured in a saloon setting, there were differences between this film and *Hearts in Dixie* and *Hallelujah* that held out some promise for better future portrayals of Afro-Americans: It was set in an urban area, St. Louis, rather than in the Deep South, the music was scored by the Afro-Americans Handy and Johnson, and the focus was on the personalities of the people involved rather than on stereotypes of characters.

If somewhat too removed from reality, *The St. Louis Blues* was nonetheless an inspired work which in turn inspired a host of other all-black musicals by independents as well as demonstrated the potential of Afro-American musical and dramatic talents to the Hollywood studios. Actually filmed as a short, Hollywood found *The St. Louis Blues* interesting and profitable enough a fantasy for Paramount to do two feature-length remakes, one in 1939 with Maxine Sullivan and a white supporting cast, and another in 1958 with an all-black cast that included Nat "King" Cole, Eartha Kitt, Pearl Bailey, Cab Calloway, Ruby Dee, Mahalia Jackson, Ella Fitzgerald, and Juano Hernandez. Of the three, the original 1929 version was the most vigorous and most enduring. Duke Ellington, Fredi Washington, and Alec Lovejoy in *Black and Tan* (RKO, 1929), again revealed the potential of sound films for Afro-American entertainers. In common with *The St. Louis Blues*, it was also directed by Dudley Murphy and it also, unlike the rural milieu of Hollywood's *Hearts in Dixie* and *Hallelujah*, had an urban setting, this one in Harlem. And it too was a serious portrayal of the lives of entertainers rather than just the presentation of entertainment. With Dudley's musicals, the tradition of the musical short was established. It would not retain the dramatic elements, however, and the musical shorts which followed were no more than showcases for Afro-American talents.

These spin-offs from the Hollywood all-black musicals were shorts which normally ranged in length from ten to twenty minutes. As with the feature-length musicals with all-black casts, the directors and producers were almost without exception Anglo-Americans. One of the earliest was *Yamacraw* (Vitaphone, 1930), directed by Anglo-American Murray Roth. Afro-American James P. Johnson did the music for it and, along with Jimmy Mordecai, acted out its subtheme of a country versus city conflict. The stereotypes of blacks surfaced quickly in this genre. *Cotton-Pickin' Days* (Tiffany, 1930), featured the Afro-American Forbes Randolph Kentucky Jubilee Singers and a plantation setting in slavery days. And still in the first year following the major Hollywood all-black musicals, Afro-Americans Aubrey Lyles and Flournoy E. Miller appeared in *Midnight Lodge* (Vitagraph, 1930). Flournoy E. Miller, who also appeared in dozens of independent Afro-American films, was a terrified watchman, as was Mantan Moreland, in *That's the Spirit* (Vitaphone, 1932). This early musical short also included Cora LaRedd, the Washboard Serenaders, and Nobble Sissle and his band. Other standard Afro-American stereotypes like crap shooting were present along with the music and dance of *Smash Your Baggage* (Vitaphone, 1932), with Roy Eldridge, Dickie Wells, and Small's Paradise Entertainers. Similar scenes were used in other musical shorts, as when Victoria Spivey plops a mophandle on the head of the King of Jazzlvania, Louis Armstrong, in *Rhapsody in Black and Blue* (Paramount, 1932), also with Sidney Easton.

A director who did many of the early all-black musical shorts was Anglo-American Roy Mack. His *All-Colored Vaudeville Show* (Warners and Vitaphone, 1935), featured Adelaide Hall and the Nicholas Brothers. Eubie Blake and Noble Sissle did several feature-length films together and each appeared in these shorts. Eubie Blake and his band, along with Nina Mae McKinney and the Nicholas Brothers were featured in Mack's *Pie, Pie Blackbird* (Warners, 1932), and Noble Sissle appeared with Bob Howard in *Howard's House Party* Century Films, 1947). Bob Howard also appeared in Al Christie's *Gifts in Rhythm* (Educational Pictures, 1936), along with the Cabin Kids.

Cab Calloway and Duke Ellington were among the most consistent performers in the musical shorts of the thirties and forties. Calloway was featured in Fred Waller's *Cab Calloway's Jitterbug Party* (1931); he appeared with Adelaide Hall, the Nicholas Brothers, and Eunice Wilson in *Dixieland Jamboree* (Warners and Vitaphone, 1935); he was featured again in Fred Waller's *Cab Calloway's Hi-De-Ho* (Paramount, 1934), along with his orchestra, and again three years later with another musical short with the same title, *Cab Calloway's Di-De-Ho* (Paramount, 1937); he appeared with Isham Jones and His Orchestra in *Meet the Maestros* (Paramount, 1938); and in the forties, Cab Calloway's scat song, "Hi-De-Hot" was featured in Anglo-American Josh Binney's *Hi-De-Ho* (All-American, 1947), an independent production with Jeni LeGon and Ida James in it as well. Among the many in which Duke Ellington appeared were *A Bundle of Blues* (Paramount, 1933), with Ivy Anderson; he was featured in *Duke Ellington and His Orchestra* (RKO, 1943), along with Johnny Hodges, Ben

Webster, Ray Nance, and Taft Jordan; and he appeared in George Gershwin's documentary for the March of Times Series, *Upbeat in Music* (1943), along with Marian Anderson and Art Tatum.

The popular Hall Johnson Choir had performed in many films of the thirties, including *The Hall Johnson Choir in a Syncopated Sermon* (Warners, 1935), *Banjo on My Knee* (Twentieth Century-Fox, 1936), and *Lost Horizon* (Columbia, 1937). In addition to these feature films and appearances in numerous musical shorts, the Hall Johnson Choir appeared in George Randol's *Deep South* (RKO, 1937), which was a runner-up for an Academy Award for the best photography. Individual actors who were or would become famous in feature-length films appeared in these musical shorts as well: Stepin Fetchit as a toned down coon and performer in *Slow Poke* (Educational Pictures and Fox, 1932); Bill Robinson in *King for a Day* (1934) with Dusty Fletcher; Frank Wilson in a short based on Stephen Foster's songs, *Melody Makers Series* (Wardour Films, 1932); Frank Wilson and Ethel Waters in *Bubbling Over* (RKO, 1934); Lena Horne and Teddy Wilson in the independent *Harlem Hotshots* (Metropolitan, 1940; Lena Horne, the Ebony Trio, and Alex Brown in *Bip Bam Boogie* (ca. 1940's); Lena Horne in *Hi-De-Ho Holiday* (ca. 1940's); and Dorothy Dandridge and Herbert Jeffries in Stillman Pond Productions' *Flamingo* (1947).

Featured bands and orchestras reflected the popular music of the era: Claude Hopkins Band and the Nicholas Brothers in *Barbershop Blues* (1932); *Don Redman and His Orchestra* (Warners and Vitaphone, 1934); *Jimmie Lunceford and His Dance Orchestra* (1936); The Ernest Hawkins Orchestra and Wilbur Bascomb in *Deviled Hams* (1937); Lee Hite and His Orchestra and June Richmond in *Murder in Swingtime* (RKO, 1937); Lee Nroman's Orchestra and Arthur White's Lindy Hoppers in *Jittering Jitter-Bugs* (1938); Count Basie and His Orchestra in *Choo Choo Swing* (Universal, 1943); Rita Rio and Her All-Girl Band in *Sweet Shoe* (ca. 1940's); Louis Jordan and His Band in *Toot That Trumpet* (1946); and Billy Eckstine and His Orchestra and Ann Baker, Micky O'Daniel, and Al Guster in *Harlem after Midnight* (1947). At the same time, the popular Bebop music of Dizzy Gillespie was featured in *Oop Boop Sh'Bam* (1947), *Ee Baba Leba* (1947) with Helen Humes and Ralph Brown, *Harlem Dynamite* (1947), and *Harlem Rhythm* (1947). Others in the forties were Ralph Brown and Ella Mae Harris in *Swing It Harlem* (1941) and Edna Mae Harris and "Rubberneck" Holmes in *Solid Senders* (ca. 1940's). On occasion these all-black musical shorts included Anglo-Americans. Anglo-American Barney Kessel, "shot in silhouette," appears in *Jammin' the Blues* (Warners, 1944), with the Afro-Americans Harry Edison, Lester Young, Illinois Jacquet, Philly Jo Jones, Sidney Catlett, Red Callender, and Marie Bryant. These shorts were to continue well into the sixties, but those which Anglo-American Will Cowan directed for Universal Interantional marked the end of an era: *Symphony in Swing* (1949) with Duke Ellington and His Orchestra and the Delta Rhythm Boys; *"King" Cole and His Trio* (1950) with Benny Carter and His Orchestra and "Scat Man" Crothers; *Frankie "Sugar Chile" Robinson--Billie Holliday--Count Basie and His Sextet* (1950); *Sarah Vaughn and Herb Jeffries/Kid Ory and His Creole Jazz Band* (1950); *Salute to Duke Ellington* (1950); *Nat "King" Cole and Joe Adams' Orchestra* (1951); *Nat "King" Cole and Buss Morgan's Orchestra* (1953); and into the mid-fifties with *Lionel Hampton and Herb Jeffries* (1955), which was also titled *Negro Marches On*.

Hollywood's all-black musical shorts did not exist in a vacuum through all these years. Hollywood made other feature-length all-black films which were, with only the two exceptions of *The Emperor Jones* (1933) and *Bright Road* (1953), in the tradition of the musicals. With only two out of hundreds of all-black musicals, features and shorts, having dramatic rather than musical content, the Hollywood record of ignoring Afro-Americans in roles other than those of entertainers was incredibly biased. The film industry may as well have been back in the early days of blackfacing both Anglo-Americans and Afro-Americans before allowing them to be minstrels. As already noted, Al Jolson's *The Jazz Singer* (1927) did not eliminate blackfacing from the screen, but it narrowed the range of its application to entertainers or comedians, with a few exceptions, rather than to exotics or villains. The initial empathy by Afro-Americans in seeing even a Hollywood imitation of their music and traditions in *The Jazz Singer*, an empathy spurred by the possibilities it represented for future representations of their culture, was quickly dissipated.

In the thirties, Warner Brothers continued to promote Al Jolson in blackface in musical feature films like the roadshow minstrelsy in *Mammy* (1930). Jolson also appeared as a blackface jockey in *Big Boy* (1930); in blackface in *Go into Your Dance* (1935), with "Snowflake" (Fred Toones) listed in the credits as Jolson's "valet"; and in blackface in *The Singing Kid* (1936), in which there was rapport other than in musical numbers between blackface Jolson and Cab Calloway. For First National, Jolson did *Wonder Bar* (1934), a burlesque of the stage production of *The Green Pastures*. Jolson had wanted to do the role of De Lawd in the all-black film version of *The Green Pastures* (1936), then in the planning stages, but he settled for a blackface act in which he sang "Goin' to Heaven on a Mule" in *Wonder Bar*.

The generation's only all-black dramatic film by Hollywood, *The Emperor Jones*, had come and gone and the return to the all-black musical features was just around the corner with *The Green Pastures*. In some ways the most gratifying film made of Afro-Americans, Dudley Murphy's *The Emperor Jones* (United Artists, 1933), was based upon the racially ambiguous play by Eugene O'Neill. It was not an entirely all-black cast--Anglo-Americans Dudley Diggs and Brendon Evans were in it--but the film is best placed in the Hollywood all-black tradition. In perhaps the finest Afro-American performances to date, Rex Ingram, Jackie Mayble, George Haymind Stamper, Gordon Taylor, and Blueboy O'Connor, along with Paul Robeson as Brutas Jones, Frank Wilson as Jeff, Fredi Washington as Undine, and Ruby Elzy as Dolly overrode the worst of O'Neill's exotic and often racially demeaning images. The production quality was not higher than the best of the independents, but the film helped make stars of Ingram and Robeson. Robeson's roguish and power hungry Brutas Jones, the Pullman portor who becomes king of a Caribbean island, was perhaps his finest role. To the delight of Afro-American audiences, Robeson as Brutas turned the tables and subjugated whites, though he pays in the end when he is hunted down and slain. Ingram went on to become one of the few Afro-American actors allowed to exhibit his full human stature in his usually small film roles, but Robeson's career slumped into well-intended but frequently ignoble roles. The Anglo-American press and Anglo-American audiences praised the film. The NAACP balked at endorcing the film and the Afro-American press was skeptical, but many Afro-Americans saw it as an achievement. The result was that the controversial film was a financial failure.

Thus, Hollywood decided to return to the all-black musical feature in hopes of finding a money-maker. The musical shorts remained popular. Fred Waller's *Symphony in Black* (1935) featured Duke Ellington, Earl "Snakehips" Tucker, and Billie Holliday in her first film appearance. *Symphony in Black* chose the urban milieu, but apparently only in the musical shorts was this to be case, for the following year Hollywood returned to the old southern mold it had used in *Hearts in Dixie* and *Hallelujah* with Marc Connelly's Pulitzer-Prize winning play *The Green Pastures* in 1936. Anglo-American audiences during the Great Depression were not yet ready to accept full characterizations of Afro-Americans, like those in *The Emperor Jones*, regardless of the quality of their roles.

Staring Rex Ingram, one of the celebrated Afro-American dramatists of the era, *The Green Pastures* (Warners, 1936), was Hollywood's first all-black box office success. It was a fantasy using religious allegory on which to metaphorically represent Afro-American culture. Its most outstanding features as a film were twenty-five spirituals and the "Great Fish Fry" in heaven. Such all-black Hollywood productions did nothing to correct the shallow Afro-American on the screen. Individual portrayals by Afro-Americans were oftentimes exceptional despite the image their roles created. Among the other members of the cast were Oscar Polk, Eddie Anderson, Frank Wilson, Ernest Whitman, William Cumby, Edna Mae Harris, Al Stokes, David Bethea, George Reed, Clinton Rosemond, and Myrtle Anderson. But the content revealed little more than entertaining quasi-interpretations of the fashionable images of laziness and zealous religiosity coveted by Anglo-American audiences.

Two more popular all-black Hollywood films, both in the tradition of shallow musicals, were made mid-way through World War Two. *Stormy Weather* and *Cabin in the Sky* were 1943 extravaganzas of Afro-American talent representative of the height of the obsession with the Afro-American as natural-born musician and perfect entertainer, to use Reddick's designations, which got underway a century earlier with the birth of Negro minstrelsy. Both films reflect a dominant Hollywood concept of the Afro-American as entertainer, called once again into service as part of the war effort, rather than as a serious participant in the war effort. Andrew Stone's *Stormy Weather* (Twentieth Century-Fox, 1943), featured Bill "Bojangles" Robinson as Corky, Cab Calloway and his band, Fats Waller, the Nicholas Brothers, Dooley Wilson, Ernest Whitman, Nicodemus Stewart, Flournoy E. Miller, Zuttie Singleton, Babe Wallace, Ada Brown, and the pert Lena Horne as Robinson's sweetheart and then wife. The film unravels as a series of flashbacks of Robinson's life as a dancer. He has just received a twenty-fifth anniversary copy of *Theater World* dedicated to him, and he fondly recalls his career in show business. *Stormy Weather's* attempt to inspire pride in the fact that an Afro-American could make it in America, in show business at least, also featured the Cakewalk, perhaps the first dance originating in the Afro-American community to be popularized in the America of the 1890's.

Similarly slight, Vincent Minnelli's *Cabin in the Sky* (MGM, 1943), revolved around a battle for the soul of Little Joe (Eddie "Rochester" Anderson) between his wife, Petunia (Ethel Waters), the temptress Georgia Brown (Lena Horne), and Lucifer (Rex Ingram). Willie Best, Butterfly McQueen, Kenneth Spencer, Ernest Whitman, Mantan Moreland, Ruby Dandridge, Buck and Bubbles (Ford Lee and John Sublette), and Oscar Polk were present, too, as was the musical accompaniment of Louis Armstrong, Duke Ellington's Orchestra, and the Hall Johnson Choir. The slim plot revolves around a heavenly battle for Little Joe's soul. Regardless of whether these two films represented what the public most wanted to see of Afro-Americans, or whether they represented what Hollywood wanted the public to see, they were popular musicals in which there was no connection between reality and ideality. They were outlandish entertainments typical of musicals in which "ersatz Negro folk culture," Donald Bogle reminds the readers of *Toms, Coons, Mulattoes, Mammies, and Bucks* (1973), "was passed off as the real thing."[1] This was, of course, part and parcel of the same tradition which spawned the earlier all-black Hollywood films such as *The Green Pastures* (1936), *Hearts in Dixie* (1929), and *Hallelujah* (1929).

There were two other Hollywood musicals which were longer than shorts but not quite feature-length that included all-black casts. With a story revolving around the creation of a black radio station, *Black Network* (Vitaphone, 1936), the cast included Nina Mae McKinney, the Nicholas Brothers, and Amanda Randolf. Katherine Dunham's famous dance troupe with Archie Savage did *Carnival in Rhythm* (Warners, 1940), which celebrated Afro-Cuban dancing. The latter was one of the few positive cultural statements allowed by Hollywood on film, even though it was done in the entertainer mode. A principle applicable to these Hollywood films and to the segregated Hollywood movies of the thirties and forties was that the larger the audience a producer sought, the more the producer was likely to reduce the film's content to commonplace and stereotypical elements. This was before the era in which Hollywood producers avidly sought specialized subcultural themes. In the case of the all-black films, and the Hollywood films in which Afro-Americans appeared in segregated scenes, it was entertainment which provided the common medium for the largest audience. And Afro-Americans were good at entertaining. The Afro-American film appearances during the thirties and forties consisted overwhelmingly of safe roles as dancers, fun-makers and musicians. Frederick Douglass once said, "Who could speak of the singing among slaves as evidence of their contentment and happiness? Slaves sing most when they are most unhappy . . . the songs of the slave represent the sorrows of his heart; and he is relieved by them, only as an aching heart is relieved by its tears."[2] Twentieth-century Hollywood all-black productions still continued this myth of the singing slave through the vehicle of the all-black light musical. The narrowness of this range of Hollywood perceptions indicates also the narrowness of the American popular mind's concepts of Afro-Americans.

It was difficult for some producers and some Afro-American actors and actresses to remember slavery days. On the eve of the *Brown* decision, when the biases from the Griffith era of filmmaking were being overturned, when it seemed that the attempts of the problem-cycle films of the late forties and early fifties to create new images were to be successful, Otto Preminger produced *Carmen Jones* (Twentieth Century-Fox, 1954). So successful was *Carmen Jones* that Preminger attempted to repeat his feat with *Porgy and Bess* (Columbia, 1959), a full five years after the *Brown* decision. A throwback to the twenties, Preminger based the latter film on the 1928 Broadway musical, *Porgy*, which in turn was based on Southerners Dorothy and DuBose Heywood's book, *Porgy* (1925). With all that was happening in America pointing to an entirely different direction, these anomalies by Preminger were representations of nothing but a fantasized slice of a Hollywood studio creation. Yet tremendous profits came from their abuse of the Afro-American culture. These movies were popular but out of touch with America; they appealed to something in the national psyche with their malignant content, but to state that they were a generation out-of-date would be too mild. They never were in-date; they never should have found a place in cinematic history. The cast gathered for *Carmen Jones* read like the honor roll of Afro-American talent in the fifties: Harry Belafonte as Joe, Dorothy Dandridge as Carmen, Joe Adams as Husky, along with Pearl Bailey, Diahann Carroll, Olga James, and Brock Peters were all piloted through *Carmen Jones* and, in the case of many of them, *Porgy and Bess*. All the old themes and myths were present, with the addition of black eroticism, and the talent was as orchestrated as was the music. Even the voices of Dandridge and Belafonte, both of whom had previously been successful in careers as singers, were dubbed in by the Anglo-Americans Marilyn Horn and LaVern Huchenson, a technique which was repeated in *Porgy and Bess*. There were losts of jobs and lots of money for the Afro-Americans who submitted to this pandering before cardboard settings complemented by a cardboard plot: Joe deserts the Army in World War Two for Carmen, they run away together, Carmen leaves Joe for a prizefighter, and Joe strangles Carmen.

The roles for Afro-American entertainers did not diminish in the thirties and forties as films like *Carmen Jones* and *Porgy and Bess* illustrate. Aside from the all-black Hollywood musicals, Afro-American independents made many similar films like *Danger in the Dark* (1932) with Adelaide Hall and Duke Ellington; *Merry Howe Carfe* (ca. 1939) with Freddie Jackson, Jeni Legon, and Monte Hawley; and *Junction 88* (ca. 1940's) with Noble Sissle, Bob Howard, Dewey "Pigmeat" Markham, and Wyatt Clark. In addition, the Afro-Americans who appeared in or did the music for other Hollywood films of the thirties, forties, and fifties are almost uncountable. Among many others were the following: Lionel Hampton in *Sing Singer Sing* (Majestic, 1933); the Mills Brothers in *20 Million Sweethearts* (First National, 1934); Allen Joskins and Nina Mae McKinney, who dubbed Jean Harlow's songs for her, in *Reckless* (MGM, 1935); Bill "Bojangles" Robinson and Fats Waller in *Hooray for Love* (RKO, 1935); Fats Waller in *King of Burlesque* (Twentieth Century-Fox, 1936); Cab Calloway and his band in *Manhattan Merry-Go-Round* (Republic, 1937); Duke Ellington and his band in *The Hit Parade of 1937* (Republic, 1937), also titled *I'll Reach for a Star*; the "King" Cole Trio in *Here Comes Elmer* (1943), also titled *Hitch-Hike to Happiness*; the Step Brothers and Lester Horton Dancers in *Rhythm of the Islands* (1943); and into the fifties, Monette Moore in *Yes Sir, Mr. Bones* (1951). Even overseas, the roles were often the same for Afro-Americans. The Mills Brothers performed in a film variously titled *Sing as You Swing*, *Swing Tease*, and *The Music Box* (England, 1937), and

Johnny Russell was featured as a jazz musician in *L'Alibi* (France, 1938), or *The Alibi*.

In the cultural context, despite the distorted images, all-black films gained for the small segment of the American populace who viewed them an exposure to Afro-Americans. Oftentimes it was an exposure to imitation Afro-American people. *In Old Kentucky* was remade as a musical in this era; two versions of Edna Ferber's novel, *Show Boat*, were filmed as musicals during this era; and *The St. Louis Blues* was remade with an almost all-white cast and then again with an all-black cast in this era. As preludes to a dominant Hollywood trend in which mixed-blood characters would be called Negroes, but would be played by Anglo-Americans, a trend that was first established with blackfacing prior to the sound era, all the versions of *Show Boat* (1929, 1936, and 1951), used an Anglo-American actress in the important role of the "mulatto," and even into the fifties this would continue with the Anglo-Americans Natalie Wood as the "mulatto" in *Kings Go Forth* (1958) and Susan Kohner as the "mulatto" in the remake of *Imitation of Life* (1959). This was done even though the Hays Office in the twenties, the film industry's Motion Picture Code of Production in 1933, and the agreements reached between the NAACP and Hollywood in 1942 forbade the presentation of miscegenation themes. In the films of this era, Hollywood avoided the distinctive qualities of Afro-American culture by relying on ever more fantastic fantasies, especially in the musicals. In these musicals, Hollywood presented the Afro-American in covert, non-specific situations that had little to do with real life. Cousin to these all-black films were the mostly white Hollywood films in which specifically segregated scenes, discussed in more detail in the following chapter, were frequently given to Afro-Americans.

In America's film culture, the only all-black film after *The Emperor Jones* (1933) which made an attempt to use drama instead of music to portray Afro-Americans was *Bright Road* (1953). It was an entire generation of neglect on Hollywood's part. *Bright Road* was so atypical that it is discussed in more detail in the chapter titled Problematic Films: The Unfinished Image. It was a hopeful title, *Bright Road*, but in 1953 the only hope on the horizon came not from Hollywood but from the soon to be won *Brown* decision.

Notes

[1] Donald Bogle, *Toms, Coons, Mulattoes, Mammies, and Bucks: An Interpretive History of Blacks in American Films* (New York: Viking, 1973), p. 131.

[2] Frederick Douglass, *Narrative of the Life of Frederick Douglass, an American Slave*, ed. by Benjamin Quarles (Cambridge: Harvard Univ. Press, 1967), p. 38.

Chapter Twelve

Segregated Hollywood Films

Jesse Owens accomplished a moral as well as a physical victory for Afro-Americans and Anglo-Americans alike when he outperformed Adolf Hitler's "superior race" of Anglo-Saxon Germans at the 1936 Berlin Olympics. Americans loved Owens, and his four Gold Medals, but on the homefront the most popular genre of the thirties in Hollywood films with Afro-Americans in them was the Jim Crow or segregated films. Afro-American players in these films were included in large numbers. Their roles were predominantly those in which they appeared only in separate scenes, as in the musicals beginning with *Fox Movietone Follies* (Twentieth Century-Fox, 1929), in which Stepin Fetchit's first film role was as a scatterbrained dancer, or in roles in which Afro-Americans were portrayed as subservient, ignorant, or comic. In the musicals, segregated scenes were common fare, using such celebrated Afro-American musicians as Duke Ellington, Louis Armstrong, and Lena Horne. In the subservient roles, the best remembered figures are Hattie McDaniel, Louise Beavers, and the "happy Negroes," Bill "Bojangles" Robinson, Stepin Fetchit, Clarence Muse, and "Sleep 'n' Eat" Willie Best. The positive factor in all this was that Hollywood provided a showcase for Afro-American "talents." The negative of all this was that the limited and stereotypical roles affected how Afro-Americans were viewed. As with many Afro-Americans working in films during the thirties and forties, the role these talented Afro-Americans were given rarely made full use of their talents. In the crowning (almost literally) experience for Afro-Americans in the thirties, Hattie McDaniel did receive the Oscar in 1939 for best supporting actress for her comic-mammy role in *Gone with the Wind*, an award which many in the Afro-American community thought she should refuse in protest of the Afro-American images Hollywood consistently presented.

Hattie McDaniel's role in *Gone with the Wind* was stereotyped but successful in the context of the film, a paradox which raises a suggestive issue concerning the adequacy of the concept of stereotyping in explaining Afro-American images in film. I.C. Jarvie contends in *Movies and Society* (1970) that "one of the most underrated strengths of the popular arts is their use of formulas," and that "the stereotype and rituals need not enslave the creator, [for] they can be exploited to challenge or surprise the audience."[1] This Hattie McDaniel successfully did in *Gone with the Wind*. Unfortunately, the potential for exploiting stereotypes was a rarity in films when it came to Afro-Americans.

Audiences, whether Afro-American or Anglo-American, obviously chose to support recurrent stereotypes by steadily attending those films which were the most formulaic without the surprise or twist on the stereotype, like the films of Will Rogers and Stepin Fetchit or Shirley Temple and Bill "Bojangles" Robinson. But the concept of stereotyping explains little more about an image than the fact that it exists in patterns of superficial deductions about groups of people. The inadequacy of this explanation indicates that further investigations into the reasons behind the development of a stereotype, reaching perhaps into the realm of archetypes, is needed. The present study only cursorily deals with this phenomenon, but other recent studies have enlarged upon these concepts. Most useful is John G. Cawelti's *Adventure, Mystery, and Romance: Formula Stories as Art and Popular Culture* (1976). Cawelti explores formulas in popular film as well as popular literature, and he provides methodological insights into such studies as that of the black image in popular American films.[2]

One of the recurrent formulas of the thirties was that which placed Afro-Americans in the setting of the rural South as slaves, domestics, or troublemakers to be put back into their place. Another was the use of segregated scenes, in deference to the South, for Afro-American entertainers appearing in films. Segregated Jim Crow sequences in Hollywood films were present throughout the thirties and forties. Afro-American and Anglo-American musicians did not usually appear together in the same scenes despite the fame and popularity of many of the Afro-American entertainers. Some exceptions occurred when Afro-Americans and Anglo-Americans met in foreign countries, as with Dooley "Play It Again, Sam" Wilson, the piano player in *Casablanca* (1942), but Afro-Americans were most frequently presented as entertainers even when their roles were not segregated.

In the first generation of sound movies, from approximately 1929 to 1949, the following were but some of the many segregated appearances of Afro-American entertainers in Hollywood films: The Mills Brothers, Cab Calloway, who does "Minnie the Moocher," and Benny Carter in *The Big Broadcast* (Paramount, 1932); Cab Calloway singing "Reefer Man" in *International House* (Paramount, 1933); Cab Calloway in David Butler's *Ali Baba Goes to Town* (1937); the Mills Brothers in both *Strictly Dynamite* (RKO, 1934) and *Rhythm Parade* (Monogram, 1942); the Nicholas Brothers as Dot and Dash in featured scenes in *Big Broadcast of 1936* (Paramount, 1935), in *Down Argentine Way* (Twentieth Century-Fox, 1940), with the Four Inkspots in *The Great American Broadcast* (Fox, 1941), in several numbers with Dorothy Dandridge in *Sun Valley Serenade* (Twentieth Century-Fox, 1944), and in *The Pirate* (MGM, 1948); Etta Moten's "Remember My Forgotten Man" in *Gold Diggers of 1933* (Warners, 1933); the performances in night club scenes of Louis Armstrong in *Pennies from Heaven* (Columbia, 1937), with Lionel Hampton in one number as well, in *Doctor Rhythm* (Paramount, 1938), in *Every Day's a Holiday* (Paramount, 1938), and in *Atlantic City* (Republic, 1945); the one number by Duke Ellington and His Orchestra in *Murder at the Vanities* (Paramount, 1934); the one sequence in which Jimmy Lunceford and his band appear in *Blues in the Night* (Paramount, 1941), also titled *Hot Nocturne*; the performances by Count Basie and his band and the Delta Rhythm Boys in *Crazy House/Funzapoppin* (1943); the performances by Count Basie and his band and Louise Franklin in *Crazy House* (Universal, 1943); the segregated sequences from *Show Boat* featuring Lena Horne and Caleb Peterson in *Till the Clouds Roll By* (MGM, 1946); Lena Horne and Avon Long in one appearance in *Ziegfield Follies* (MGM, 1946); Avon Long's one song in *Centennial Summer* (Twentieth Century-Fox, 1946); Avon Long's one dance in *Romance on the High Seas* (Warners, 1948); and Lena Horne's appearance in *Words and Music* (MGM, 1948). There were others, like Jeni LeGon's one dance routine with Les Hite and His Orchestra in the background in *Fools for Scandal* (Warners, 1938), and those in which Hattie McDaniel, Willie Best, Bill Robinson, and Eddie Anderson, all people to be discussed in greater detail shortly, appeared: the "Specialty Dancer" in the credits of *Dixiana* (Radio Pictures, 1930), was Bill Robinson; Eddie Anderson and Katherine Dunham did an act together in *Star-Spangled Rhythm* (Paramount, 1942); and Hattie McDaniel and Willie Best's one number in *Thank Your Lucky Stars* (Warners, 1943).

There other films in which both kinds of segregation were present, that of isolated appearances as well as of the segregation of subservience. In the Fred Astaire and Ginger Rogers film, *Flying Down to Rio* (RKO, 1933), Etta Moten is segregated when she sings the title song, but Clarence Muse appears in other scenes; similarly it was Clarence Muse and other Afro-Americans as servants, waiters, and tap dancers in *Night and Day* (Warners, 1946), in which Hazel Scott appears only as herself. Muse frequently appeared as a domestic, at times as a coon, and often as a sidekick to an Anglo-American. Many of his films have already been mentioned, as well as the many screenplays he wrote and the Afro-American independent films he appeared in. Among his other films is an impressive and, unlike the other major actors to be discussed in this chapter, varied collection.

Clarence Muse's appearances included his role as Clarence in Frank Capra's Antarctic thriller, *Dirigible* (Columbia, 1931); in a featured role in the murder mystery, *Secret Witness* (Columbia, 1931), also titled *Secret Wilderness*; as the blind begger and an advisor during the filming of *The Cabin in the Cotton* (Warners and First National, 1932), a film that also had Fred "Snowflake" Toones in it; as Horace in *Is MY Face Red?* (RKO, 1932); as Jeff in the courtroom drama, *Attorney for the Defense* (Columbia, 1932); as James Cagney's trainer in the boxing film, *Winner Take All* (Warners, 1933); as Sam who teams up with an ostracized Indian in *Massacre* (First National, 1934); as co-star with Anglo-American Warner Baxter in a race track film, *Broadway Bill* (Columbia, 1934); as Jeff in an exceptionally good performance in *O'Shaughnessy's Boy* (MGM, 1935); as Deacon in a combination boxing film and musical, *Laughing Irish Eyes* (Republic, 1936); as Tiger in *Secrets of a Nurse* (Universal, 1938); as Evans in a Bela Lugosi mystery, *The Invisible Ghost* (Monogram, 1941); as a Pullman porter in an Alfred Hitchcock thriller, *Shadow of a Doubt* (Universal, 1943); as Jasper in the comedy, *Heaven Can Wait* (Twentieth Century-Fox, 1943); and again as a porter in *Two Smart People* (MGM, 1946). Muse also had bit parts in *Rain or Shine* (1930); *The Woman from Monte Carlo* (First National, 1931); *The Mind Reader* (Warners, 1933); *Alias Mary Dow* (Universal, 1935); *Muss 'Em Up* (RKO, 1936); *Joe Palooka in the Knockout* (1947); *An Act of Murder* (Universal, 1948); and an appearance in *Broken Earth* (ca. 1940's).

A talented performer whose roles were much more stereotyped than Muse's was Bill "Bojangles" Robinson, best remembered for his formulaic characterizations in the Shirley Temple children's classics. His was a copasetic (a term he coined with the attendant definition of "capital, snappy, prime"), attitude that nothing could ruffle. He was the epitomy of the "happy Negro" in films. The Robinson/Temple performances were in David Butler's *The Little Colonel* (Twentieth Century-Fox, 1935), *The Littlest Rebel* (Twentieth Century-Fox, 1936), and *Just Around the Corner* (Twentieth Century-Fox, 1938), and *Rebecca of Sunnybrook Farm* (Twentieth Century-Fox, 1938), in which half of Robinson's scenes involved both singing and dancing. Their performances together almost always included the "stair dance" which Robinson took with him from tap dancing days in vaudeville to his stint on Broadway in Lew Leslie's *Blackbirds* (1927), and then to his movies with Temple, the last of which was *Curly Top* (1938). In David Butler's *The Little Colonel* and *The Littlest Rebel*, the old southern milieu is present again as it was in so many films of the thirties. In the first of these, Robinson is the butler, Walker, and Hattie McDaniel is a rather weak mammy. Little Shirley keeps the pickaninnies in line. In *The Littlest Rebel*, Robinson is a patient and trustworthy tom, Uncle Billy. Willie Best appears as the irresponsible coon and Shirley fits in a blackface scene. Robinson's other roles in these films were similar whether he was Aloysius or Corporal Jones the doorman. Unique among American film images, Afro-American Robinson and Anglo-American Temple were allowed to develop a childish love relationship on the screen which Donald Bogle in *Toms, Coons, Mulattoes, Mammies, and Bucks* (1973) refers to as "the perfect interracial love match."[3] Miscegenation was a standard topic for Hollywood, but the acts which produced the miscegenation were not. It took another thirty years for an Afro-American male, Jim Brown, to become involved in a mature and explicit interracial sex match with an Anglo-American female, Raquel Welch, in *100 Rifles* (1968).

Prior to a brief appearance in *Road Demon* (1938), Bill Robinson had appeared with Fredi Washington and Eddie Anderson in *One Mile from Heaven* (Twentieth Century-Fox, 1937). The form of segregation which put Bill Robinson in subservient roles except when he danced with a young white girl was present in many of the films of Eddie Anderson. He played the entertainer, the coon, and the foil to Jack Benny. Among his more prominent roles were in the comic role as Mose in *Three Men on a Horse* (Warners, 1936); as comic relief in *Melody for Two* (Warners, 1939); as Donald, along with Robert "Smokey" Whitfield and Lillian Yarbo as Rheba, in Frank Capra's *You Can't Take It With You* (Columbia, 1938); as "Cheerful" of the circus in W.C. Fields' *You Can't Cheat an Honest Man* (Universal, 1939); as a featured performer in *Kiss the Boys Good-Bye* (Paramount, 1941); as Lovey, a musician, along with Ruby Elzy whose only other film role was in *The Emperor Jones*, in *Birth of the Blues* (Paramount, 1941); as one of a group who turn a ghost town into a resort in *What's Buzzin' Cousin* (Columbia, 1943); and as Jackson in *Brewster's Millions* (United Artists, 1945).

Eddie Anderson is probably best remembered for his films with Jack Benny. As Rochester, Anderson often "stole the show" in *Man About Town* (Paramount, 1939), with Teresa Harris, *Love Thy Neighbor* (Paramount, 1940), the comedy western *Buck Benny Rides Again* (Paramount, 1940), and *The Meanest Man in the World* (Twentieth Century-Fox, 1943). Among Anderson's other film appearances were *The Music Goes 'Round* (Columbia, 1936); *On Such a Night* (Paramount, 1937); *White Bondage* (Warners, 1937); *Bill Cracks Down* (Republic, 1937); *I Love a Bandleader* (1945); *The Sailor Takes a Wife* (MGM, 1946); *Memory for Two* (Columbia, 1946), with Louise Franklin; and *The Show-Off* (MGM, 1946). Anderson's career in films ended shortly after World War Two, but he did appear as a cabbie in *It's a Mad, Mad, Mad World* (United Artists, 1963).

The man who could dance like Bill "Bojangles" Robinson, act as the foil to a white man like Eddie "Rochester" Anderson, and shuffle his way through the thirties as the definitive coon was Lincoln "Stepin Fetchit" Perry. When he provided the humor, it was comic relief at its worst. Because of his notorious film image, Stepin Fetchit became the most famous and most maligned of the Afro-American actors in the thirties. In *Dimples* (Twentieth Century-Fox, 1936), it was Stepin Fetchit instead of Bill "Bojangles" Robinson who performed as Shirley Temple's dance partner. The plot of *Dimples* involves the putting on of a production of *Uncle Tom's Cabin* in New York City prior to the Civil War. Fetchit's successful portrayal of the subservient and comical "darkie" who was so short on intellect in *Dimples* that as Cicero he was confused over the reason firemen wear red suspenders became a norm by which many Anglo-Americans could measure Afro-Americans. Popular because of his deficiencies, Fetchit's screen image was Jim Crowism personified. The American public, excluding those Afro-Americans who had been warned off by civil rights groups, loved his antics both on and off the screen. When he was not being fired or hired by a studio, he was being advertised by a studio as a flamboyant gadabout who wore $2,000 suits and drove a pink Cadillac or a pink Rolls Royce. Similarly, Bill Robinson was the idol of Harlem, and at one time the Honorary Mayor of Harlem, who sported about in a chauffer-driven Deusenberg with the licence number "BR6."

Today, television reruns often cut out Stepin Fetchit sequences when showing a film in which he appeared. There had been a change in what was considered acceptable Afro-American images, although proud Fetchit maintained that "I was a 100% black accomplishment." Similar examples of such changes were television's refusal to keep *Amos "n" Andy* on the air in the early fifties and to not show D.W. Griffith's *The Birth of a Nation* when it was proposed to do so in the late fifties. In each instance, it was pressures from the Afro-American community and from civil rights groups which achieved these notable gains in the television medium, gains which had not been possible with America's movie industry. Harry Menig gives a summation of what he considers the most informed Anglo-American attitudes concerning Stepin Fetchit's roles in the movies:

> It is one of the unfortunate aspects of the nostalgia of these films that the Black actor often had to take the brunt of the "good natured" fun. If for a moment one can forget the image, one may find Stepin Fetchit one of the funniest men in show business.[4]

The censorship of Fetchit's film images may backfire in the long run. In the minds of both Afro-Americans and Anglo-Americans, interest has been rekindled concerning the dichotomy between Fetchit as an artist and Fetchit as an unfortunate victim of Anglo-American control of the Afro-American image in films.

The films in which Stepin Fetchit was paired with Will Rogers were *Steamboat 'Round the Bend* (Twentieth Century-Fox, 1935), *Judge Priest* (Twentieth Century-Fox, 1935), *The Country Chairman* (Fox, 1935), and, discussed earlier, *David Harum* (Fox, 1934). These films further reflected popular attitudes toward Afro-Americans by presenting a master/servant relationship between Will Rogers and Stephin Fetchit similar to that of Robinson Crusoe and Friday. Donald Bogle describes Rogers/Fetchit relationship as the *huckfinn fixation*. It is, states Bogle, a phenomenon which "perhaps represents the white liberal American's dream of lost innocence and freedom," and it is "closely aligned to the master-servant syndrome yet with far deeper connotations."[5] Films like *Casablanca* (Warners, 1942), in which Dooley Wilson as Sam the piano player is an associate of Humphrey Bogart's Rick, are related to the *huckfinn fixation*, Bogle asserts, for

> The essential scenario for the exploration of the *huckfinn fixation* is quite simple: A good white man opposes the corruption and pretenses of the dominant white culture. In rejecting society, he (like Huck Finn) takes up with an outcast. The other man (like Nigger Jim) is a trusty black who never competes with the white man and who serves as a reliable ego padder.[6]

While this is true, it dismisses the essential dignity of the character Jim and fails to take into account the very crux of the Huck Finn/Jim relationship--that of Huck's conscientious efforts to come to grips with the essential issue of Jim's humanity. The film versions of Twain's *The Adventures of Huckleberry Finn* have, to be sure, complied with the *huckfinn fixation* as Bogle describes it. But Twain's novel is the source of the relationship between Huck and Jim and it presents a far more serious view. More befitting of the Will Rogers and Stepin Fetchit relationship is the analogy to Daniel Defoe's *Robinson Crusoe* (1719) and its presentation of the relationship between Crusoe and Friday. In this relationship the master/servant status is never questioned by the exiles/outcasts. The films which have been made from Defoe's work have also altered certain elements of the original, but the essence of the relationship between a white and a non-white remains intact.

In the first film version, *Robinson Crusoe* (1922), pal Friday was another black exotic in exile from Africa, just as were Afro-Americans in America by implication. This was contrary to Defoe's original work in which Friday is a light-skinned Caribbean, not a black-skinned African, though Noble Johnson, who played

Friday in this version, could have been either. The island fantasy where white supremacy is carried out far from civilization reflected America's isolationist views which were particularly strong in the twenties. Noble Johnson also appeared in *Little Robinson Crusoe* (1924), though this time as a cannibal chief. Jackie Coogan was the little Robinson who did what was expected: he finds a way to rule the island by becoming the war god of the cannibals. The dominance which the white character exerts because of the black character's superstitions is evident in the Rogers/Fetchit relationship. More interesting were the French versions, the first of which was like a mature Robinson/Temple relationship. In *Cain* (France, 1932), the white man, Cain (Crusoe), reaches an island near Madagascar where he battles the natives for, and wins, Zouzour (Friday) for his loyal companion. Luis Bunuel's *The Adventures of Robinson Crusoe* (France, 1953), was the best representation of the Defoe storyline, though Friday was again played by an Afro-American, James Fernandez. While actor Dan O'Herlihy was Crusoe. Americans have still to find a happy medium in dealing with Crusoe/Friday on film. The latest version, Jack Gold's *Man Friday* (Avco Embassy, 1970), presented Richard Roundtree as Friday and Peter O'Toole as Crusoe in a farcical reversal of the traditional roles which accomplished nothing in regard to alleviating the superior/inferior premises of white/black relations in America.

Thus, the Crusoe/Friday relationship in which Crusoe is the white missionary bending the will of the black native to his own ends. This manipulation of the master/servant relationship is far closer to the mark than the *huckfinn fixation* in regard to the Rogers and Fetchit films. Instead of an island isolated from civilization the setting is the South isolated from the North. Unlike the Huck/Jim relationship, in the Rogers/Fetchit relationship the white man reigns supreme in every way just as does Crusoe with Friday. These views were best represented by the southern settings of *Steamboat 'Round the Bend* and *Judge Priest*. The latter film was based on the stories of Kentucky in Irvin S. Cobb's *Old Judge Priest* (1915). Cobb was born in Paducah, Kentucky, on the Ohio River, and the theme of *Steamboat 'Round the Bend* is similar to Cobb's stories. Cobb, in fact, appears in *Steamboat 'Round the Bend* as the rival riverboat captain to Captain Will Rogers.

In one scene from *Steamboat 'Round the Bend*, the only Afro-Americans present at a marriage ceremony for an Anglo-American couple were humming throughout the scene. Afro-Americans were rarely shown as the bride and groom in wedding scenes of the thirties; the closest they ever seemed to get to a wedding was through the side, or perhaps the back, door as the accompaniment providing the music. It was the sort of image the Marx Brothers pictures portrayed throughout the decade, beginning with *Animal Crackers* (Paramount, 1930), in which four African natives give Groucho his grand entrance by carrying him into a grand ballroom that might metaphorically have been the decade of the thirties. In the Marx Brothers' *A Day at the Races* (MGM, 1937), Ivie Anderson, Leon James, Etta Moten and, perhaps Dorothy Dandridge as a child, are at the other extreme of the background hummers for they are presented as blacks singing their souls out in wild abandon. And, fittingly, at the end of the decade in *At the Circus* (MGM, 1939), it is a black crowd which applauds the musical antics of the Marx Brothers. It was a Crusoe/Friday decade which began with African natives, eased into the southern stereotype of the good-time Negro, and ended with Afro-Americans as the audience for the white man's circus. Stepin Fetchit was not an anomaly; he was the norm for the thirties.

In another scene from *Steamboat 'Round the Bend*, the wax figure of Robert E. Lee was unveiled as a stage attraction before a riotous group of Southerners. Accompanying the figure of Robert E. Lee, the revered leader of the southern cause in the Civil War, was a mechanized band cranked by a toothy Stepin Fetchit as Jonah the Janitor. Jonah, of course, makes his entrance by skidding from the mouth of a wax whale. The mechanized band is all-black. Not necessarily distorted portrayals of Afro-American realities, but unpleasantly common realities, were the jail scenes in *Steamboat 'Round the Bend* in which most inmates shown were Afro-Americans. In the sixties, the controversial Black Muslim militant, Malcolm X, stated that Afro-Americans do not get into a prison; they were born in a prison. Certainly, in many such prison scenes, Afro-Americans appear as if they had always been there.

The larger concept Malcolm X expressed was of America as a prison. It was precisely the sort of film treatment blacks were receiving in the thirties that led to the formulations of Elijah Muhammad which led to the founding of the Black Muslim religious movement in the thirties. Certainly America's film culture alone provided justification enough, though of course films were but one provocation, for the Black Muslim's strange conglomeration of Islam, hatred, and even the Protestant Ethic. At the same time it was an indigenous creation of the Afro-American community and one of its major recruiting grounds was America's prisons where a disproportionate number of Afro-Americans were confined. Given the overwhelming southern orientation in film culture and the Crusoe/Friday relationship that made people like Stepin Fetchit and Willie Best popular, the program of the Black Muslim's was a mild one indeed. Reflecting its roots in the Garveyism of the years just following World War One, the Black Muslims propagated the idea that white skin was a mutation from the black skins of the world's original inhabitants. Until Allah chose to eliminate the devil (white people), the goal of all Afro-Americans should be the creation of a separate state, the Nation of Islam, which Elijah Muhammad persistently called for until his death in 1975. The black power and black separatism themes of the Black Muslims, as well as the programs of the civil rights groups formed prior to the Second World War, would have a substantial and divisive impact on both Afro-Americans and Anglo-Americans in the sixties.

It was not just the coon images of Stepin Fetchit and Willie Best that represented through film culture what the Black Muslims objected to in America. The female counterparts of Fetchit and Best were the maids and mammies of Afro-Americans like Hattie McDaniel and Louise Beavers who were, the Black Muslims felt, in the employ of the devil by working for whites. On a less metaphorical level, McDaniel and Beavers represented another form of segregation or Jim Crowism found in film culture. In the Will Rogers and Stepin Fetchit film, *Judge Priest*, the South versus North theme is present and Hattie McDaniel is present too as a bossy mammy. Both Fetchit and McDaniel were repeating the roles they played in the Old South picture, *Carolina* (1934), that matched a Southerner and Northerner in marriage. The roles were typical of those Fetchit and McDaniel made a career by playing.

Fetchit's career included a small part in the important anti-war film, *The World Moves On* (Fox, 1934), and he was not even credited for his small appearance in *One More Spring* (Fox, 1935). Most of his film appearances were as a comic coon, as in his exaggerated fright at ghosts in *Helldorado* (Fox, 1935), which included Afro-American Lucky Hurlic for comedy as well. As Chan's chauffer, Snowshoes, in *Charlie Chan in Egypt*

(Warners, 1935), he was typically amazed when the ghost appeared in the pyramid. He was also typical Fetchit in the musical, *On the Avenue* (Fox, 1937), and as Percy in *Fifty Roads to Town* (Twentieth Century-Fox, 1937). Fetchit was Kokey, the comic, and Gertrude Howard was Naomi, in *The Southerner* (MGM, n.d.). He appeared in *36 Hours to Kill* (Twentieth Century-Fox, 1936), and *Elephants Never Forget* (1939). In the forties, he performed with Dorothy Dandridge in *Moo Cow Boogie* (1943) and made occasional appearances in all-black independent films, but his career was essentially at an end prior to World War Two.

The other major coon figure of the thirties, Willie Best, also appeared with Shirley Temple in *Little Miss Marker* (Paramount, 1934). His career was like a shadow to Stepin Fetchit's. He began appearing in films a few years after Fetchit and his career ended a few years after Fetchit's. Best did not have the talents of Fetchit, who could have been more than a coon, but he was successful in his carbon copies of Fetchit's antics. Best played roles like that of a porter in *Blondie* (Columbia, 1938), and *Vivacious Lady* (RKO, 1938); a stable hand and groom in *Home in Indiana* (Fox, 1944), and *Red Stallion* (Eagle-Lion, 1947); and a valet named Euclid White in *Whispering Ghosts* (Twentieth Century-Fox, 1942). Best was Pompay in *The Arizonian* (RKO, 1935), Eph in *Two in Revolt* (1936), Drowsy in *Thank You, Jeeves* (Twentieth Century-Fox, 1936), and Sambo in *I Take This Woman* (MGM, 1940). Typical of the terrifying settings in which he finds himself is the haunted mansion in *The Smiling Ghost* (Warners, 1941). The others were similar: *Make Way for a Lady* (RKO, 1936); *Racing Lady* (1937); *Super Sleuth* (RKO, 1937); *Breezing Home* (1937); *Gold Is Where You Find It* (Warners, 1938); *Merrily We Live* (Hal Roach, 1938); *Spring Madness* (MGM, 1938); *Youth Takes a Fling* (Universal, 1938); *Nancy Drew, Trouble Shooter* (Warners, 1939); *Who Killed Aunt Maggie?* (Republic, 1940); *Nothing but the Truth* (Paramount, 1941); *The Body Disappears* (Warners, 1942); *The Hidden Hand* (Warners, 1942); and *Pillow to Post* (Warners, 1945). In one of his last film roles, Best co-starred in *Hold That Blond* (Paramount, 1945).

Hattie "Hi Hat" McDaniel appeared with many of the big-name Anglo stars during her career. She had learned her acting in roadshows and, along with Louise Beavers, became the model substitute mother, the mammy, of the thirties. McDaniel was big, jolly, tidy, energetic and, at times, a comic. She sometimes approached social equality in her roles, especially late in her career. By the forties, the redundancy of her roles had taken its toll and the vibrancy of her earlier roles rarely surfaced. In her early roles she was the loyal maid. She evolved her role into an assertive presence, like that of comic but successful Queenie for *Show Boat* (Universal, 1936). Her crowning success was her Oscar for Best Supporting Actress in *Gone with the Wind* (1939). Among her many roles as a maid or mammy not discussed in more detail elsewhere were the following: *The Gold West* (1937); Joseph von Sternberg's *Blonde Venus* (1932) as helpmate to Marlene Dietrich; *The Story of Temple Drake* (Paramount, 1933); *Operator 13* (MGM, 1934), also titled *Spy 13*, which included Anglo-American Marion Davies as a blackface mulatto; *Little Men* (Mascot, 1934); *Lost in the Stratosphere* (Monogram, 1934); *Babbitt* (1934); *Alice Adams* (RKO, 1935), as a saucy maid who undercuts the white family; *Anniversay Trouble* (MGM, 1935); *Another Face* (1935); *China Seas* (MGM, 1935), as Jean Harlow's wisecracking maid; *Music Is Magic* (1935); *Valiant Is the Word for Carrie* (Paramount, 1936); *Postal Inspector* (1936); *Reunion* (Twentieth Century-Fox, 1936); *Star for a Night* (Twentieth Century-Fox, 1936); *Hearts Divided* (Warners, 1936), which also included the Hall Johnson Choir, Phillip Hurley as a stableboy, and Sam McDaniel as a butler; *High Tension* (Twentieth Century-Fox, 1936); *Arbor Day* (MGM, 1936); *The Bride Walks Out* (RKO, 1936); *Can This Be Dixie* (1936); *The First Baby* (1936); *Gentle Julia* (Twentieth Century-Fox, 1936); *Nothing Sacred* (United Artists, 1937); *Saratoga* (MGM, 1937), again as helpmate to Jean Harlow; *True Confession* (Paramount, 1937); *45 Fathers* (Twentieth Century-Fox, 1937); *The Shopworn Angel* (MGM, 1938); *The Mad Miss Manton* (RKO, 1938), as helpmate to Barbara Stanwyck; *Battle of Broadway* (Twentieth Century-Fox, 1938); *Maryland* (MGM, 1940); *The Great Lie* (Warners, 1941), with Sam McDaniel as a loyal servant; *Affectionately Yours* (Warners, 1941), with Butterfly McQueen in another "Prissy" role as maid; *George Washington Slept Here* (Warners, 1942); *The Male Animal* (Warners, 1942); *They Died With Their Boots On* (Warners, 1942); *Johnny Vagabond* (United Artists, 1943), also titled *Johnny Come Lately*; *Janie* (Warners, 1944); *Since You Went Away* (United Artists, 1944), as the loyal maid to Claudette Colbert; *Margie* (Twentieth Century-Fox, 1946); and *Family Honeymoon* (Universal International, 1948). In many of these roles, McDaniel was called Cleota, Beula, Fidelia, or Agatha. Whatever the name, the role came to be known as the "Aunt Jemima" stereotype.

Louise Beavers was another "Aunt Jemima," and her names in films varied from Pearl and Bedelia to Celestine and Niagara. As with all of the major figures discussed in this chapter, Beavers did a movie with Will Rogers. It was titled *Too Busy to Work* (Fox, 1932), and Beavers was the mammy. She appeared as Mauree in *West of the Pecos* (RKO, 1934), another film in which Willie Best appeared and was put in the credits as "Sleep 'n' Eat." As Jenny, she appeared in *Brother Rat* (1938) with a future president of the United States, Ronald Reagan. She too was one of Mae West's maids, in *She Done Him Wrong* (Paramount, 1933), and she appeared briefly in the Mae West film in which Gertrude Howard was the maid, Beulah, *I'm No Angel* (Paramount, 1933). Like McDaniel, she too played the maid to Jean Harlow, in *Bombshell* (MGM, 1933), also titled *The Blonde Bombshell*. Her most famous role was as the mammy in *Imitation of Life* (1934), but she had other prominent roles: as Madame Nellie La Fleur who heads the rackets in Harlem for *Bullets or Ballots* (Warners, 1936); as Mammy Lou in *Belle Star* (Fox, 1941), who tells the tale which forms the film's plot and who tells Randolph Scott that "You better get out of here right now, white man!"; and as Gussie the maid who makes famous an advertising slogan that saves an executive's job and dreamhouse, "If you ain't eatin' Wham you ain't eatin' ham," in *Mr. Blandings Builds His Dreamhouse* (RKO, 1948).

The other roles of Beavers were numerous and almost entirely as either maids or mammies: *Coquette* (United Artists, 1929); *Sundown Trail* (1931); *The Expert* (Warners, 1932); *Unashamed* (MGM, 1932); *Girl Missing* (Warners, 1933); *In the Money* (1933); *Cheaters* (Liberty Pictures, 1934); *Annapolis Farewell* (Paramount, 1935); *Wings Over Honolulu* (Universal, 1937); *The Last Gangster* (MGM, 1937); *Love in a Bungalow* (1937); *Make Way for Tomorrow* (Paramount, 1937); *Lady's from Kentucky* (Paramount, 1938), one of the Kentucky revival films of the thirties which also had Lew Payton in it as Sixty; *Peck's Bad Boy with the Circus* (RKO, 1938); *Reckless Living* (1938); *Scandal Street* (1938); *Made for Each Other* (United Artists, 1939); *I Want a Divorce* (Paramount, 1940); *No Time for Comedy* (Warners, 1941); *Shadow of the Thin Man* (MGM, 1941); *The Vanishing Virginian* (MGM, 1941), with Leigh Whipper as Uncle Josh; *Virginia* (Paramount, 1941), with Beavers and Leigh Whipper as loyal slaves in a pre-Civil War setting; *Holiday Inn* (Paramount, 1942), with Bing Crosby in blackface; *Reap the Wild Wind* (Paramount, 1942); *Seven Sweethearts* (MGM, 1942); *Top Man* (Universal, 1943), with Count Basie and His Orchestra; *The Big Street* (RKO, 1943); *DuBarry Was a Lady* (MGM, 1943); *Jack London* (United Artists, 1943); *Delightfully Dangerous* (United Artists, 1945); and *Barbary Coast Gent* (MGM, 1946). Beavers also appeared in many films by Afro-American independents and she was most consistently an ever-happy cook or maid or mammy. As early as 1931 she was playing roles similar to the confidante roles of later years, as in *Good Sport* (1931). Like McDaniel, Beavers developed a stoicism and resignation that her ready smile belied.

The thirties films in which these coons and mammies and entertainers appeared were romantic escapist films for the most part. They were far removed from the militancy of the Black Muslins. Many of the films in which they appeared were popular by contrast to the depressing cultural situation brought on by the Great Depression. The ability to laught, to forget, to sneak into another life--all were reasons sufficient to guarantee the popularity of these films among a demoralized American public. The Hollywood films of the thirties were also representative of the inconsistency of the national sentiment toward Afro-Americans. The hardships of the Great Depression were finally countered by the liberal New Deal, but few Afro-Americans were a position to benefit. In Will Rogers' films the home and family were the germs from which a new society would spring. But Stepin Fetchit and Willie Best rarely had a real family in their screen roles with Rogers or in any of their other films. Instead, they were usually portrayed as the servant half of a black/white team, or as perpetual wanderers, characterizations which were as far as could be from the truth concerning most Afro-Americans. The implication was that Afro-Americans, having no home and no family, would not be part of the new society which Will Rogers envisioned over and over again in his films and in his nationally syndicated newspaper columns. As far back as 1919, Rogers did a silent film, *Jubilo*--the remake, *Jubilo* (ca. 1932), included Louise Beavers in her mammy role--in which he portrayed himself as the conscience of the "darkeys." Outside of his film roles, Rogers was a high-minded humorist and a high-souled humanist. He was quick to remind Americans during the Mississippi flood of 1927 that "you don't want to forget that water is just as high up on them [Afro-Americans] as it is if they were white."[7] But his once-spoken platitudes failed to offset the impact of his numerous films. Rogers was capable of playing a role in the race track film, *David Harum* (1934), in which he nonchalantly traded away a horse . . . along with Stepin Fetchit.

By the time the contemporary Afro-American comedian Bill Cosby made *Black History: Lost, Stolen or Strayed?* (1965), there were over six thousand films in which Afro-Americans had appeared. Most of these "characterizations" of Afro-Americans were hardly noticeable, for they came under the genre just discussed, the segregated or Jim Crow Hollywood films. Just as *The Birth of a Nation* evoked a rebuttal film, Scott's *Birth of a Race*, so these racist images exemplified by Stepin Fetchit, Willie Best, Louise Beavers, and Hattie McDaniel, among others, were accompanied by a handful of films in the first round of a new Hollywood genre, the social commitment films.

Notes

[1] I.C. Jarvie, *Movies and Society* (New York: Basic Books, 1970), p. 164.

[2] For an additional discussion on this topic see my article, "Cawelti's Methodology and Popular Culture Studies," *Magazine of the Faculty of Arts* [Sana'a, Yemen] (Fall 1979), pp. 81-84.

[3] Donald Bogle, *Toms, Coons, Mulattoes, Mammies, and Bucks: An Interpretive History of Blacks in American Films* (New York: Viking, 1973), p. 63.

[4] Harry Menig, "A Guide to the Will Rogers Film Festival," p. 12. Paper accompanying the film festival at the American Studies Association National Convention in San Francisco, California, 18-20 October 1973.

[5] Bogle, pp. 198 and 199.

[6] Bogle, pp. 197-198.

[7] Menig, p. 3.

Chapter Thirteen

Social Commitment Hollywood Films

"Star Dust" was a popular 1929 song which reflected the dreams of the twenties. By 1933 the mood had changed to "Stormy Weather." For nearly everyone in America, the thirties began as an era in which economic survival at home was as pressing as political turmoil abroad. The cause celebre of the thirties for Afro-American civil rights groups and Anglo-American liberals, including the American Community Party, was the 1931 frame-up of nine young Afro-American men known as the Scottsboro Incident. It was one notorious large-scale example of the cultural reality that Afro-Americans were usually non-entities in America. As allies, the Afro-American community was sought after whenever it was politically expedient, but Anglo-American attitudes of supremacy were predominant as the North absorbed attitudes born in the South to a striking degree. The NAACP began its legal battles over segregation in education before the Supreme Court by losing its first case on a technicality in 1933. For yet another decade, both in film culture and in American culture, Afro-Americans were Jim Crowed and relegated to the lowest social status in the nation.

Hollywood went through a cycle of prison films in the early thirties which included Afro-Americans as convicts. Louise Beavers was Ivory, for instance, an inmate at the big house in *Ladies of the Big House* (Paramount-Publix, 1931); Clarence Muse was an inmate on death row in *Last Parade* (Columbia, 1931), a convict on a chain gang in *Laughter in Hell* (Universal, 1933), and, in another chain gang feature, Muse was Rascal, a character who finds that mules are more important to white people than are men, in *Hell's Highway* (RKO, 1933); Daniel Haynes was Sonny Jackson, a convicted murderer, in the statement on capital punishment titled *The Last Mile* (1932); Madame Sul-te-Wan was an inmate in a women's prison in *Ladies They Talk About* (Warners, 1933); Allen Hoskins (in the credits he is "Farina," his nickname from the *Our Gang Series*) was Smoke, one of the boys at the reformatory run by James Cagney in *The Mayor of Hell* (Warners, 1933); Stepin Fetchit was the prisoner in *Virginia Judge* (Paramount, 1935); and, even late in the thirties, Bill Robinson was Memphis Jones, an inmate in a prison with a football team, in the comedy *Up the River* (Twentieth Century-Fox, 1938).

Such images were not new to the thirties, but the trend in portraying Afro-Americans as criminals turned to a fad with such pictures as the above. They did not go unnoticed:

> Lester Granger, executive secretary of the National Urban League, among others, has said: "One of the greatest handicaps that the Negro has to face in his fight for complete integration into the American social scene is the persistent American stereotype which portrays him as a criminal, potential or actual, or as a stupid, doltish clown.[1]

The antics of such clowns as Willie Best in films like *Murder on a Honeymoon* (RKO, 1935), and *Murder on a Bridle Path* (RKO, 1936), are discussed elsewhere. But the image of the Afro-American as a criminal is treated here through those films which made the most serious attempts to explore this subject. Also discussed here is one of the few films of the thirties which attempted to go beyond the normal stereotypes of blacks in films, *Imitation of Life* (1934). These films were neither segregated, in the manner discussed in the previous chapter, nor all-black. If they at times lacked explicit presentations of just what it was they were attempting to commit themselves to, they were clearly the antithesis of Stepin Fetchit as tradeable object. Along with *Imitation of Life*, four of these social commitment films shall be cited in some depth to illustrate the most significant aspects of this genre: *I Am a Fugitive from a Chain Gang* (1932), *Fury* (1936), *They Won't Forget* (1937), and *The Black Legion* (1937). The last three constituted a conscious wave of attacks upon the biases perpetrated in films like the pro-lynching stance in *Barbary Coast* (1935) and *The Frisco Kid* (1935) which had further evolved the essence of D.W. Griffith's themes friendly to the Ku Klux Klan. As rarities agitating not just against a crowd but against a significant portion of the nation, the social commitment films must be seen as an acceptance of a considerable risk on the part of both the producers and the studios which backed them. With the exception of *Imitation of Life*, such films were usually neither popular nor entertaining. But they pointedly made instructive statements through America's film culture about race relations in the thirties.

Universal's *Imitation of Life* (1934) presented the apotheosis of Alain Locke's "New Negro" demanding a "real new deal." The financial success of this movie was attributable to the superb acting, including that of the Afro-Americans Fredi Washington as Peola and Louise Beavers as Aunt Delilah, to the renown of the Fanny Hurst romance on which it was based, to the direction of John M. Stahl of a well-made film, and to the ingratiating presentation of what Donald Bogle calls the "archetypal tragic mulatto" as a theme which explored what it is like to be an outsider caught between the cultures of Afro-America and Anglo-America. The movie reflected the liberal spirit of the New Deal in the characterization of the mulatto, Peola, who seeks liberation by "passing." People not only rejects her Afro-American heritage, but she seeks the Anglo version of the American Dream.

Social issues were raised, but *Imitation of Life* was also the premier "Aunt Jemima" film in which patient Aunt Delilah gratuitously gives away her potential fortune, during America's Great Depression Era, by revealing to the enterprising Miss Bea (Claudette Colbert) the recipe for grand homemade pancakes. Beavers' mammy accepts her inferior social status when she declares that instead of a twenty per cent interest in the new pancake business she would much prefer to remain a cook for Miss Bea! Her only wish is for a glorious funeral, the kind which would make "those colored folks' eyes to bulge out" when the procession rolls through Harlem.

While *Imitation of Life* was a positive ethnic statement, taken as a whole, the commercial considerations that made it a big success at the box office demanded a shift away from a too-serious hearing of the racial issues. The close friendship between the widows, Aunt Delilah and Miss Bea, ultimately seemed to mean that the Afro-American was present only to make life better for the Anglo-American, both financially and familially. The imitation was shifted from the Afro-American lives to the conflict between the Anglo-American mother and daughter, Miss Bea and Jesse, for love of the same man.

A 1959 remake of *Imitation of Life* by Universal

was even less liberal. It featured Afro-American Juanita Moore as Annie Johnson (Aunt Delilah) but Anglo-American Susan Kohner played Sarah Jane (Peola), apparently in an attempt to build up more Anglo-American sympathy for the mulatto who is most frequently considered Afro-American rather than Anglo-American. Deprecating lines weakened the impact of both versions of *Imitation of Life*. The reply which Beavers gave in the original version when Miss Bea stated that Beavers' daughter was smarter than her own daughter was not atypical: "Yessum. We all start out that way; we don't get dumb until later." Sterling Brown complained in the Urban League's *Opportunity* of the famous comment in the film, that "Once a pancake, always a pancake"; he saw it as indicative of how the film reinforced negative aspects of Afro-Americans. The NAACP's *The Crisis*, on the other hand, focused on praising the superb acting of Louise Beavers. Whatever the varied opinions of the Afro-American community of the day, the original *Imitation of Life* carried hopeful signs for the future. Beavers had demonstrated that even a mammy role could be imbued with humane dimensions and Washington showed how the "archetypal tragic mulatto" had relevance to Afro-Americans and Anglo-Americans alike in an era when most Americans sought a new and better life.

More poignant and less compromised was Mervyn LeRoy's production for Warner Brothers, *I Am a Fugitive from a Chain Gang* (1932). The theme of this film was lucidly presented: The Afro-American and the Anglo-American against the oppressive laws of the South. Everett Brown played the part of the Afro-American prisoner who was portrayed as having "a good brain, a friendly nature and a clear philosophy . . . an ordinary human being, capable of great friendship, loyalty and courage," according to the earliest history of blacks in films, Peter Noble, in *The Negro in Films* (ca. 1948).[2] Brown and Anglo-American Paul Muni's escape from the chain gang together put them on equal terms, for to be successful both had to desire freedom.

Twenty-five years later, during yet another cycle of social commitment films, Stanley Kramer took up an identical theme in *The Defiant Ones* (1958) with Sidney Poitier and Tony Curtis as the pair of escapees. Kramer made it evident that he was following in LeRoy's footsteps, for he dealt with an Afro-American and an Anglo-American chained together as prisoners on another chain gang. When they escape, they too must escape together. They also had no choice but to work together in spite of racial differences if they wanted their freedom. Kramer's statement was as explicit as LeRoy's: Afro-Americans and Anglo-Americans alike remain in chains and, without cooperation between all peoples, humankind will remain in chains. The universality of this theme raised the issue above one of Afro-American versus Anglo-American and focused it instead on the limits of authority, whether individual or social, with which all humans must contend.

Kramer's film was controversial but, in 1932, LeRoy's *I Am a Fugitive from a Chain Gang* had the impact of a Lady Godiva. LeRoy was presenting anti-fascist themes during an era in which Americans were bewildered over the rise of fascism in Europe and the germination of fascism at home. Such frank treatments of these themes must have pricked the social consciences of those who were aware that fascism, in the form of oppressive laws imposed by Anglo-Americans, was more than just a far-across-the-seas threat to America's national security. Such films made it clear that fascism could be a threat locally as well as nationally in America, especially in the South.

Fritz Lang's *Fury* (1936) was MGM's foray into the social commitment genre. Spencer Tracy, who has often been featured in ethnic protest films, made an early appearance in the genre with *Fury*. Afro-Americans were portrayed in only one scene in the film, a scene in which an Afro-American woman was singing and several Afro-American men were loitering. The scene established the mood through which the complexity of mind of the Anglo-American characters was to be viewed. In *From Sambo to Superspade* (1975), Daniel J. Leab indicates that the only scene with Afro-Americans in it came at the end of this film and that it was cut before the film was released. The version seen for this study had the initial scene just described. Apparently there was an attempt to use Afro-Americans as a framing device, before and after the story itself, to make clear that the film was concerned with more than just the violence of Anglo-American against Anglo-American, especially since the focus was on a traditional method of killing Afro-Americans: lynching. Thus, the major theme of *Fury*, like the theme of the 1943 classic, *Ox-Bow Incident*, was clear: an attack on vigilantes and lynching. Discrimination was the second theme and in this case the discrimination was against an Anglo-American outsider, a man whose only "crime" was that he was a stranger. Because Americans could not help but see a reflection of themselves or their culture in the mob scenes, the film was not popular.

With *They Won't Forget* (1937), Warner Brothers again allowed LeRoy to spearhead a controversial theme. Less effective, and less popular, *They Won't Forget* followed Fritz Lang's *Fury* in delving into the subject of lynching. As an attack on southern intolerance, *They Won't Forget* blatantly pitted northern ideals against southern realities. In the LeRoy films, *I Am a Fugitive from a Chain Gang* and *They Won't Forget*, the major Afro-American characters were presented as a prisoner on a chain gang, Everett Brown, and a janitor who who suspected of murdering an Anglo-American girl, Clinton Rosemond, respectively. Because of the essence of the Afro-Americans' characterizations, however, their less than admirable occupations were not meant as slights perpetrated upon Afro-Americans. They instead represented the dilemma of down-and-outers caught in the "twoness" of being Afro-Americans and of being outsiders to the justice metted out in the South.

Because of its anti-Klan bias, the film *The Black Legion* (1937) was another of the few exceptions to the neglect by Hollywood of taking up challenging issues even though no Afro-Americans were featured in it. The state of mind which produced the Red Hunts--which occurred during World War One and recurred during the thirties and the Korean War--was by implication being attacked in Archie Mayo's *The Black Legion* which starred Humphrey Bogart. At the sentencing of the Black Legionnaires to life imprisonment for their hooded deeds, the judge delivers a long speech on the "true" meaning of Americanism which rhetorically, at least, laid to rest the concept of the Ku Klux Klan and the Black Legion's "America for Americans" of a particular hue and culture. Certainly it was easier for the Hollywood studios to make the many pro-Klan, or at best neutral-Klan, propaganda films than it was for a studio (in this case, Warner Brothers again), to produce a novel film like *The Black Legion* to challenge prevalent American attitudes. *The Black Legion* was the last major exception by Hollywood in the thirties, however, in producing films involving a social commitment to Afro-Americans.

The controversial themes presented in the thirties films by Mervyn LeRoy, Fritz Lang, and Archie Mayo were a "white blacklash." These themes now appear to be fatherly attempts by Anglo-Americans to help Afro-Americans wave the banner of their identity, though they were liberal acts in the context of the thirties when Afro-Americans either did not or usually could not do it for themselves in America. The films are, nonetheless, praiseworthy efforts to realign the Afro-American image in films. Indeed, the thirties cycle of social commitment films as a whole represent an opposite extreme in social commentary from that presented by D.W. Griffith and continued into the late thirties by David O. Selznick in *Gone with the Wind* (1939). Further, *I Am a Fugitive from a Chain Gang*, *Fury*, *They Won't Forget*, and *The Black Legion* were the predecessors of the problem films in the late forties and early fifties. This later cycle of films, by such producers as Stanley Kramer and Darryl Zanuck, is treated in the chapter on "Problematic Films: The Unfinished Image." By then, the era of the *Brown versus the Topeka Board of Education* Supreme Court decision in 1954 was just around the corner.

Hollywood films of the thirties normally presented Afro-Americans in all-black light musicals, in segregated sequences for entertainers, or in Willie Best fashion. Louis Armstrong and his band were segregated in their first feature film early in the decade, *Ex-Flame* (1931), for instance, and Willie Best was beginning to be featured as "Sleep 'n' Eat" in such films as *The Monster Walks* (Mayfair, 1932). Afro-American independent filmmakers were productive but not successful at the box office, despite the infiltration of Anglo-American money and technological skills. Only a handful of films in the thirties challenged the existing order in America, but other films made their mark. Busby Berkeley's *Hollywood Hotel* (1937) presented the first integrated band in a Hollywood film with Afro-Americans Lionel Hampton and Teddy Wilson appearing with the Benny Goodman Quartet. Goodman and Hampton were at the height of their careers as the "kings of swing." In Paramount's *Artists and Models* (1937) Louis "Satchmo" Armstrong and Martha Raye performed together. A black man and white woman performing together was a landmark, as well, though it was muted by the fact that Raye appeared with Armstrong in blackface.

Other positive factors for Afro-Americans during the thirties included the conciliatory attitudes of the new Congress of Industrial Organizations, the American Negro Theater, and the still fruitful, if more dispersed, Harlem Renaissance. The noticeable improvements for the talented and middle-class elements of the Afro-American community did not affect the Afro-American community as a whole. Benjamin O. Davis, Jr., became the first Afro-American West Point graduate of the twentieth century in 1937. But there were only two Afro-American line officers in the United States Army in 1939, the Davis, father and son. Already stagnated in a deplorable economic condition--reflected in Afro-American claims that they were "the last to be hired and the first to be fired" and slogans like "Don't buy where you can't work"--the nonavailability of jobs for Afro-Americans would continue far beyond 1954.

The thirties was also an era of maturing ideological panaceas. The panaceas were no less prevalent among the hardworking, yet rarely visible civil rights groups. The Supreme Court mustered up a redundant 1938 ruling that each state must provide equal education facilities for Afro-Americans. Sensing that this was simply the shoring up of the fragile legal precedent of *Plessy versus Ferguson* (1896), the NAACP in 1939 founded a separate organization called the NAACP Legal Defense and Educational Fund. This group of activists soon brought winning cases before the Supreme Court on behalf of Afro-Americans and other ethnic groups. The torrents emanating from both the prevailing ideologies and the civil rights groups were to flood America in the decade to follow. Before going on to these ideological issues of the forties, however, the images of Afro-American women in American films shall be considered.

Notes

[1] Lawrence Reddick, "Of Motion Pictures," in *Black Films and Film-Makers: A Comprehensive Anthology from Stereotype to Superhero*, ed. by Lindsay Patterson (New York: Dodd and Mead, 1975), p. 21.

[2] Peter Noble, *The Negro in Films* (London: Skelton Robinson, ca. 1948), p. 71.

Chapter Fourteen

Invisible Women: Afro-American Women in Films

A woman's place is in the home raising a family, advocates Anglo-American Jackie Davis.[1] Her Happiness of Womanhood (HOW) was a movement of anti-liberationists for the seventies, though most American women have always been where Davis wants them--and they have been there both in reality and in films. The Afro-American community, to be sure, has traditionally been a matriarchal subculture in America. This chapter is an overview of the treatment of these Afro-American women in films. In culling information, the chapter cuts across chronology and focuses on examples drawn from films discussed elsewhere in this study. Only in this manner can the totality of the negative or invisible images of Afro-American women, fostered still in reality by Jackie Davis and HOW, be gauged.

When asked about her consistent stereotyping as a maid, Hattie McDaniel reportedly remarked that she would rather play the role of a maid for $7000 a week than be one for $7 a week.[2] At times, perhaps, McDaniel did earn such an extraordinary salary. But today her success is measured in terms of the immortality she has gained as one of the most familiar and best loved women in American films, even though she was confined to scores and scores of film roles as mammy and maid. The volume of such roles is not so startling when put in the context that the dominant image of Afro-American women in American films has been that of mammy and maid and that, indeed, these roles outnumber several times over all others played by Afro-American women.

In contrast to the mammy/maid, there is the new image of Afro-American women which began its emergence in the sixties with such actresses as Ruby Dee and Cicely Tyson. Along with several others, these two actresses issued a statement in 1973 with which Hattie McDaniel and all Afro-American actresses in American films would probably have agreed. Their statement read, in part, that "the characterizations forced upon [Afro-American actresses] had nothing to do with Black or human reality." American film, because it is "essentially a medium for the promotion of fantasy," is conducive to exclusionary practices, these Afro-American actresses stress, and, for Afro-American women, this exclusion arises from the fact that "just the presence of a Black woman in a film negates illusion because she is not the blue-eyed, blonde-haired goddess that Americans have been trained to buy."[3] Theirs is but one of many rationales for the invisibility of Afro-American women resulting from the frequent exclusion of Afro-Americans from the movie industry and from the relative invisibility of Afro-American actresses like Hattie McDaniel who, though included in films, had roles which were downplayed as much as possible. Indeed, the thought of Bee Freeman, known as the "Sepia Mae West," starring in place of the real Mae West in a film like *She Done Him Wrong* in 1933, does jar the fantasy of the American filmviewer's universe.

Images of Afro-American women in film began to appear as quickly as film became a popular medium after the turn of the century. During the period of film shorts before World War One, the image of the Afro-American woman was the creation primarily of Anglo-Americans who held firm control as producers and directors, a situation which has remained essentially the same for seventy-five years. The early screen representations of Afro-American women were played by blackfaced Anglo-American actresses. Only upon occasion did Afro-American women actually appear in roles portraying Afro-American women and, most often, this was limited to film shorts produced by Afro-American filmmakers. This exclusion from films of scores of Afro-Americans because of black-faced imitators was utilized by D.W. Griffith in *The Birth of a Nation* in 1915. Right up to his retirement in 1930, Griffith never veered from his practice of blackfacing; and so too with the film industry as a whole, which assured that the blackface would contribute the most frequent so-called image of Afro-American women in the pre-thirties period. Because of the exaggerated images necessary for successful silent films, these early film images of Afro-American women are still potent.

The introduction of sound made it more feasible-- as well as more realistic-- to utilize Afro-American actors and actresses in roles portraying Afro-Americans. Because it is one of the first sound movies, *The Jazz Singer*, in 1927, is representative of a turning point in the trend of blackfacing Anglo-Americans like Al Jolson to play Afro-American roles. But it was only after 1929, the year in which Hollywoodwood rushed into production three all-black musicals, that the practice of blackfacing diminished, although it did not lose its appeal until the fifties. Just as D.W. Griffith was one of the most prominent advocates of the imitation Afro-American, so his films, particularly his early feature-length *The Birth of a Nation*, simultaneously developed, as well as carried to their most grotesque frontiers, the prototypes of all the most influential Afro-American film images--including the mammy, the menial, the entertainer, the hang-around, the mulatto, the brute, and the coon.

The topical possibilities for investigating the Afro-American women in films become immense when confronted with such an array of images. There are, for instance, no young, mature Afro-American women in Griffith's *The Birth of a Nation*, and the only love matches between Afro-Americans and Anglo-Americans are between mulattoes and degenerates. There are both Hollywood productions and independent productions of all-black films, and there are, among the independents, both Anglo-American producers like the Goldberg brothers and Afro-American producers like Oscar Michaeux. There are individual cases like that of Butterfly McQueen's as well. She finally refused to play "handkerchief head" parts and, unfortunately, she was not offered other roles. There are the exotic Afro-American females like Dorothy Dandridge in the fifties' films *Tamango* and *Tarzan's Peril* who might be juxtapositioned with the rare portrayals of an Afro-American woman interested in a lover, in a marriage, or in a family.

There is an entire genre of Anglo-American women paired with Afro-American men, beginning with the innocuous Shirley Temple and Bill "Bojangles" Robinson pair, through the hesitantly developed Sidney Poitier with any young Anglo-American girl, to the first love-making scene between an Anglo-American woman and an Afro-American man (outside of sexploitative films) with the raucous bedding down in 1968 of Raquel Welch and Jim Brown in *100 Rifles*. There is the process of Jim Crowing--in other words, of cutting out for some southern audiences--entire segments of entertainment films before the fifties; in this manner, Afro-American entertainers like Hazel Scott and Lena Horne were censored by what have become known as segregated interludes in films, interludes in which no Anglo-Americans appears and which were not usually related to the film's plot so that they were easily deleted.

Having noted some of the possibilities both for lengthy and for fascinating studies in the image of Afro-American women in films, the perspective is now narrowed so that several of these topics may be looked at in more depth. Some images which focus on traditional and representative treatments of Afro-American women are the mammy/maid image, the image of the mulatto, and the image of the entertainer in the all-black casts of Hollywood films. After looking at some of these, a brief critique will be undertaken of some of the critical works which continue to reinforce, in yet another way, the invisibility of Afro-American women in films.

In *The Birth of a Nation*, the old mammy of the Cameron household continues to be loyal to her former Anglo-American master after the Civil War. Her most memorable scene is the one in which she kicks the Afro-American carpetbagger in the seat of his pants after he ogles the generous dimensions of her body. Her loyalty, her husky physique, and her member-of-the-family relationship to the Camerons are traits of the mammy/maid which have come down to the present through numerous progeny. Reinforcements for the mammy/maid image came in droves, as in Afro-American Bessie Toner's portrayal of Jane Porter's nanny in *Tarzan of the Apes* in 1918, the original of over forty feature-length Tarzan films. She too is loyal to an Anglo-American family, the Porters; she too is buxom and has the capacity to grin her delights and fears; and she too plays mammy to an Anglo-American child, in which employment she intercedes between the villain and "her child," Jane Porter.

The maturation--the term "maturation" is not entirely appropriate--of the mammy/maid image in American films came in the thirties and forties. Mae West, for instance, made it a point to always have an Afro-American maid who also served as trustworthy friend and confidante to her, the Anglo-American goddess. Serving this function was Gertrude Howard as "Beulah" in *I'm No Angel* (1933), and Libby Taylor as

"Jasmine" in *Belle of the Nineties* (1934). Louise Beavers, one of the most famous mammy/maids, is "Pearl" (sometimes called "Eightball"!) in Mae West's *She Done Him Wrong* (1933). In the latter film, after a reprimand by West for not being immediately available, Beavers responds that "I ain't been no place." West caps this with, "no, you ain't been no place; you just been lost!" Of course, dark-skinned Beavers was not lost, but her film image, as well as the image of most Afro-American women--as the wit of West foreshadowed--was in danger of becoming lost.

In the all-female film *The Women* (1939), there is a socially conscious capitalization upon the cliches of the thirties concerning the behavior of Anglo-American women. The Afro-American women in the film are revealing contrasts. They appear as dogkeeper, kitchen help, and maids--one maid being Butterfly McQueen who has been asked to surreptitiously prepare a meal for an Anglo-American woman's boyfriend. The invisible or hidden image of the Afro-American female is epitomized by the quip that, "because Lolla [Butterfly McQueen] is dark, [the boyfriend] won't be able to see her!" This invisibility in the vicinity of Anglo-American women is also in later films with a message, like the powerful *Diary of a Mad Housewife* (1970) in which the only two Afro-American women are a housecleaner and a maid. In the genre of mock-liberation films, there is *Kisses for My President* in which Polly Bergen becomes the first female president. The only sighting of Afro-American women in this 1964 film is when Bergen is introduced to the White House staff, nearly all several dozen of whom are Afro-American servants and maids.

There have been some strong portrayals of women who were also film mammies. In *To Kill a Mockingbird* in 1962, Calpurnia sheds some of the normal associations with the mammy. She is a generous human being with natural apprehensions and natural enjoyments. In contradiction to the image of the excited or fearful mammy, Cal remains calm, collected, and in control, even when a mad dog approaches her and the children. She increases the power and drama of this film because she is somewhat more than an ornament in an Anglo-American southern household. She is the exception, however, as is the stoicism sometimes present in the mammy roles of Louise Beavers and Hattie McDaniel. Hattie McDaniel, for her mammy role in *Gone with the Wind*, was the only Afro-American before the sixties to win an Oscar. It is unfortunate that fuller, more humane, images of Afro-American women would have jarred the filmic fantasy desired by, and rewarded by, American audiences. But the ability to overcome the limitations of the stultifying tradition of mammyism indicates an Afro-American presence which is important when so much else in the Afro-American character is not present in American films.

Mammy

Another strong mammy is Louise Beavers in *Imitation of Life* (1934 version), the role in which Afro-American actress Juanita Moore won an Academy Award nomination in the 1959 remake, showing plainly that Americans in 1959 were still rewarding the mammy image. Both the 1934 and 1959 versions of *Imitation of Life* start out as commentaries on the themes of youthful rebellion and passing for white, but both degenerate to the more attractive and acceptable love affair in which there is competition for the same man between the Anglo-American mother and her daughter. The themes dealing with the Afro-American mother and her daughter are nearly forgotten as the plot unfolds. More so than the producers realized, *Imitation of Life* is a fitting title, for this film is, in miniature, a chapter of the plight of Afro-American women in films who have not been allowed to tell their own stories, or act their own roles, or exhibit their true abilities, or rise to the status which any human being ought to have. Instead, theirs is the imitation of life, heightened by the fact that the mulatto daughter is Afro-American actress Fredi Washington in the 1934 version, while in the 1959 version the mulatto role is acted by Anglo-American actress Susan Kohner.

Using Anglo-American actresses to play mulatto roles goes back even further than the Anglo-American actress who played the mulatto Lydia Brown, a villainess in *The Birth of a Nation*. This has, in fact, most often been the case, despite the irony that American cultural mores concerning ethnic status clearly relegate mulattoes to the category of Afro-American, not Anglo-American. In the landmark film *Pinky* in 1949, in which many still-volatile social issues are taken up, the role of the mulatto is again played by an Anglo-American actress, Jeanne Crain; the effect of the rare portrayal of an Afro-American/ Anglo-American romance in *Pinky* is substantially diminished because the audience knows that the romance is actually between two Anglo-Americans. On the other hand, an Anglo-American actress in the role of the mulatto may have evoked more sympathy from the primarily Anglo-American audience and allowed for more empathy between the mulatto and that audience.

Ethel Waters received an Academy Award nomination in what was for her a most unusual role as the mammy in *Pinky*. *Pinky* also included the last role of a firey Afro-American actress who started out twenty years before as the "Black Garbo," Nina Mae McKinny. In 1929, in *Hallelujah*, McKinny's career as an Afro-American love goddess was born. Sadly, it was still-born in the film, for seductress McKinny is killed by the preacher Zeke and, as it turns out, this is a symbolic moral vindication which eliminated for a generation--until Hazel Scott and Lena Horne in the forties--the prospect of successful Afro-American goddesses on the screen. In *Pinky*, McKinny is a violent and wild bitch who drinks excessively, insults everybody, and carries a stiletto gartered to one of her shapely legs.

McKinny's star-to-bitch career is not atypical of what is faced by all actresses, and particularly by Afro-American actresses. While Anglo-American women worry over the type of role they actually get, Afro-American women worry over whether or not they will get a role as mammy or, less frequently, as mulatto or entertainer. The names Victoria Spivey and Fannie Belle DeKnight may now by forgotten by many, but they were among the stars in the all-black Hollywood musical *Hallelujah* which, along with *Hearts in Dixie* and *St. Louis Blues*, was part of the first significant cycle of all-black Hollywood musicals in 1929. The next cycle came as a war-time effort and included the all-black musicals *Cabin in the Sky* and *Stormy Weather*, both in 1943. From *Stormy Weather*, only Lena Horne perhaps is remembered among the actresses who appeared. Most of the other women, as with most of the women in the 1929 musicals, were only in Hollywood for one film. *Cabin in the Sky*, however, was an obvious exception, a roll-call film in which many of the Afro-American women who approached star status were included, women like Ethel Waters, Butterfly McQueen and, of course, Lena Horne. These films are good-time entertainment; they are occasionally exotic, always rhythmic, but they are never serious about anything, especially not Afro-American culture.

The roll-call method was taken up by Otto Preminger in two all-black musical productions in the fifties which culminate the tradition. Both films, *Carmen Jones* in 1954 and *Porgy and Bess* in 1959, starred Dorothy Dandridge, Pearl Bailey and Diahann Carroll. Like most Preminger films about Afro-Americans, these two were a mixed blessing upon their heads, despite their renowned casts, because they continued all the faulty, narrow, and unrealistic stock characterizations. For the women, this meant primarily mammies, mulattoes, and entertainers. After the Preminger spectaculars, all-black musicals once again went out of fashion, and they have yet to re-emerge on a similar scale. There is no comparison in the quality of Afro-American presentations between these all-black musicals and, say, *The Lady Sings the Blues* in 1972, a film which wrenches apart the stock Afro-American characterizations and replaces them with strong and humane portraitures of real Afro-Americans.

The invisibility of Afro-American women in films is still in fashion, however, and it is aggravated by the critical writers who are recording the history of Afro-American women in films. Two competent works of film criticism which include discussions of the image of Afro-American women are Afro-American author Donald Bogle's *Toms, Coons, Mulattoes, Mammies, and Bucks* (1973) and Anglo-American author Thomas Cripps' *Slow Fade to Black* (1977). But Daniel J. Leab's *From Sambo to Superspade* (1975) is disappointingly limited in its coverage. In his history of Afro-Americans in films, Leab contributes to the invisibility of Afro-American women by failing to discuss many of the films in which Afro-American women appear, including *St. Louis Blues, I'm No Angel, She Done Him Wrong, Belle of the Nineties, The Women, Tarzan's Peril, Hurry Sundown, To Kill a Mockingbird* . . . the list could grow lengthy. A specialized book like Gabe Essoe's *Tarzan of the Movies* (1968) also illustrates the problem. Although Afro-American women in Tarzan films are abundant, there certainly are more than the two Afro-American women Essoe mentions--Bessie Tomer from *Tarzan of the Apes* and Dorothy Dandridge from *Tarzan's Peril*. Dozens of Afro-American did appear in the Tarzan jungle films, and Essoe's citation of only two is another example of the problems concerning both the exclusion and documentation of the Afro-American women in films.

It is not just the male authors who are contributing to the invisibility of Afro-American women. Two additional symptomatic expressions are found in recent books which purport to convey the image of women in American films. Marjorie Rosen's *Popcorn Venus* (1973) and Molly Haskell's *From Reverence to Rape* (1974) are critical studies by Anglo-American women which, because of their exclusionary practices, indicate that hundreds of Afro-American females have passed before the floodlights of Hollywood only to become invisible women. Rosen's women in *Popcorn Venus*--which book has the subtitle, *Women, Movies and the American Dream*--are almost entirely Anglo-Americans, while Haskell's coverage of Afro-American women in *From Reverence to Rape* is limited to the mentioning of six Afro-American actresses.

Numerous examples of this exclusion could be cataloged, but the unavoidable and overwhelming point seems to be that, with the exception of Bogle and Cripps, there is no coverage--there is no visibility given to Afro-American actresses by the writers on women in films. Haskell's book, nonetheless, provides a revealing statement: "At present, the [Hollywood film] industry, such as it is, is giving women the same treatment that it gave blacks for the half-century after *Birth of a Nation*: a kick in the face or a cold shoulder."[4] With that ironical recognition on Haskell's part, one wonders why there is still a "cold shoulder" toward the invisible women--the Afro-American women--not only among the movie-makers, but among all but two of the men and women writing books today about the female image in films. Each of these books, it is necessary to add, is in its own way a valuable contribution to understanding the image of women in film; but, what they exclude explains as much as what they include about the film industry and critical establishment in relation to American culture.

Thus, there is invisibility in exclusion as well as in the way in which Afro-American women are included in films. These Afro-American images, if they are not a reflection of cultural reality, are certainly a refraction and illumination of cultural myths, particularly for Afro-Americans who are often negative values as well as negative images in American culture. Myths have their bases in reality and one predominant myth is that films portraying Afro-Americans are to be identified interchangeably with films about Afro-Americans, about Afro-American problems, and about Afro-American culture. This just is not so. The sheer facelessness of the most important stereotype of all--the seven or eight thousand films in which Afro-Americans have appeared but disappeared--further enhances the conclusion that not only have Afro-American women been left out of the Hollywood dream factory, but out of the American Dream as well.

As one corrective, the irresponsibility of critics should not be allowed to go unchallenged when they regularly cite as facts such unsubstantiated statements as Marjorie Rosen's when she writes that the film *The Last Angry Man* (1959) was "totally devoid of females."[5] The concept of a female, visible or invisible, being used by Rosen is elusive because, in actuality, *The Last Angry Man* included Betsy Palmer, Joanna Moore, Nancy R. Pollock and Helen Chapman. *The Last Angry Man* also introduced to films the Afro-American actresses Claudia McNeil and Cicely Tyson![6]

Notes

[1] Jackie Davis, Speaker for Happiness of Womanhood (HOW), before Paul Vanderwood's "History through Film" class, San Diego State Univ. (25 October 1973).

[2] Donald Bogle, *Toms, Coons, Mulattoes, Mammies, and Bucks* (New York: Bantam Books, 1973), pp. 114-115.

[3] Barbara Smith, "Reader's Forum: Black Women in Film Symposium," *Freedomways*, 14 (1975), p. 268. The symposium took place in April 1973 and was sponsored by Boston University's Afro-American and American Studies Departments. The panelists noted here include Susan Bateson, Cynthia Belgrave, Ruby Dee, Beah Richards, and Cicely Tyson.

[4] Molly Haskell, *From Reverence to Rape* (Baltimore: Penguin, 1974), p. 370.

[5] Marjorie Rosen, *Popcorn Venus* (New York: Avon, 1973), p. 265.

[6] This chapter is a revised text of a paper delivered as chair of a panel titled "Images of Blacks in Popular Culture" on 22 October 1976 at the Midwest

Popular Culture Association Meeting, Bowling Green State University.

Chapter Fifteen

World War Two and Humanitarian Dilemmas

Humanitarian declarations made in the heat of World War Two were often both intellectually sincere and popularistically oriented. Intellectuals were generally in agreement with the movement among the Allied Powers to guarantee basic human rights for all people. The popular mind was eager to drench itself in the concept as well but not to apply it whole-heartedly at home. Afro-American Richard Wright's *Native Son* was a best seller in 1940, although few Americans read deeply enough to understand that this book exploded the myths and images normally held by Anglo-Americans about Afro-Americans. *Native Son* was a harsh propaganda statement in an era of unprecedented propaganda battles fought to sway the popular mind. Wright's book was aimed generally at American culture and specifically at film culture and other mass media. But for Anglo-Americans, printed words were as easy to reject as the visual images of films were easy to accept when it came to Afro-Americans.

Mediocre in its unbelievable characterizations, whether Afro-American or Anglo-American, *Home in Indiana* (1944) also attempted but did not achieve a satisfactory propaganda statement. Willie Best, another graduate of the Shirley Temple classics, received considerable attention in the film as Mo, the Afro-American groom and stablehand for the little horse ranch in Indiana. Originating with Stepin Fetchit in the sound films of the thirties, Best carried on the tradition of the easily frightened, wide-eyed darky whose witless fear of a "vicious" horse was played off against the young Anglo-American to whom the same horse was "tame." As this film demonstrates, the underlying assumptions of Hollywood's film culture did not change even at the height of the greatest twentieth-century challenge, World War Two, to America's existence.

The major fear of the forties, for Afro-Americans

and Anglo-American alike, was the fear of myriad conflicting ideologies. In *Home in Indiana* an Anglo-American foreman "defects" to another ranch to be on the victorious side of a competition between race horse breeders. It was an era of ideas to be faced up to, reflecting a sentiment in American culture to "face the music, falling about you like rain."[1] Inundation with the fluid aligments between Christianity, democracy, fascism, militaristic governments, communism, the specter of the atomic bomb, and an emerging world-wide revolution of non-Anglo peoples, combined to create the battlefronts for the war of ideas throughout the forties. The outward commitments of America appeared solid, but internal conflicts tore at the thoughts of many Americans whose loyalties to American policies were not as strong as they seemed.

The Nazi-Soviet Non-Aggression Pact in 1939 crushed the hopes of the left-wing intellectuals in America by identifying fascism on the right of the political spectrum with communism on the left. Their earlier radicalism, brought to a peak by the Great Depression, mollified somewhat by participation in the creative outlets of the Federal Theater and the Federal Writer's Project, many intellectuals were forced into a reaffirmation of American culture by the Soviet's betrayal of those ideals they had held up for the world and by the onslaught of World War Two. The social disorganization brought on by the war again raised the expectations of Afro-Americans, duplicating to some degree the World War War patterns. Again hundreds of thousands of Afro-Americans and Anglo-Americans migrated to the North to meet the drastically increased manpower needs of farm and industry which had to support an American Army of twelve million.

Hundreds of thousands more Afro-Americans voluntarily enlisted in the military, offering both their services and their lives side by side with Anglo-Americans. Messman Dorie Miller's heroism in shooting down four Japanese planes during the attack on Pearl Harbor earned him the first Navy Cross for an Afro-American and the pride of the Afro-American community. Six months later, the first commission in the Navy was granted to an Afro-American, and by late 1944 Afro-American women were admitted into the Women's Naval Corp. The particular fears of Anglo-Americans, however, kept the situation inequitable for most Afro-Americans in both military and civilian life.

Intellectuals recognized and were more troubled than the citizenry at large over the blatant duplicity which existed in the treatment of Afro-Americans. In *Home in Indiana*, Mo (Willie Best) was ordered around not by the foreman or the owner of the ranch, but by Tuppy. Tuppy was a hired hand like Mo, though Anglo-American. Films like *Tennessee Johnson* (1944) continued to give the glaring implication that Afro-Americans were inferior, in spite of the enlightened United States Supreme Court decision of the same year, *Smith versus Allwright*, which ruled that Afro-Americans must be allowed to vote in southern primary elections. One of the most protested films ever, *Tennessee Johnson* became a focal point for civil rights groups, led by the National Association for the Advancement of Colored Peoples (NAACP), concerned with the image of Afro-Americans in films. Immediately after World War Two an attempt to lapse back into the old situation was again exemplified by the growth of yet another Ku Klux Klan movement. In the popular mind, the anxiety of the forties was matched only by the promise of affluence held out by the war industry's healthy priming of the economy.

To both the intellectual and to the popular mind, humanitarianism became an ideal which applied to others much more than it applied to one's self. This transcendental application was made all the more forceful by the contrast of a real war. Throughout the war, the NAACP led the lodging of protests with governmental agencies, charging that the American press reported domestic Afro-American crime but not the achievements of Afro-American combat units overseas. Pressure from civil rights groups during the war to eliminate the stereotyping of Afro-Americans in films led to fewer roles for Afro-Americans, which in turn led to the establishment of the Institute of Progressive Artists in America. Humanitarianism became a platitude to justify the past and present rather than a course of action to be pursued in the future.

Pressure from the Afro-American community was growing as its resources grew and its ideas coalesced. Membership in the NAACP went from 50,000 to 450,000 during World War Two. Afro-Americans too were fighting in a war which entailed a thrust against Nazi racism and a second war against brown people in the

Pacific. In *Home in Indiana* the Anglo-American youth and Mo pitch in their own resources, and borrow the rest on bonds, to win a horse race. Like the Afro-American community, Mo reached for the lure of democracy which, without his positive efforts in conjunction with Anglo-Americans, might not be perpetrated. Afro-American fears were reinforced by the specter of internment when the Japanese-Americans in California were concentrated into camps in 1942 under the recently passed Smith Act (1940). The initial defeat at Pearl Harbor led many Afro-Americans to question both the superiority of Anglo-America and its potential to win the war, doubts which became positive factors later as Afro-Americans contributed their share and more to the war effort.

Total commitment to the war by the American culture created a higher level of tolerance than had existed during World War One. Afro-Americans and Anglo-Americans fighting for and against the same things produced a potent situation which was not ignored by the Afro-American leadership. This leadership groped for the means to construct suitable tools to give the situation a leverage on their behalf. They did not always succeed as they had hoped. Although considered a victory at the time, a Supreme Court decision in 1941 actually reinforced the "separate but equal" doctrine by ruling that railroad facilities had to be "substantially equal."

Intellectuals were hard at work after 1945 debating the merits and direction of the new United Nations while the attitudes of the majority of Americans toward Afro-Americans verged on a backward scramble. The emergency of the issue became academic. In 1946, Eugene Talmadge was re-elected to the governorship of Georgia on a platform to "show the nigger who is boss!" Many Americans wanted to forget the pledges of wartime and move to the promise of prosperity in a consumer culture soon to be supplemented by large Cold War budgets. Harry Truman, rising to the presidency after the death of Franklin Roosevelt in 1945, was as difficult to move on civil rights issues as was his predecessor. Much of Truman's energies were, in fact, being absorbed by the Cold War. The American nation, like the Uncle Sam figure (Walter Brennan) in *Home in Indiana*, was being maneuvered into a global corner of a universe in which it was unsure of its best course of action. The choice for both America and Uncle Brennan was between withdrawal into isolationism, or a frantic reformism thrust upon the globe which would leave no doubt as to the leadership and power of their respective roles in the universe. Like America, Uncle Brennan had sulkingly passed through a twenty-year period between "wars" and was now rejuvenated.

In *The Strange Career of Jim Crow*, C. Vann Woodward relates that Gunnar Myrdal, in looking at America in 1944, stated that "segregation is now becoming so complete that the white Southerner practically never sees a Negro except as his servant and in other standardized and formalized caste situations."[2] Southern Democrats, also in 1944, managed to replace the liberal Vice President Henry Wallace who had the backing of many in the Afro-American community. Henry Wallace split the Democratic Party in 1947 by forming the more liberal Progressive Party with a strong civil rights platform. The efforts of young Hubert Humphrey, also a man with views on civil rights more liberal than those of most Anglo-Americans, created waves at the 1948 Democratic convention which resulted in the alienation of the Southern Dixiecrats who, like the Progressives, broke away and formed a splinter party.

However, the strains of war had given the Afro-Americans other openings. The wartime appeals for unity had been accepted by the Afro-American community and a growing Afro-American press, numbering nearly hundred newspapers and periodicals by the mid-forties, disseminated the information. By endorsing these pronouncements, the Anglo-American community could no longer rest easily in its exclusion of Afro-Americans from American culture. As if to emphasize the point, in the summer of 1943 Detroit, Harlem, and several other cities experienced ethnically motivated convulsions similar to the St. Louis riot during World War One. Even more serious riots were to break out in Cicero, Illinois, at the height of the Korean war in 1951, a pattern which would again prevail in the mid-sixties when the Vietnam police build-up coincided with the Los Angles riot in 1965 and the long hot summer of 1967. But unlike the situation during World War One, the country was in the midst of the New Deal, of new systems of thought, of the war against fascism and of the social consciousness of young writers. Amid it all was the necessity of at least keeping the Afro-Americans neutral along with the hope that Afro-Americans could be put to use in the war effort. Each of these pressures, along with the riots in places like Detroit and Harlem, contributed in the short-run to more sympathy toward the Afro-American causes.

The Congress of Racial Equality (CORE) was founded midway through World War Two. Essentially an Anglo-American liberal organization emphasizing the pacifism of Ghandi, CORE began under the leadership of James Farmer. It was not until the early sixties that it gained national prominence during the "Freedom Rides," still under Farmer's leadership. The philosophy of CORE had its greatest impact upon the destiny of a young man named Martin Luther King, Jr. Using sit-down and sit-in strikes, CORE launched an attack on segregation not in the South but in the domain of the Anglo-American liberals: the North. W.E.B. DuBois spoke of the "history of a dream" in 1944; in the sixties, King took the dream out of history by making famous the phrase, "I have a dream." King's notorious but effective use of the boycott which made him well-known in the mid-fifties was first used by CORE in Chicago in 1946 and 1947.

Sympathy toward the Afro-American cause translated into new opportunities for Afro-Americans, albeit quite limited and discriminatory opportunities. In World War One, with the exception of messmen in the Navy, Afro-Americans served only in one branch of the military, the Army, and only in segregated units. By 1940, America had its first Afro-American general, Benjamin O. Davis, Sr.; of the 776 generals who served during World War Two, Davis was the only Afro-American. At the beginning of the war, Afro-Americans still served either as messmen in the Navy or in one of the Army's four Afro-American units. By the end of the war, over one million Afro-Americans had served in all branches of the military. Again, as in World War One, no Afro-American received the Congressional Medal of Honor. Again, as in all previous wars, Afro-Americans still served in segregated units.

The significant contributions of Afro-Americans to the precise goals of the nation, that is, to the winning of the war and to the creation of a more humane post-war world, were seemingly accepted by the American popular mind as a war effort only. The dichotomy was most obvious overseas where Europeans could not reconcile the image of Afro-Americans they gained from American films and the image they received through personal contact with Afro-Americans. James

Baldwin's account of his first visit to Sweden in "Stranger in the Village" (1953) reflects this dichotomy in the post-World War two era,[3] and so does Nevil Shute's novel with its symbolic title of *Chequerboard*. After the war, humanitarian gestures continued to be goals without means of implementation. *The Kerner Report* (1968), in searching for causes for the riots of the sixties, gave a vivid example of this duplicity of thought in America from the post-war era. The example concerned the American Red Cross which, "with the government's approval, separated Negro and white blood in banks established for wounded servicemen--even though the blood banks were largely the work of a Negro physician, Charles Drew."[4] Drew's story became one of the most tragic examples of Anglo-American prejudice against Afro-Americans, for he died after an accident in 1950, from loss of blood, when an Anglo-American hospital refused to take him in.

An early attempt to utilize the leverage being acquired by the Afro-American community came in 1941. Asa Philip Randolph advertised the possibility of a massive march on Washington if President Roosevelt failed to take steps to secure federal employment opportunities for Afro-Americans. The rhetorical leverage Randolph applied was that the majority of the Afro-American community had supported the president in his successive bids for the presidency and now the Afro-American community was helping to support America against the emerging threat of foreign wars. The demonstration being arranged by the March on Washington Movement was unnecessary as Roosevelt was pressured by the threat of it to sign Executive Order 8802, which barred racial discrimination in war-related programs and industries, and to establish the federal Committee on Fair Employment Practices which attempted, unsuccessfully in the long run, to implement federal laws protecting Afro-Americans from employment discrimination.

Similar pressures were brought to bear on President Truman when the Afro-American community demanded full integration within the armed forces. Again it was Asa Philip Randolph who came into the limelight with his argument before the president in 1947 that Afro-American people would not fight in Asia against brown people if the military continued to segregate its units. To further dramatize the issue, Randolph gave his support to Afro-Americans resisting the draft by participating in the creation of the

League for Non-Violent Civil Disobedience Against Military Segregation. Randolph ran a considerable risk. The country was in a reactionary mood as the battlelines of the Cold War solidified and, like the ritualization after World War One of nationalistic measures requiring the saluting of the American flag and the pledging of allegiance to America, the new loyalty program was in full swing. In the late forties, the United States Attorney General published the first list of so-called subversive organizations, a list which was in effect until after the Vietnam War. In response to Randolph's pressure, gratifyingly, the Truman administration appointed a commission which produced the report titled *Freedom to Serve*. Shortly thereafter, Truman began the slow process of desegregating the military. Yet, at the time of the Communist victory in China in 1949 and the Korean War in 1950, when the issue of colored fighting colored was forced, only the Navy and Marine Corps afforded equal treatment and opportunity to Afro-Americans.

International concern mounted as the non-Anglo envoys to the new United Nations, afforded the finest accomodations and protocol of the United States Government, experienced the shocking squalor and unfair treatment of Afro-Americans in New York City. The official stance of the United States Government was ambivalent: "The international reason for acting to secure our civil rights now is not to win the approval of our totalitarian critics. . . . we are more concerned with the good opinion of the peoples of the world."[5] Through an application of domestic pressure from civil rights groups, and international pressure from what were soon to be called Third World nations, the process of desegregation in all branches of the military was nearly complete by the end of the Korean War. Outside of propagandistic films, Hollywood made little effort to reflect in American film culture the far-ranging changes which World War Two and the Cold War were bringing about for Afro-Americans.

Notes

[1] Christopher Morley, *Morley's Magnum* (Philadelphia: J.B. Lippincott, 1935), p. 187.

[2] C. Vann Woodward, *The Strange Career of Jim Crow*, 2nd. rev. ed. (New York: Oxford Univ. Press, 1966), p. 118.

[3] James Baldwin, "Stranger in the Village," *Notes of a Native Son* (New York: Bantam, 1972), pp. 135-149.

[4] *Report of the National Advisory Commission on Civil Disorders [The Kerner Report]* (New York: Bantam, 1968), p. 223.

[5] *To Secure These Rights: The Report of the President's Committee on Civil Rights* (Washington, 1947). Cited from Nelson Manfred Blake, *A History of American Life and Thought* (New York: McGraw-Hill,

Chapter Sixteen

Propagandistic Films and Buckling Stereotypes

During the forties, cinema was one of America's largest industries and for a time it was ranked third largest. As in other industries, however, labor organizations had taken hold in Hollywood. After World War Two the contract system between the studios and the actors, actresses, and writers declined. Just after the war there were over one hundred independent filmmakers in Hollywood itself and this group produced approximately thirty per cent of the total film output. Anti-trust suits during the forties helped dismantle the Hollywood studio empire and give impetus to an even larger wave of new independents.

For Afro-Americans there were more conspicuous film roles after World War Two began. By the time the war ended this trend had reversed and only in the fifties would significant Afro-American portrayals on film pick up again in greater numbers. Pressures from the Afro-American community were to a remarkable extent responsible for both the upsurge and the decline in the numer of these roles for Afro-Americans. Controversy raged during the war between Afro-American, headed by the NAACP, who demanded better film parts or at least an elimination of the negative roles and the film producers who often wrote out Afro-American roles altogether as a result of these pressures. Responsible also for the upsurge during the early years of the war were the catering attitudes on the part of Anglo-Americans who wished to retain the Afro-American community's allegiance and support in the war effort. The result was that Afro-Americans appeared most conspicuously in propagandistic films and entertainment spectacles, both of which will be discussed in this chapter.

In spite of the increase in roles for Afro-Americans in these contexts, their total numbers remained small in this large industry, indicating the force of the exclusionary practices which still existed.

Furthermore, the images of the Afro-Americans who did appear in other contexts were essentially the same as they had been for generations. The following is the complete listing of the most pervasive stereotypes of Afro-Americans in media as of 1944 which Lawrence D. Reddick formulated in "Educational Programs for the Improvement of Race Relations: Motion Pictures, Radio, The Press, and Libraries":

1. The savage African
2. The happy slave
3. The devoted servant
4. The corrupt politician
5. The petty thief
6. The irresponsible citizen
7. The social delinquent
8. The vicious criminal
9. The sexual superman
10. The superior athlete
11. The unhappy non-white
12. The natural-born cook
13. The natural-born musician
14. The perfect entertainer
15. The superstitious churchgoer
16. The chicken and watermelon eater
17. The razor and knife "toter"
18. The uninhibited expressionist
19. The mental inferior[1]

Although it draws from several of these stereotypes, what might have made Reddick's list an even twenty is distinctive enough to be mentioned: The childhood comrade. The childhood comrade is the stereotype found in films similar to the *Our Gang Series* in which the playful relationship between the races is confined to youngsters. Ernie "Sunshine Sammy" Morrison as Scruno in *Mr. Wise Guy* (Monogram, 1941), for instance, or Morrison with the Bowery Boys in *Spooks Run Wild* (Monogram, 1941). Besides the publication of Reddick's important list in 1944, there were other significant dedevelopments that year. In addition to their efforts earlier in the war to influence Hollywood, the NAACP, in conjunction with the International Film and Radio Guild (IFRG), initiated an enormous effort in 1944 directed toward correcting the most out-of-line images of Afro-Americans in film. It produced mixed results, but it was another important step in the process of critically examining the black image in films. Reflecting similar interests, the year 1944 also saw the creation of the anti-Jim Crow Independent Citizens Committee of the Arts, Sciences and Professions instigated by President Roosevelt and the creation of the United Negro College Fund. Throughout the forties, however, the two most dominant images of blacks in films remained those of the perfect entertainer and the devoted servant. Some roles managed to combine both, like Pearl Bailey as the singing maid in *Isn't It Romantic* (Paramount, 1948), but most fell under either one or the other of the two categories.

Among the individual Afro-Americans presented in the mode of the perfect entertainer in the forties are the following: Ella Fitzgerald as Ruby and the group of uncredited black jitterbug dancers in the Abbott and Costello comedy, *Ride 'Em Cowboy* (Universal, 1941); the smooth dancing of the Nicholas Brothers in *Orchestra Wives* (Twentieth Century-Fox, 1942); Dooley Wilson's music in *Take a Letter Darling* (Paramount, 1942); The Mills Brothers in such musical westerns and comedies as *He's My Guy* (Universal, 1943), *Chatterbox* (Republic, 1943), and *Cowboy Canteen* (1944); the ever-popular Cab Calloway in *Sensations of 1945* (United Artists, 1945); Nat "King" Cole in the comedies *See My Lawyer* (Universal, 1945), and *Breakfast in Hollywood* (1946); Louise Franklin in *Hollywood Canteen* (Warners, 1946); Louis Jordan in the musical comedy *Swing Parade of 1946* (Monogram, 1946); "Sugar Chile" Robinson and his "boogie-woogie" piano work in *No Leave, No Love* (MGM, 1946); Ben Carter as old John Henry the railroad builder in the musical comedy *The Harvey Girls* (MGM, 1946); Jo Jones as the jazz drummer in *Kiss of Death* (Fox, 1947); and Pearl Bailey in her first singing role in the musical *Variety Girl* (Paramount, 1947).

The devoted servant stereotype of the forties had undergone changes begun by Louise Beavers and Hattie McDaniel in the thirties. Teresa Harris' maids were generally no longer subservient and Rex Ingram's domestics were no longer servile or patronizing. The Afro-American man was now frequently portrayed as a "right-hand man" to the protagonist or as a lacky for a fighter or gangster. But the roles were still in the tradition of the domestic, for the relationship between whites and blacks--who was giving and who was receiving the paychecks and the orders--amounted to the same thing. Such roles, safe for the time being from the scrutiny of the NAACP and IFRG, picked up again at the end of World War Two though they were never absent in the forties. Among these typical roles for the forties were Fred "Snowflake" Toones as the domestic in the feature for kids, *The Biscuit Eater* (Paramount, 1940); Clinton Rosemond as Zeke and Teresa Harris as Cleo in *Blossoms in the Dust* (MGM, 1941); Teresa Harris as the witty maid and confidante to Marlene Dietrich in *Flame of New Orleans* (Universal, 1941), and as the lively maid in *Smooth as Silk* (Universal, 1946); Sam McDaniel in *Louisiana Purchase* (Paramount, 1941), and as Boatright in *Flamingo Road* (Warners, 1949); Benny Carter as the "colored assistant" in *Scattergood Baines* (RKO, 1941); Dorothy Dandridge as the maid in *Lady from Louisiana* (Republic, 1941), also titled *Lady from New Orleans*; Rex Ingram as Tilney in *The Talk of the Town* (Columbia, 1942), as Charles in *Fired Wife* (Universal, 1943), and as Pearson Jackson in *Dark Waters* (United Artists, 1945), in which Nina Mae McKinney also appeared; Nina Mae McKinney in *Without Love* (MGM, 1942), and *Night Train to Memphis* (Republic, 1946); Sir Lancelot as Edward, the confidante to a white girl wrapped up in a fantasy world, in *The Curse of the Cat People* (RKO, 1944); James Edwards as the butler in *Manhandled* (Paramount, 1944); Butterfly McQueen as maid and helpmate to Mildred in *Mildred Pierce* (Warners, 1945), and in a strong performance as the maid, Vashti, in *Duel in the Sun* (Selznick, 1947); "Smokey" Whitfield in *Three Little Girls in Blue* (Twentieth Century-Fox, 1946); Ernest Whitman as Mr. Mordecai, along with Lillian Yarbo, in *My Brother Talks to Horses* (MGM, 1946); Bill Walker as Sam, along with Davis Roberts, in a boxing film based on a Hemingway story, *The Killers* (Universal, 1946); and Josh White in *The Walking Hills* (Columbia, 1949).

In addition to the general images of Afro-Americans as perfect entertainers and devoted servants, there were still the descendents of Stepin Fetchit and Willie Best from the thirties, most notably the coon stereotype of Mantan Moreland in the forties. The same popular Anglo-American attitudes toward the ersatz in Afro-American culture were easily registered in jokes with blacks in roles as servants and coons. A collection of such jokes from the early forties may have left some wondering about the appropriateness of its claim to be *2500 Jokes for All Occasions*.[2] From a total of eighty-one "Negro Jokes" in this volume by Powers Moulton, one sampling provided the gist of the image projected upon the Afro-American character and mentality: a recruiting officer says to Rastus, "Don't you want to joing the cavalry? That's a fine branch of the service." Rastus replies, "No, sah! Ef Ah has to retreat, Ah doesn't want to be bodered draggin' along no horse."

The cowardly assistant in films, Mantan Moreland, was Rastus wrapped in the trim of the forties. The eighty-one jokes indicated that the following were the employments and situations of Afro-Americans: nine preachers; six defendents in court (one of whom was the only "black gentleman" mentioned in the jokebook); eight butlers (bellboys, porters, cloakroom attendants, and so on); three each of maids, farmers and church elders; two witnesses in courts (one of whom was testifying for an Afro-American friend, the other of whom was testifying for an anonymous person). There was, in addition, one citation each for maintenance man, military man, circus roustabout, hack driver, waiter, insurance solicitor and attorney. In general, these jokebook images paralleled the major images of Afro-Americans in films in the forties with the one exception of the perfect entertainer which films exploited far more thoroughly.

With the possible exception of the attorney, whose plea to his client was that he could get her marriage annulled because her father did not have a license to carry a gun, there were no jokes portraying an intelligent, professional, hardworking, or monied Afro-American man or woman. There were no watermelon jokes either, but there were thirteen direct references to criminality on the part of Afro-Americans, and an additional seventeen references to Afro-Americans being lazy and/or poor; the poorness, it is implied, being the result of the laziness. Like the all too familiar movie scenes of Bill "Bojangles" Robinson muttering "polo bears" for polar bears, there were thirty-one direct assaults upon the intelligence of Afro-Americans, not including their numerous attributed grammatical mistakes. The content of these jokes further illustrates the state of the popular mind in regard to Afro-Americans. Since they were generally portrayed misconceptions about the nature of Afro-Americans, misconceptions reflected in other media as well, then it follows that Jim Crow treatment would be acceptable, for Afro-Americans have little in common with other Americans.

The major example of these images in the films of the forties came from the appearances of Mantan Moreland. Again a composite of many of Reddick's stereotypes, his coon image was reminiscent of the Stepin Fetchit/Will Rogers team. Indeed, during the years of the Fetchit/Rogers films, Moreland appeared in films by independent Afro-American filmmakers and in musical shorts made in Hollywood. In the late thirties, he began appearing in Hollywood feature-length films like *Millionaire Playboy* (1937), *Irish Luck* (1938), *The Next Time I Marry* (RKO, 1938), and *Frontier Scout* (Franklyn Warner, 1938). In the forties, he came into his own as the premier coon with the rolling eyes--he was "Smoke Eyes" in *Treat 'Em Rough* (Universal, 1942)--and convulsive frights that he would be the last to make a career out of performing. One of several films in which Moreland's hair turns white with fright was *The Strange Case of Dr. RX* (Universal, 1942). Moreland was the sunshine friend, the coon who turned coward at the first sign of distress , or the coon who could not motivate his feet when the rest of him was shivering.

In one of several series in which he appeared, Moreland was teamed with Anglo-American Frankie Darro as crime fighters in *Amateur Detective* (1940), *Chasing Trouble* (1940), *Farewell to Fame* (1941), *In the Night* (1941), *Up in the Air* (1941), and *You're Out of Luck* (1941). He also made an appearance as Lightnin' in one of the *Mexican Spitfire Series*, a film titled *Mexican Spitfire Sees a Ghost* (RKO, 1942), by which time his coon character was established and in demand. Often he appeared in detective, gangster, or mystery films which would best show off his coon antics. He appeared, for example as Roy in *Ellery Queen's Penthouse Mystery* (Columbia, 1941), as Alistair in *Eyes in the Night* (MGM, 1942), paired with Anglo-American Frank Graham in *Crime Smasher* (Monogram, 1943), and as Henry in *The Spiders* (Fox, 1946).

Moreland's most famous series of films, the Charlie Chan mystery comedies, was one in which Stepin Fetchit and Willie best had performed similar functions: Stepin Fetchit in *Charlie Chan in Egypt* (Warners, 1935), and Willie Best in *The Red Dragon* (Monogram, 1946). In the *Charlie Chan Series*, Mantan is Birmingham Brown, Chan's sidekick, driver, servant, and fall guy. The series was even more popular in the forties than in the thirties, and Moreland appeared in over a dozen of them, all produced by Monogram, between 1944 and 1949: *Charlie Chan in the Secret Service* (1944), *The Chinese Cat* (1944), *The Jade Mask* (1945), *The Scarlet Clue* (1945), *The Dark Alibi* (1946), in which Ben Carter also appeared, *Shadow over Chinatown* (1946), *The Trap* (1946), *Chinese Ring* (1947), *The Docks of New Orleans* (1948), *The Golden Eye* (1948), *The Feathered Serpent* (1948), *The Shanghai Chest* (1948), and *The Sky Dragon* (1949), which was a composite of the earlier

Charlie Chan films with Mantan Moreland.

Moreland also appeared in *Laughing at Danger* (1940), *Law of the Jungle* (1942), *Footlight Serenade* (Fox, 1942), *Melody Parade* (Monogram, 1943), *Wrong Girl* (Monogram, 1943), *South of Dixie* (1944), and, with Ben Carter as No-More, in *Bowery to Broadway* (Universal, 1944). Except for the Chan films, his career was over by the end of World War Two, though he did appear in a few films as late as *The Comic* (Columbia, 1969) and *Watermelon Man* (Columbia, 1970). The changes brought about by World War Two, along with the achievements of the NAACP and IFRG, killed the coon as a staple in films.

Earlier attempts to alter the image of blacks in film had been sporadic and usually unsuccessful. The option was to go overseas, as Paul Robeson did in the thirties. In addition to their traditions of jungle films, important films with prominent roles for blacks had been made by filmmakers in several overseas countries. Victor Trivas' *Niemandsland* (Germany, 1932)--variously titled in English as *No Man's Land*, *Hell on Earth*, and *War Is Hell*--presented the black actor Louis Douglas as the first soldier to discard his uniform in this anti-war film set during the World War One fighting in "no man's land." But Douglas was also portrayed as a tap dancer and as a saviour of the whites, carry overs from traditional stereotypes that would also haunt the overseas productions in which Paul Robeson appeared. Robeson's films set in Africa were discussed in the chapter on jungle films, "America, The Dark Continent." He also made three other foreign films, none of which were widely distributed in the United States, beginning with Kenneth Macpherson's *Borderline* (Switzerland, 1930). This art film was made by an international group involved with the avant-garde magazine, *Close Up*, who formed Pool Films to produce a statement on racism in Switzerland. Paul Robeson played Pete and Robeson's wife, Esmeralda Goode Robeson, played Adah. As a black couple in a foursome, they are scapegoated when trouble arises. Because of its experimental nature, the film was not widely circulated even in Europe.

In Lion-Hammer's *Big Fella* (England, 1938), based on the novel *Banjo* (1929) by black author Claude McKay, Paul Robeson, Esmeralda Goode Robeson, and the black actress Elizabeth Welch are featured. Paul Robeson is portrayed as a renegade in Marseilles who cares for a white boy, a theme similar to the Huckleberry Finn/Jim pairing found so frequently in American films. His last overseas film was more important, but not for the reasons Robeson would have liked. Ealing's *Proud Valley* (England, 1940), also titled *The Tunnel*, is a strong statement on the plight of Welch coal miners. Robeson stars as David Goliath, the leader of the miners bent on reopening a coal mine. As the only black in the film, the black-as-savior theme is used again as Goliath gives his life for the miners' cause. The film was a statement on class rather than racial distinctions, however, and it brought to a close the attempts on Robeson's part to find a foreign avenue of expression that would square more with reality than the images of blacks found in American films. The ten-year effort had brought prominence to Robeson as an actor, but it had failed to provide better models on which to base black images in films.

After this, Robeson appeared in only one more feature film made in American, Julien Duvivier's *Tales of Manhattan* (Twentieth Century-Fox, 1942). It was a major production based on a series of intertwining tales tied to an elusive coat. The film featured the Anglo-Americans Rita Hayworth, Edward G. Robinson, and Charles Boyers, along with the Afro-Americans Paul Robeson, Ethel Waters, Eddie Anderson, Cordell Hickman, Clarence Muse, George Reed, and the Hall Johnson Choir. The roles overall were not positive. Eddie "Rochester" Anderson portrayed an opportunistic preacher and Robeson and his film wife, Ethel Waters, came out looking like gullible and superstitious sharecroppers. For Robeson, disgusted over the way the film was slanted, it was his last feature film. The NAACP's Walter White liked the film, but when other civil rights groups protested, Robeson picketed the film's opening along with them. The film was indicative of the plight of Afro-Americans in films generally, and Robeson in particular.

Robeson turned to more civil rights work. He narrated and sang the songs for a documentary based on the hearings of the Senate Civil Liberties Committee in 1938, *Native Land* (Frontier Films, 1942), in which violations of the Bill of Rights in America were emphasized. He also concentrated his talents as a singer and dramatic reader on such efforts as the narration of another documentary, *My Song Goes Forth* (Ambassador Films, ca. 1947). With talents transcendent of race, Robeson could not only fulfill all expectations for the role of the Moorish general in Shakespeare's

Othello, but he could render "Joe Hill" and "Old Man River" into moving tributes to various aspects of American life; despite his interest in propagandizing communism as well as the Bill of Rights, activities which cost him many potential appearances, his "Ballad for Americans" is among the most patriotic of American songs.

At the other extreme, another famous actor, patriot, propagandist, and former football player whose career overlapped Robeson's was Anglo-American John Wayne, who illustrates the reactionary ideas about Afro-Americans circulating in Hollywood. Wayne had little in mind ever, but he certainly did not have Robeson in mind when he stated that "I believe in white supremacy until the blacks are educated to a point of responsibility." He flippantly added that slavery was "just another fact of life, like the kid who gets infantile paralysis and has to wear braces so he can't play football with the rest of us."[3] Like the film images of Afro-Americans in American films, Wayne's reactionary pronouncements represented no more than what many Americans wanted to know or hear about Afro-Americans.

Also a fact of life, most film roles for Afro-Americans during World War Two were in musical revues and variety shows directed at servicemen. Among these films were Hazel Scott's first, *Something to Shout About* (Columbia, 1943), which also featured Teddy Wilson and his band; *Reveille with Beverly* (Columbia, 1943), with Duke Ellington, Count Basie, and The Mills Brothers; *Stage Door Canteen* (United Artists, 1943), with Count Basie and Ethel Waters; *The Hit Parade of 1943* (Republic, 1943), or *Change of Heart*, with Count Basie, Dorothy Dandridge, and The Harlem Sandman; *Two Girls and a Sailor* (MGM, 1944), with Ella Fitzgerald and Lena Horne; *Jam Session* (Columbia, 1944), with Louis Armstrong and His Orchestra and Clarence Muse in comic relief; *Follow the Boys* (Universal, 1944), with Louis Jordan, Louise Beavers, and Nicodemus Steward in the role of a black officer; *Carolina Blues* (Columbia, 1944), with Marie Bryant, Harold Nichols, The Step Brothers, and Louise Franklin; and *Dixie Jamboree* (PRC, 1945), with Louise Beavers, Ben Carter, Cab Calloway, and Adelaide Hall.

Although it continued to be the Afro-American male entertainer who was inserted most conspicuously in Hollywood musical inteludes--scenes as unconnected to the theme or plot of the film as Wayne's notions of Afro-Americans were to Afro-Americans--Lena Horne and Hazel Scott began their film careers during World War Two with many segregated appearances. Excellent entertainers with established careers in the entertainment world, Horne and Scott were both militant in their ideas about civil rights and films. They refused degrading roles in films, choosing to appear in films only if they portrayed themselves. The NAACP encouraged Horne, in particular, feeling that she was finally breaking free of the shallow female roles heretofore assigned to most Afro-American women. Nonetheless, many of the help-the-war-effort movies in which Horne and Scott appeared were still Jim Crow.

As the first Afro-American female entertainers to appear regularly in other than all-black musicals, Horne and Scott were featured in separate scenes unrelated to the plot of the following movies: in the Red Skelton and Ann Southern musical comedy, *Panama Hattie* (MGM, 1943), Lena Horne is featured with one song along with the Berry Brothers, Nyas, James, and Warren; in the Red Skelton and Eleanor Powell musical comedy, which also had a role for Butterfly McQueen, *I Dood It* (MGM, 1943), or *By Hook or by Crook*, Lena Horne and Hazel Scott perform several numbers; in *Thousands Cheer* (MGM, 1943), or *As Thousands Cheer*, Horne, Scott, and Benny Carter's Band perform; in *Swing Fever* (MGM, 1943), Horne sings "Indifferent"; in both *The Heat's On* (Columbia, 1943) and *Rhapsody in Blue* (Warners, 1945), Scott has segregated appearances; and along with Eddie Anderson, Horne and Scott have segregated appearances in *Broadway Rhythm* (MGM, 1944).

Servicemen loved Horne and Scott, and Horne became the first renowned Afro-American pin-up girl but, in deference to popular Anglo-American attitudes on the homefront, their scenes were often cut when the films played in the South. In 1946, Scott left the movies to marry the first Afro-American Congressman from the East, Adam Clayton Powell. Horne, a friend of Paul Robeson's, shared his fate in the blacklisting purges in film and television during the early fifties. When asked about blacklisting, the Anglo-American purist John Wayne stated that "there was no blacklist . . . That was a lot of horse----. . . . The only thing our side did that was anywhere near blacklisting was just running a lot of people out of the business."[4] John Wayne's "side" was the Hollywood which did a rather thorough job of chasing the "bad guys," regardless of race, creed, or ethnic origins, right out of the American Dream. The same sentiment exists today. In the early seventies a popular pro-Vietnam song by Merle Haggard, "The Fightin' Side of Me," declares about America that, "If you don't love, leave it."

The propaganda of the Second World War was more interested in keeping everyone, particularly ethnic groups, in America on the side of the United States Government. Numerous documentaries were made for and about Afro-Americans in an attempt to inspire not only race pride but pride in the war effort America was engaged in. The most significant of these documentaries was *The Negro Soldier* (1943) sponsored by the War Department. Frank Capra supervised the production, but Afro-American Carlton Moss did the screenplay and was responsible for many of the production decisions. The film presented scenes of Afro-American participation in previous wars as well as World War Two. Moss did the narration and played the minister of the church in which the story unravels as the mother of a soldier relates the news he has sent her. Afro-American Bertha Wolford was the mother and Afro-American Lt. Norman Ford was the son. This was the best of the documentaries of the war era that dealt with Afro-Americans. Unlike a generation before, during World War One, the use of propaganda at least partially controlled by Afro-Americans was possible during World War Two.

The documentaries about Afro-Americans during World War One had shown their contributions as well, but they did not include the social commentary that set *The Negro Soldier* apart. Some of the documentaries from the First World War were *Our Colored Fighters* (1918), *Our Hell Fighters* (1918), *Doing Their Bit* (1918), *From Harlem to the Rhine* (ca. 1918), and *Our Hell Fighters Return* (1919). Some of those made during World War Two to show the Afro-American contribution were *Henry Brown, Farmer* (1942), a documentary narrated by Canada Lee on the contributions of Afro-American farmers to the war effort; *Fighting Americans* (1943), a fifty-minute newsreel which featured Afro-American men and women in training for the war; *Wings for This Man* (1944), a documentary on Afro-American participation in the Army Air Corps; and *The Negro College in Wartime* (1945).

A dramatic short, *Shoe Shine Boy* (MGM, 1943), was one of Hollywood's contributions and it featured a young Afro-American who wants to go from shining shoes to learning to play a horn so that he blow it for Uncle

Sam. Afro-Americans Joe Louis and Ralph Metcalfe back up the message of Paul Robeson's narration concerning how to avoid venereal disease in an Army training film titled *Easy to Get* (n.d.). Leigh Whipper and Joel Fluellen appeared in the War Department's *The Negro Sailor* (1944). After the war, documentaries on Afro-American contributions continued with Alexander Productions' *The Highest Tradition* (1946) and *The Call of Duty* (1946). In another documentary by the Army, Sidney Poitier is a soldier learning to readjust in *From Whence Cometh My Help* (1949).

In the years just prior to and just after World War Two both Hollywood and independent filmmakers produced documentaries on George Washington Carver: *Story of Dr. Carver* (MGM, 1939); Bryant Productions' *George Washington Carver* (1940); *Dr. George Washinton Carver* (MGM, 1945); and Consolidated Pictures' *Peanut Man* (1947). Carlton Moss did the short documentary titled *Frederick Douglass: The House on Cedar Hill* (1953). What all of these documentaries had in common was the intention to build race pride. With only one exception that came just prior to World War Two, these documentaries did not deal with civilian and domestic problems for Afro-Americans. The one exception was Henwar Rodakiewiecz' *One Tenth of Our Nation* (1940) and it went to the root of the problem which the Supreme Court would deal with in the *Brown* decision of 1954: the poor quality of education for Afro-Americans in the South.

Afro-American problems existed prior to their appearance on film in the late forties, to be sure, but few attempts had been made by Hollywood or by independents to unravel these problems. A great leap backwards, in fact, was taken just after World War Two ended. While the United States Supreme Court outlawed segregation on interstate bus travel in 1946, Walt Disney filmed the Afro-American folk tales of Joel Chandler Harris in *Song of the South* (RKO and Disney, 1946), with Hattie McDaniel and James Baskett. Uncle Remus' tales, as told by Baskett, were alive in the American culture but, as Hollywood came to see it, not coming across so well as he used to. Disney may have acquired a more significant place in film history than that of a successful producer, as Bogle makes clear, because "*Song of the South* glaringly signaled the demise of the Negro as fanciful entertainer or comic servant . . . Neither the songs nor the servants had worked. Afterward Hollywood ignored them both."[5] Hollywood did not entirely ignore them, despite protests by the NAACP, for this capitalization on the Afro-American as perfect entertainer did make money. The rage in black entertainers was submerged slightly in deference to the cycle of late forties problem films only to surface again in the mid-fifties.

Notes

[1] Lawrence D. Reddick, "Educational Programs for the Improvement of Race Relations: Motion Pictures, Radio, The Press, and Libraries," *Journal of Negro Education*, 13 (Summer 1944), p. 369.

[2] Powers Moulton, *2500 Jokes for All Occasions* (New York: New Home Library, 1942), pp. 298-299.

[3] Jack Kroll, "John Wayne: End as a Man," *Newsweek*, 93 (25 June 1979), p. 46.

[4] Kroll, p. 46.

[5] Donald Bogle, *Toms, Coons, Mulattoes, Mammies, and Bucks: An Interpretive History of Blacks in American Films* (New York: Viking, 1973), p. 136.

Chapter Seventeen

Problematic Films: The Unfinished Image

There were powerful culture-wide influences in the forties which inhibited the developement of socially conscious films. With the introduction of social security numbers, the serial number syndrome epitomized further bureaucratization in the federal government. The G.I. (Government Issue) complex experienced by tens of millions fed both the hope for security and the fear of depersonalization in the militarized culture of America during World War Two. This state of mind detracted from general concern for Afro-Americans, except as allies in the war effort. It also detracted from concern for the images of Afro-Americans presented to the public through the media, except for the propagandistic films discussed earlier. Gnawing at Anglo-Americans during the forties was the possibility that American culture was headed toward depersonalization and loss of identity, a view of the forties that was worked out in literature by a British writer only at the end of decade with George Orwell's *Nineteen Eighty-Four* (1949). Films like *Grapes of Wrath* (1940), based on John Steinbeck's epic proletarian novel, had pointed in that direction even before World War Two. Such films, however, excluded Afro-Americans from such situations as the migration from Oklahoma to California in the thirties when historical accuracy demanded they be there. During the forties, Afro-Americans continued to search for a means to integrate their culture with the shifting perspectives of American culture generally. A few steps in that direction did occur, beginning in the same year that *Gone with the Wind* (1939) reaffirmed all of the old avenues of expression for Afro-Americans.

It was another of Steinbeck's works that showed an Afro-American more prominently. *Of Mice and Men* (United Artists, 1939), based on Steinbeck's experimental prose drama, revealed the loss of the American Dream for Anglo-Americans Lenny and George when they reach the last frontier of America's hope, the West Coast ranch in Salinas Valley. But the cripple Crooks, played by Afro-American Leigh Whipper, is portrayed as an intelligent and contemplative man sharing in the impossible dreams of Lenny and George and showing himself to be the ranch community's conscience. That same year Clifford Odets' play was put on film in *Golden Boy* (Columbia, 1939). It challenged the assumption that all Americans are equal under the law when an Anglo-American boxer kills an Afro-American boxer in the ring. In one of his best roles, Afro-American Clinton Rosemond is the dead boxer's father. He seeks justice, but the white boxer goes free. These films presaged the problematic films which appeared during World War Two and then developed more fully in a cycle of films coming at the end of the forties and early in the fifties.

Films based on the works of other liberal writers, like Lillian Hellman, failed to make so much as a symbolic gesture toward including Afro-Americans in the struggle to find new directions for America in the years after the Great Depression put prior to World War Two. Her story for *The Little Foxes* (Samuel Goldwyn, 1941), reinterpreted the early twentieth-century decay of southern aristocracy through the Hubbard family. The Afro-Americans in the film are sprite when not simply in the background, but their duty is clearly to lend support by covering up and making excuses for the members of the Anglo family. Far from being a liberal, or even condescendingly sympathetic, portrait of Afro-Americans, the best that can be said today is that the Afro-Americans in this film, none of whom are listed in the credits, repeatedly uttered the point that they did not relish what they were doing for the Anglo family. Hellman's work provided the basis for *Watch on the Rhine* (Warners, 1943), a pre-World War Two story about Nazi Germany. It included only one role for an Afro-American, Frank Wilson as Joseph, which did not deviate from standard stereotypes. After the war, another of her works was used as material for *Another Part of the Forest* (Universal International, 1948). It continued the Hubbard family saga, but returned it to pre-Civil War days. The portrayals of Afro-Americans as domestics are typical, if a bit more feisty than usual through the efforts of Afro-Americans Libby Taylor and Robert "Smokey" Whitfield.

Hellman was not out of step with the times, for stronger statements on domestic relations between the races were few. Perhaps the most realistic handling of ethnic discrimination during the early years of the war appeared in Warners' *In This Our Life* (1942), an adaptation of Ellen Glasgow's 1941 Pulitzer Prize-winning novel. Set in the South, Bette Davis plays the spoiled belle who attempts to frame a black youth for an auto accident she had. The youth, played by Afro-American Ernest Anderson in his first film role, speaks standard English, goes to law school, and stands up to Anglo pressures to make him a scapegoat. Anderson's non-stereotypical performance was highly praised, and Hattie McDaniel was in her best form as his supportive mother, a laundress. While some minor Afro-American roles fell back on old coon stereotypes to some extent, the film was placed on the Honor Role of Race Relations for 1942.

Another domestic setting, this one in the Old West, was William Wellman's *Ox-Bow Incident* (Twentieth Century-Fox, 1943), also titled *Strange Incident*. In it, Sparks, the sensitive Afro-American preacher played by Leigh Whipper, stands out as the possessor of a social conscience the Anglo-American lynching party lacks. The lynched men are white, further magnifying the revulsion which Sparks signified. Sparks spoke not just for the hanged men, but for himself and for all Afro-Americans, when he choked on the phrase from a hymn, "you got to go there by yourself." The same year, Twentieth Century-Fox and Teaching Films Custodians released a shortened version of *Ox-Bow Incident*, titled *Due Process of Law Denied* (1943), which focused on Leigh Whipper's role as the mob's conscience. *Ox-Bow Incident* was yet another example of an important social statement accurately translated to film from a classical work of literature, Walter Van Tilburg Clark's in this case, which was financially unsuccessful. Partially for this reason, there were few of these strong social commitment films concerning Afro-Americans set in America itself until the latter years of the forties.

Leigh Whipper also appeared in one of the World War Two films which made a point of including Afro-Americans in prominent roles on foreign soil. These films--*Mission to Moscow* (1943), *Bataan* (1943), *Lifeboat* (1944), *Crash Dive* (1943), and *Sahara* (1943)--could be included under propagandistic films. Their blatant anti-Fascist statements were similar in tone to *The Negro Soldier* (1943) but, unlike the propaganda films discussed earlier, these were made as feature films and intended as entertainment for homefront audiences. The first of these, in fact, Michael Curtiz' *Mission to Moscow* (Warners, 1943), was commissioned by the Office of War Information. Leigh Whipper in one his most impressive roles was featured as Haile Selassie, the leader of Ethiopia.

In John Huston's *Bataan* (1943) and Alfred Hitchcock's *Lifeboat* (1944), the latter based on yet another work by Steinbeck, the social concerns of war, democracy and, to a lesser extent, Afro-Americans were explored. As part of the war effort, the American movie industry was showing a marked, if occasional, change toward freeing Afro-Americans from their enculturated image in films. But because of their propagandistic intent, these films often dwelled on the point that being an Afro-American in America was perhaps not such a bad lot when compared to Fascist societies. Afro-American Kenneth Spencer is the soldier Wesley Epps in MGM's *Bataan*, a film lauded by the NAACP despite the rather stereotyped role Spencer was given. The main point, though, is that he is symbolically on an equal footing with the Anglo-American soldiers as they live, fight, and die in the last heroic days of resistance to the Japanese invasion of the Philippines. Twentieth Century-Fox's *Lifeboat* featured Canada Lee as a dignified, if primarily in the background, Afro-American steward afloat on the lifeboat, a little America, along with other survivors of the Nazi torpedoing of their ship. These Hollywood films were obviously creating token symbols by including lone Afro-American characters.

Similarly, Archie Mayo's *Crash Dive* (Twentieth Century-Fox, 1943), portrayed Afro-American Ben Carter as Oliver Cromwell Jones, a messman in the Navy whose film heroism is reminiscent of the Afro-American hero of Pearl Harbor, Dorie Miller. In Zoltan Korda's *Sahara* (Columbia, 1943), Rex Ingram is a strong and intelligent Sudanese non-commissioned officer named Tambul. Fighting with the Allies in Libya, represented by Humphrey Bogard and Lloyd Bridges in this film, Ingram's departure from the stereotypes include his having a white Italian prisoner of war as his servant and his killing a Nazi in the Sahara. This killing, which could not have been committed in a film set in America, is an act for which he is heroized in the film. As did Epps in *Bataan*, Tambul sacrificed his life for the "free world." Ingram's role was noticed, for "a special award from the Motion Picture Committee for Unity" was given to him as the "most outstanding black actor of the year."[1]

There were other roles of this nature, as in *None Shall Escape* (Columbia, 1944), "in which a black was one of the judges in a war crimes trial."[2] Mervyn LeRoy did a short film dealing with ethnic intolerance, *The House I Live In* (1945), which starred Frank Sinatra and won a Special Academy Award. The popular post-war film, Edward Dmytryk's *Till the End of Time* (RKO, 1946), touched on the ethnic discrimination faced by a returning Afro-American soldier played by Ernest Anderson. It was not a forceful presentation of the theme, but it pointed the way to other post-war efforts like the documentation and exposure of the activities of the Ku Klux Klan in *The Burning Cross* (1947), discussed in an earlier chapter, and ethnic discrimination as it was developed in *Gentleman's Agreement* (1947) and *Crossfire* (1947). These two films dealt with anti-Semitism and in so doing prepared the way for cinematic attacks on prejudice against Afro-Americans.

The first of this new crop of films was *Moonrise* (Republic, 1948), a presentation of the issue with more potential that it actually developed. It presents Rex Ingram as Mose, an outcast who lives in the woods. Anglo-American Dave Clark is Danny, another outcast, who joins Mose. Mose learns that Danny is running from society because he committed a murder and, while he himself cannot do it as a black man, Mose convinces Danny to stand up and face what he did in order to retain his self-dignity. It took another film, in which the counselor was white and the patient black, to open up the issue of racism through film. Filmed under cover as *High Noon*, the film was made as an independent venture by Stanley Kramer and released by United Artists as *Home of the Brave* (1949).

Originally a Broadway play with an anti-Semitic theme similar to *Gentleman's Agreement* and *Crossfire*, the major character was altered to make the film a comment on Afro-Americans in America. James Edwards plays Peter Moss, the black soldier who is traumatized by the racism he experienced from fellow soldiers while fighting the Japanese. His closest white companion is killed and Moss has a breakdown. The heavy-handed message contains ambiguities, for it is clear that the white doctors do not understand the perspective of a black man fighting for survival not just against the Japanese but against fellow Americans. Also ambiguous is the ending in which a one-armed Anglo-American, Mingo, symbolically offers a non-existent hand to the mentally traumatized Moss. Neither is a complete human being, this ending suggests, and there is but little hope held out for the image of a black and a white working together being fulfilled.

In a major turnabout from the World War Two films in which token Afro-Americans exist harmoniously with Anglo-Americans, *Home of the Brave* was more straightforward since the war was over. It presented the realities of racism in the military as well as in civilian life. As such, it was the first of the major problem pictures of the years 1949 and 1950. Edward's characterization of Moss was not entirely successful--he came across as somewhat cowardly despite the obviously traumatic experiences which would do the same to anyone--but the movie was an overwhelming success with the public. On the bright side, the film did open up access to the screen for something new for Afro-Americans: the opportunity to seriously attempt to interprete their experience with American culture. More cynically, it also opened up new opportunities for Anglo-American producers to profit from problem pictures concerning Afro-American themes, which is what Kramer admittedly did.

The next film in the cycle went to the heart of the South to dissect racism. It took the issue about as far as it could be taken in a film that depended on audiences expecting entertainment. Based on the novel by William Faulkner, Clarence Browne's *Intruder in the Dust* (MGM, 1949), featured an Afro-American character who did not fit the normal stereotypes or even variations on the normal stereotypes. The Afro-American character, Lucas Beauchamp, was portrayed by Juano Hernandez from Puerto Rico in his first film. Beauchamp is presented in a complex and humane manner as a man revolting privately, he thinks, against the southern social and legal systems. Accused of murder, he barely escapes being lynched. The theme of justice for some only in the South is then thoroughly explored. As Beauchamp, Hernandez was too independent, too proud, and too defiant for Anglo-American audiences, making the film a less than moderate success at the box office. The following year, Hernandez appeared in Michael Curtiz' *The Breaking Point* (Warners, 1950), yet another film based on Ernest Hemingway's novel, *To Have and Have Not* (1937). About a black and white team of charter boat operator's run-ins with the law, the movie was, Hernandez claimed, the first to portray an Afro-American as the equal of an Anglo-American.

The themes of justice and equality, highlighted by the conflict and then racial riot between "Beaver Canal" and "Niggertown," also motivated Joseph Manckiewicz' *No Way Out* (Twentieth Century-Fox, 1950). In his first feature film, Sidney Poitier is the star. Newcomer Ossie Davis also appears, along with Ruby Dee, Dotts Johnson, Mildred Joanne Smith, Frederick O'Neill and J. Louis Johnson. Poitier plays an aspiring young doctor, Luther Brooks, whose career is threatened when a white patient dies under his hands while the patient's bigoted brother watches. Accused of murder, only an exhumation and autopsy of the dead man's body proves Brooks' innocence. Yet the brother of the dead man seeks revenge and nearly kills Brooks before being subdued. It is at this point that Brooks' most powerful line struck deep into the social consciousness of Anglo-America. After tending to the wounds of the bigot who tried to kill him, Poitier testily tells him, "White boy, you're going to live," meaning essentially that the bigot must live with himself.

Criticisms of *No Way Out* abounded. I.C. Jarvie informally notes in *Movies and Society* (1970) some of the observations of a critical study of *No Way Out* by two social scientists:

> The apparently liberal surface of the film conceals: ambiguity about black murdering white; negroes initiating violence against white, including women; theme of violating a white body to save a negro; dependence of the negro on whites to fight his battle . . . negroes are shown eating heartily; eating is rare in films and this emphasizes the stereotype of negroes preoccupied with bodily pleasures; even the title is ambiguous.[3]

Thus, despite sincere efforts, this example of the new breed of liberal Hollywood films about Afro-Americans had major shortcomings.

Poitier also came under fire as portraying a new stereotype, now referred to as "ebony saint," and for being, in retrospect, "a hero for an integrationist age"; in other words, he is portrayed as a clean-cut, ambitious, hard-working doctor with bourgeois aspirations who earns his standing as an equal to whites. True no doubt, but Poitier's was indeed a new image, one that America desperately needed and one that Poitier made a career portraying. While a few other films attempted a conscious, and at times conscientious, examination of Afro-American themes, it was Poitier's roles in the fifties which most consistently suggested that solutions to some of the ethnic crises were possible. The important point about his role in *No Way Out* remains that it was a praiseworthy attempt to come to grips with at least a few aspects of racial realities in America.

An old theme in American films, "passing," was the basis for yet another important film of this era, Louis de Rochemont's *Lost Boundaries* (Film Classics, 1949). It was based on a true account of an Afro-American family posing for a generation as Anglo-Americans in New England. The family members, including Dr. Scott Carter [Dr. Albert H. Johnston in real life], his wife, and their two children, were all played by Anglo-Americans. Afro-Americans Canada Lee and Bill Greaves, who later became an important documentary filmmaker, also appeared in the film. Again the rationale used to justify Anglo-Americans playing Afro-Americans was that white audiences would respond to people "like themselves" being in a predicament of this nature. It apparently worked, for the critics reviewed the film glowingly with mostly Afro-Americans questioning the use of whites to play the mulattoes. The film revolves around the discovery of the Carters' secret. Denied a commission in the Navy in 1941, Dr. Carter was rejected for not being of pure Anglo blood. The rejection was couched in terms of not "meeting the physical requirements." His heritage revealed, the Carters are ostracized by the community they had endeared themselves to previously. Important as a statement on the hypocrisy of basing a person's worth on "blood" rather than performance or character, the film goes slightly further in treating the immediate effects on the children who must reinterprete their lives as a result of this "accident of Nature."

Another "passing" film appeared the same year. Darryl F. Zanuck's *Pinky* (Twentieth Century-Fox, 1949), was directed by Elia Kazan. The title character, Pinky, is a mulatto "passing" in the North while studying nursing. When Pinky returns to the South, leaving behind her white fiance, she is trapped into caring for an old white woman who soon dies, leaving Pinky her estate. A long struggle within herself and with her grandmother, Aunt Dicey, ensues over whether or not she should accept her "roots." She decides to stay in the South as a nurse, using the estate she inherited to serve the community. Aunt Dicey was played by Ethel

Waters and, though a typical mammy role to begin with, she brought a multifaceted strength and aura of command to her performance. Pinky was judiciously understereotyped, in large part because the young woman who starred in the role was Anglo-American Jeanne Crain. Because of this, the effect of her "interracial" romance with an Anglo-American, who she gives up when she stays in the South, was diminished. It was the first serious treatment of such a romance by Hollywood and it came to a Hollywood end. Nina Mae McKinney, in one of her last film appearances, had a small role as a nasty "high-yeller girl" and Afro-Americans Frederick O'Neal and Kenny Washington appeared too.

Kenny Washington also had a role in *The Jackie Robinson Story* (Eagle-Lion, 1950), certainly not part of the problematic cycle of films, but a film which, like *Lost Boundaries*, involved the portrayal of real incidents of racism. It was a poorly made film, despite the efforts of director Alfred E. Green, but Jackie Robinson put in a fair appearance of himself. Ruby Dee as his wife, and Louise Beavers as his mother lent needed talent to the low-budget production, as did Joel Fluellen as Jackie's brother and Howard Louis McNeely in a small role. A race-pride movie, it did tackle the race issue faced by major league baseball players which Robinson was the first to successfully overcome in his career with the Dodgers.

While the cycle of major problematic films in America ended in 1950, three foreign films made shortly thereafter seemed to fall into the short-lived tradition. Richard Wright's classic novel, *Native Son* (1940), had been produced on Broadway by Orson Welles with Canada Lee in it. But the novel was brought to the screen only when Wright went to Argentina, garnered foreign money and personnel, and put himself in the role of Bigger Thomas. Because of this lack of cohesiveness, *Native Son* (1951) was a substandard film. It remains important, nonetheless, for its attempt to further the new gropings which the social commitment films had undertaken to explore. *The Respectful Prostitute* (France, 1952), based on a story by Jean Paul Sartre, used an American background by having a southern Senator's nephew murder a black man played by Walter Bryant. A prostitute is pressured to admit that the black man was trying to rape her, but she earns her title of "the respectful prostitute" by refusing to be intimidated. And in Zoltan Korda's *Cry, the Beloved Country* (England, 1952), Alan Paton's novel is translated into a powerful, if somewhat slow-paced, drama about South Africa's new apartheid policies. The effects of poverty and the reliance on Christian values to forebear are brought poignantly to the screen by two Afro-Americans: Canada Lee in his last film role as the minister Stephen Kumalo, and Sidney Poitier as a priest. Afro-American Edric Connor also appeared in this film, along with the black actors Lionel Ngakane and Albertina Temba. This new view of colonial Africa not only clashed with the jungle genre of films, but presented striking parallels with conditions in America's South.

Other American films tentatively took up similar issues, but the thrust of the major pictures portraying racial issues was over. In Leo C. Popkin's *The Well* (United Artists, 1951), also titled *Deep Is the Well*, the old circumstance of black males being a threat to white females is turned around. In this film, an Afro-American girl is last seen with a white man and the suspicion as to what has happened to her leads to the build-up of hostility between the races, the blacks being portrayed by Afro-Americans Ernest Anderson, Maidie Norman, Bill Walker, Alfred Grant, and Gwendolyn Laster. The problem is settled when the girl is found in a well, and the conclusion of the film is the expected: the races work together to save her. As also might be expected, the riot scenes were deleted before the film was shown in cities like Atlanta. Similarly, Atlanta had banned entirely the showing of *Imitation of Life* (1934) and *Lost Boundaries* (1949) because "passing" seemed to be condoned; the equally controversial film, *Pinky* (1949), was not banned in Atlanta for Pinky's "passing" was not condoned in the picture's message.

A similar hatred turned to friendship in race relations occurred in Mark Robson's *Bright Victory* (Universal International, 1951), also titled *Lights Out*. James Edwards plays the veteran in a hospital for blind patients where, aside from Edwards, all the patients are Anglo-Americans. When the white who befriends Edwards finds out that his companion is black, he reacts in a typically bigoted manner. The white man later comes to see his hypocrisy and accepts Edwards as a friend, suggesting that intolerance can be overcome.

Stanley Kramer's *Member of the Wedding* (Paramount, 1952), made a bid to continue the cycle of problematic films dealing with race, but the film actually focused on the alienation of a white girl, Frankie Adams. The film was built upon the Broadway production of Carson McCuller's play and revolved around another mammy as ward to a white girl. Ethel Waters is Berenice Brown, the mammy, cook, et al., of the new mammy tradition, who is also raising a son, Honey Brown, played by James Edwards. It is Berenice's tutelage which brings Frankie to a better understanding of the world. Despite an other strong performance by Waters, in which she sings "His Eye Is on the Sparrow," the title of her autobiography, *Member of the Wedding* was not as dramatic or as successful as *Pinky*.

The messages became less relevant in other war-related films. As a medic in a pre-*Bright Victory* film, James Edwards does little more than recite anti-communism scripture in *The Steel Helmet* (Lippert, 1950). Arch Oboler's *Five* (Columbia, 1951), is set is the wake of nuclear holocaust. One of the five survivors is a black, played by Charles Lampkin, but instead of directing the theme toward the obvious possibilities for realigning racial attitudes in a new order, the black is simply killed off by a racist member of the surviving party. *It's a Big Country* (MGM, 1951), attempted to show ethnic contributions to World War Two but, in relation to Afro-Americans at least, it was shallow and ineffective. In *Red Ball Express* (Universal International, 1952), Sidney Poitier, who had important roles in earlier problematic pictures, played a black soldier in the quartermaster corps during World Two. While he retained his dignified bearing in this supporting role, the minor racial incidents in the film are not turned to meaningful statements. Indeed, as in films like *Bataan* (1943), the historically inaccurate suggestion that such troops were integrated is fostered. But the same ahistorical situation would permeate most war films made in America after World War Two.

Afro-American Frank Silvera played in two films which had minor themes which could have been made relevant, *The Fighter* (United Artists, 1952) and *Fear and Desire* (1953). In *The Fighter*, Silvera is Paulino, father of a boxer and revolutionary in Mexico. In Stanley Kubrick's *Fear and Desire* Sergeant Mac, one of four soldiers on a World War Two mission which Mac sees through to the finish because of his dedication. In both films, Silvera demonstrated his competence as an actor, but in neither case were the important themes of racial or social upheaval developed by the producers.

One interesting result of the message pictures was

that a film like *Bright Road* (MGM, 1953), also titled *See How They Run*, could be made. It was Harry Belafonte's first film, and he played a school principal to Dorothy Dandridge's role as a teacher. Afro-Americans Maidie Norman and Philip Hepburn also appeared in this film which featured the problem of straightening out a wayward young boy. No social statement was intended or made in this film, but what makes the film important is that it is one of the few all-black Hollywood films (there was one minor role for a white) that gave dramatic rather than musical roles to Afro-Americans. It was also remarkable for its natural portrayal of Afro-Americans as teachers, principals, and students with no attempt to fit them into the stereotypical tradition. A film like *Bright Road* could not have been made in America prior to the cycle of problematic films which preceded it.

The reasons for the production of problem films in the late forties and early fifties went much deeper than differences between Afro-Americans and Anglo-Americans. In quick succession in the late forties the Red scare was fanned as China became Communist, the Berlin blockade was instituted to check Russian aggression, and the Russians announced their possession of the atomic bomb. Frustration and confusion were amplified by the new kind of war being waged in Korea, made immediate to Americans by television. It's objectives were limited, there was no declaration of war, and the entrenchment of a "peace-time" draft resulted in a discriminatory casualty rate for Afro-Americans, twice as high as the rate for Anglo-Americans. Disillusionment and helplessness in face of fears of communism and nuclear holocaust triggered and then intensified the House Un-American Activities Committee (HUAC) investigations of both government figures and Hollywood personalities. In light of these crises, Hollywood's film criticism of the social order was curtailed somewhat after 1950 by the terror HUAC and Senator Joseph McCarthy instilled in the movie industry.

Beginning in 1947, HUAC investigations in Hollywood had resulted in prison terms for some people suspected of being Communists or Communist sympathizers. In competing with McCarthy, HUAC focused on minorities. In the movie industry it was the Hollywood Ten. The careers of Afro-Americans James Edwards, star of *Home of the Brave* (1949), and Paul Robeson were caught up short in 1952 when they both refused to testify before HUAC. Edwards still appeared in films during the fifties, but his roles were few and by the late fifties they had degenerated to appearances in films like *Tarzan's Fight for Life* (1958). Robeson, whose career could have been as a star in athletics or as a scholar in academia, had long been an admirer of the Soviet Union, which he visited in 1934. Robeson was conspicuously absent from the films of the fifties, not only because of HUAC but because of his personal decision not to work in Hollywood. His other activities were hampered by the stigma of the HUAC investigations, however. When the Supreme Court in 1958 reinstated his passport privileges, revoked in 1950, Robeson promptly fled the country, returning only in retirement five years later.

The HUAC purges in Hollywood affected outspoken Anglo-American critics of the Afro-American situation like Dalton Trumbo who was blacklisted for many years although he worked surreptitiously under pseudonyms. Carl Foreman, the Anglo-American scriptwriter for *Home of the Brave*, was also purged along with director Martin Ritt who took the Fifth Amendment when appearing before HUAC in the early fifties. Ritt was back in the waning controversy in 1957 when he co-directed with David Susskind a Poitier-Cassavetes reversal of normal Afro-American and Anglo-American film roles in *Edge of the City* (MGM and United Artists, 1957), also titled *A Man Is Ten Feet Tall*. He remained a provocative and unpredictable director even after HUAC faded away. To alleviate the social issue of the Afro-American and Anglo-American conflict, for instance, Ritt changed the Afro-American characterization of Alma, as she appeared in the novel, to that of an Anglo-American in *Hud* (Paramount, 1963). Alma, it may be recalled, was the one woman who got away from Anglo-American Paul Newman who played *macho* Hud. Ritt's greatest success in dealing with an Afro-American theme was *Sounder* (Twentieth Century-Fox, 1972), but his follow-up was a financial failure. *Conrack* (Twentieth Century-Fox, 1974), was an attempt to seriously show the real experiences of a white teacher in an underdeveloped area populated by blacks. It was a condescending portrayal of that experience on film, relying as it did on the goodwill and devotion of a white man as a secular missionary. The film was boycotted by civil rights groups.

The problems with characterizing race relations would exist even a generation after the *Brown* decision (1954) but, by then, Afro-American filmmakers were back in business in a big way as competition. In the

Hollywood films of the fifties, however, it was still Anglo-American filmmakers handling the image of Afro-Americans, though changes in the film industry were underway. Specialized theaters like art houses and drive-ins boomed after World War Two, reflecting in part an increase in amateur art buffs and in part the desire for semi-private places in which the returning G.I. anxious to begin a family could take his or her spouse. Competition from non-studio foreign films resulted in increased filming on location in Southern California. The studio system in Hollywood found itself suffering from mismanagement, union padding, and the high costs of maintaining the studios and the studio-supported theaters. All of these factors made the Hollywood productions more expensive than necessary and contributed to the rise of more independents. Perhaps taking their cue from the success of Disney's and then Hitchcock's productions, many new filmmakers sought to appeal to specialized audiences. Rather than standardized movies which attempted to attract the largest general audiences, movies were soon being made more than ever for teenagers, housewives and, in a limited realm, for or about ethnic groups like Afro-Americans.

Another of these specialized audiences was young adults. There were two million college students like Pinky in degree programs by the end of World War Two, eight times as many as in 1900. The number of junior colleges multiplied as the necessity of having a college degree was propagandized as increasing potential income by $100,000 over a lifetime. As technical expertise rather than the accumulation of property came to represent the new power base, the university became intertwined with the rapidly accelerating technology. Booker T. Washington's dilemma in finding that Afro-Americans were not allowed into entrepreneurship because they lacked the necessary training was being repeated once again as Afro-Americans were denied access to the era's passport into society, a college degree. Washington sought an answer in the creation of Afro-American vocational schools like Tuskegee Institute and by the forties there were nearly a hundred Afro-American vocational institutes and liberal arts or teachers colleges. The early years of the post-World War Two education boom yielded little immediate benefit for Afro-Americans. Despite the new training many Afro-Americans were receiving, or had received while in the military, America was not yet ready to accept them on an equal footing in the economic or social realms.

In *In This Our Life* (1942), Hattie McDaniel spoke in a moment of weakness of her law-student son who had just had a conflict with Anglo-Americans: "Ah knew this would happen if he tried to better himself. His place is with us, with the servants; he shouldn't try to make himself better than he is!" It was an Anglo-American script, but it pointed out that there was a long way to go yet before attitudes toward education for Afro-Americans would change. The inroads that would influence the changes that resulted in the *Brown* decision in 1954, however, were becomming more numerous as the fifties approached.

Beginning in the late forties when the problem pictures were being made, the United States helped unshackle the colonies belonging to Germany and Italy; these colonies, in turn, were quickly emerging as prospective independent nations along with the colonies of the decaying British Empire like South Africa. The new status for non-Anglo nations could not but have an affect on the still unsatisfactory status of Afro-Americans. Again, the contradiction between the ideal and the real was placed in the lap of America. As the colonies of colored peoples especially were being freed, the irrepressible question of the freedom of Afro-Americans in America was raised all the louder. In an effort to gain these new foreign markets, Hollywood would find itself undergoing some changes in its presentation of the Afro-American image in film culture in the years to come. The changes did not occur quickly, however, and even the impressive efforts of the problematic films of the forties and early fifties left the black image in films unfulfilled. America itself was a microcosm of a world quickly dividing politically along color lines into the first world of America and its allies, the second world of Russia and its allies, and the third world made up of the remaining unaligned countries, many of them newly created on the continents of Africa and Asia.

Notes

[1] Lindsay Patterson, ed., *Black Films and Film-Makers: A Comprehensive Anthology from Stereotype to Superhero* (New York: Dodd and Mead, 1975), p. 278.

[2] Daniel J. Leab, *From Sambo to Superspade: The Black Experience in Motion Pictures* (Boston: Houghton Mifflin, 1975), p. 30.

[3] I.C. Jarvie, *Movies and Society* (New York: Basic Books, 1970), p. 363.

Chapter Eighteen

War and Peace at Home

Spectacular revolutions with their roots in the forties--television, Korea, and McCarthyism--had a tremendous impact on American life in 1950 and provided the bases for the cultural strains of the early fifties in American culture. The crises in American culture were further precipitated when the National Association for the Advancement of Colored People (NAACP) brought three successful suits before the United States Supreme Court in 1950: *Henderson versus The United States* which held that Jim Crow was illegal on interstate dining cars; *Sweatt versus Painter* which held that equal education requires more than equal buildings; and *McLaurin versus Oklahoma State Regents* which held that no school could segregate Afro-American students from Anglo-American students once they had been admitted to previously all-white schools. In each of the three cases the Supreme Court avoided ruling specifically on the "separate but equal" doctrine but, taken together, the decisions greatly strengthened the legal arguments on which the *Brown versus The Topeka Board of Education* decision to overturn *Plessy versus Ferguson* would be based four years later.

Also in 1950, an attempt to remake *The Birth of a Nation* with sound failed; the NAACP protested the appearance of the *Amos "n" Andy Show* on television and it was withdrawn; Paul Robeson's passport was revoked because of his boycott activities and because he was "too controversial" in expressing Marxist sympathies; the first book on the Afro-American image in films by an American, *The Negro in Hollywood Films*, was published by the Marxist author, Victor J. Jerome; the Korean police action broke out; the U.S. Army propaganda machine started up again, producing films like *National Folk Festival, Part Two*, which included Afro-American and other ethnic contributions to music; Senator Joseph McCarthy gave voice to his conspiracy theory by presenting a list of Communists employed by the United States Government; the McCarran Internal Security Act was passed; Edgar Rice Burroughs, author of the twenty-six volumes of "Black Peril" Tarzan jungle tales, died; Gwendolyn Brooks became the first Afro-American to receive the Pulitzer Prize for poetry; and Afro-American Dr. Ralph J. Bunche received the Nobel Peace Prize. Bunche's accomplishment was not duplicated until Dr. Martin Luther King, Jr., won it in 1964; the Nobel Peace Prize was only given thirteen times in the intervening years and the competition was world-wide.

The impact of films on the youth of American increased significantly in the fifties. As they continued to attend the movies regularly, the youth market grew to be of prime importance for the movie industry at the same time that the images monopolized by Hollywood were being challenged from many quarters, including television. The era of the big Hollywood studios was further along the road in its decline. Admission prices were hiked as fewer films were being made and fewer theaters remained open. Anti-trust suits in the late forties broke up theater chains controlled by large studios. Producers became more autonomous and underground filmmaking became popular. Hollywood suffered setbacks as large numbers of other countries developed their own movie industries. The attempt to counter this competition was short-lived, but it resulted in bigger thematic schemes and the "big picture" which focused on spectacles and spectaculars in new wide-screen variations with Cinema-Scope and Technicolor, technological epics which neither the foreign producers nor television could match: Darryl F. Zanuck's *All About Eve* (Twentieth Century-Fox, 1950); John Huston's *The African Queen* (United Artists, 1951); Cecill B. DeMille's *The Greatest Show on Earth* (Paramount, 1952); Henry Koster's *The Robe* (Twentieth Century-Fox, 1953); and Elia Kazan's *On the Waterfront* (Columbia, 1954).

Afro-Americans faced problems in the television medium similar to those first faced in films. At a recent popular culture conference, television producer Alan Manning reported that "in the fifties there were no blacks on television, not even maids."[1] This was slightly overstated, but it reflected the fact that while only three per cent of American households in 1953 employed domestics, Hollywood's Afro-American film images told a different story. Some of the stale stereotypical maid roles in this era were those of Afro-Americans Collette Lyons as Beulah in *Wabash Ave* (Twentieth Century-Fox, 1950), Marietta Canty as Tillie in *Valentino* (Columbia, 1951), Ruby Dee as Rachel (who was not only a maid in this film but a suspect in an attempted assassination of the newly inaugurated Abraham Lincoln) in *The Tall Target* (MGM, 1951), and Amanda Randolph in the maid role Hattie McDaniel had in the *The Male Animal* (1942) in its remake, *She's Working Her Way Through College* (Warners, 1952). Louise Beavers was also back in the fifties as a maid in *My Blue Heaven* (Twentieth Century-Fox, 1950), but her career was nearly over. Her name was still a powerful attraction and she made appearances in *I Dream of Jeannie* (Republic, 1952), *Teenage Rebel* (1956), *You Can't Run Away from It* (1956), *Tammy and the Bachelor* (1957), and then after a long lapse and late in her life in *All the Fine Young Cannibals* (1960) and *The Facts of Life* (1961). Beavers' brand of mammy was nearly dead as her diminishing number of roles show. While the maid tradition continued in films, there were no new "stars" to replace the mammy she and Hattie McDaniel made famous in the thirties and forties. Hollywood and the American public were slowly changing their views on and forms of racial discrimination.

A brief filed before the Supreme Court by the Attorney General in 1952 noted that

> it is in the context of the present world struggle between freedom and tyranny that the problem of racial discrimination must be viewed . . . Racial discrimination furnishes grist for the Communist propaganda mills, and it raises doubts even among friendly nations as to the intensity of our devotion to the democratic faith.[2]

The increased importance for American ethnic relations of both exclusion and inclusion of images in the audio-visual media was reflected in both domestic and international arenas. Racial discrimination in the form of exclusion continued, however, for the same year as the Attorney General's statement no Afro-Americans were included in the credits of *Ruby Gentry* (Twentieth Century-Fox, 1952). They were there, if only behind the counter and waiting table at a resort. The inclusion in typically small ways in the background continued too with minor roles for Afro-Americans like Robert "Smokey" Whitfield in *Right Cross* (MGM, 1950), Joel Fluellen as Sam in *Sitting Bull* (United Artists, 1954), Hilda Simms as a waitress in *Black Widow* (Twentieth Century-Fox, 1954) and, in a continuation of her consistent appearances over the years in minor roles, Maidie Norman as

Camilla in *About Mrs. Leslie* (Paramount, 1954).

Television brought about a cultural revolution often compared to that generated by the printing press. But television was unique as a medium in that its impact and popularity were nearly immediate. In consonance with the rapid technological advances of the era, television, like film, speeded through the normal steps in the cycle that most new sports and media previously had passed through: from plaything of the rich, to serious utilization by the middle class, to popularization among the masses. Wrestling and governmental investigations became national sports overnight; the dramatic growth of violent professional football was coupled to the development of television. Because of their exposure through television, the country took years to recouperate from the traumatic McCarthyism, the impact of the Rosenbergs' trial for betraying atomic secrets, the testimony of Whittaker Chambers, the Kefauver crime investigations, the Alger Hiss trial, and the zealous new politician, Richard Nixon. Meanwhile, the much older issue of status for Afro-Americans sneaked up on the perpetually preoccupied American public mind.

The impact of the cultural revolution brought on by television was acute in the Afro-American community. The affluence of the Anglo-American culture was visualized on television for the Afro-American community and, to some extent, the affluent in the Anglo-American community were suddenly exposed to the Afro-American *kraals*, or ghettoes. The popularization of installment buying did little to increase the standard of living for many Afro-Americans who remained unemployed. Attempts by those who were employed to obtain the living conditions of the rest of America often failed because they were underemployed. Increased intercourse between Anglo-American merchants and Afro-American patrons resulted in increased discrimination when many Afro-Americans either could not purchase the items television indicated were available in America or could not sustain the purchases when they were made on credit.

With their traditional disdain for the film medium, intellectuals were skeptical of the new television medium. Fearful of its power, intellectuals were critical of television's assistance in displaying the unpredented influence of the demagogue McCarthy, despite the fact that it also led to his downfall during the Army hearings. To many Americans from all ethnic groups, the potential power of the new medium was terrifying. Radio had contributed a Father Coughlin as well as a Roosevelt in the thirties; television in the fifties was to open with a McCarthy and close with a Kennedy.

The demonic proportions of the Red scares during World War One, and again in the thirties, were expanded upon by McCarthy's crystalization of the issue over whether America was most in danger of a Communist takeover from within or from without the country. Communist sympathizers in the government were present but latent in the thirties and forties and had been almost entirely eliminated by the time of Mao Tse Tung's revolution in China. By defying the larger historical trends in posing this moot issue, McCarthy fanned the burned-out coals by "identifying" Communists in the government [not a single accusation of McCathy's was ever documented] and by pointing to the unjustifiable loss of Mainland China to the Communists. In spite of the limited war being fought in Korea against the Communists, McCarthy continued to shout unprovable and slanderous charges of Communist infiltration in official American agencies. McCarthy made himself the center of attraction and through a manipulation of the media he managed to fire the fear and/or the imagination of nearly every media-watcher or media-listener at home and abroad.

Other important changes were taking place at the same time. With the stardom of Elvis Presley, American youth encouraged the growth of rock music, which had its roots in the music of the Afro-American community. Afro-American entertainers returned in droves to Hollywood in the early fifties. *Ebony* magazine wryly titled an August 1951 article, "Movie Musicals: Ranking Negro Performers Given Musical Bits in Half-dozen Coming Hollywood Productions." Aside from the all-black musicals, there were dozens of other films in which Afro-Americans were cast as entertainers, among them Louis Armstrong who did the soundtrack for *The Strip* (MGM, 1951) and contributed to the music for *Here Comes the Groom* (Paramount, 1951), Dorothy Dandridge as herself sang (and an uncredited Afro-American played Ben, the janitor), in *Remains to be Seen* (MGM, 1953), Benny Carter and his band were featured in *Clash by Night* (RKO, 1952), and Nat "King" Cole performed the title song in *The Blue Gardenia* (Warners, 1953). As musicians in *Young Man with a Horn* (Warners, 1950), the talented Juano Hernandez co-starred and Louis Armstrong and

Sammy Davis, Jr., appeared in this story of a white musician, Rick Martin. Segregated, or the politer word by the fifties, cameo, roles occurred now and again for Afro-Americans, but they too were on the wane. In appearances as themselves Lena Horne sang one song in *Duchess of Idaho* (MGM, 1950), Nat "King" Cole performed in one scene in *Small Town Girl* (MGM, 1953), and Louis Armstrong played his jazz in one "sequence" in *The Glenn Miller Story* (Universal, 1954).

Two professional entertainers made a partial transition from entertainers to dramatists in film. Until *Bright Road* (1953), in which Harry Belafonte and Dorothy Dandridge engage in a love affair, the careers of both were as nightclub singers. In the following year, however, they were to repeat their entertainer roles in the all-black musical, *Carmen Jones* (1954). In addition to the reinforcement of the entertainer stereotype, there were reinforcements of other old images of Afro-Americans. The film roles of Afro-Americans as subservient background characters did not diminish much during the fifties although there were also a few progressive portrayals of the Afro-American image in the previously discussed problematic films. Stepin Fetchit made a comeback attempt as a comic in Anthony Thann's western set on the Oregon Trail, *Bend of the River* (Universal International, 1952), but it led to only one further appearance in a remake of *Judge Priest* (1934), *The Sun Shines Bright* (Argosy, 1954), in which he again played the role of Jeff. Clarence Muse appeared as a faithful servant in the role of a room in the remake of *Broadway Bill* (1934), Frank Capra's *Riding High* (Paramount, 1950). That these roles were also on the decline is illustrated by the fact that Muse made few films in the fifties and sixties. He resurfaced late in his life for minor roles in *Buck and the Preacher* (Columbia, 1972) and *Car Wash* (Universal, 1976).

Nearly always assigned to women in Hollywood films, the mulatto image was blatant in the films of the fifties. The image became all the more infuriating because the "mulatto" character was in most cases played by Anglo-American actresses while in the reality of American culture a mulatto was considered to be an Afro-American. There were occasional mulatto portrayals by Afro-American actresses. Dorothy Dandridge, for instance, played the title role in *Carmen Jones* where all of the characters were Afro-Americans. But with films like George Sidney's technicolor version of

Show Boat (MGM, 1951), with Joe E. Brown, Hollywood continued to come almost full circle since the days of blackfacing Anglo-Americans to portray Afro-Americans. This latest version of *Show Boat* cast an Anglo-American, Ava Gardner, as the mulatto Julie; the same had occurred in both the 1929 and 1936 versions. Afro-Americans William Garfield and Frances Williams played Joe and Queenie, both relatively minor roles again. The miscegenation theme was still present, but this version did delete most references to "darkies" and "niggers."

Immediately after the 1949-1950 cycle of Hollywood's problematic films, there followed several films depicting real-life Afro-American athletes. There had been few earlier attempts by Hollywood to depict on celluloid this aspect of real Afro-American achievement. Hollywood preferred to confine the roles of Afro-Americans to entertainers, domestics, comics, and propaganda figures even in sports films like *Glory Alley* (MGM, 1952), a boxing film in which Louis Armstrong had a poor role as the comic, Shadow Johnson, that was salvaged only by his jazz performances. In the same era, though, Hollywood also turned to the semi-truthful presentation of Afro-Americans in sports roles through exploitive race-pride films that attempted to appeal primarily to Afro-American audiences. Interest in boxing had never been absent, but it was revived in the late thirties when Joe Louis won the world championship. His portrayal of himself in the independently produced *The Spirit of Youth* (1937) had been a box office flop. The Joe Louis story without the real Joe Louis in it, except through footage of his fights, was remade by Hollywood as *The Joe Louis Story* (United Artists, 1953). The Hollywood version with Afro-Americans Coley Wallace as Joe, Hilda Simms as Joe's wife, and James Edwards as his trainer, fared little better than the independent *The Spirit of Youth*. Anglo-American audiences were not more than mildly interested in such achievements.

This exclusionary attitude toward outstanding Afro-American athletes was expressed during the fifties, although popular Afro-American personalities like Sugar Ray Robinson and Joe Louis had been accepted into the Anglo-American sporting establishment long before. In the fifties, an Afro-American was successful in overcoming the system if he was not a Communist and if he was successful in professional football. In some cases professional football players made the transition to film. Woody Strode, a pre-Jim Brown phenomenon with both an impressive physique and demeanor, went from playing football for the Los Angeles Rams to such diverse film roles as Josh in *The Gambler from Natchez* (Twentieth Century-Fox, 1954), a lion in *Androcles and the Lion* (RKO, 1952), and small parts in *The Ten Commandments* (Paramount, 1956) and *Tarzan's Fight for Life* (1958). Before Afro-Americans were allowed into the ranks of professional football, Paul Robeson had been the first Afro-American All-American college football player.

The low-budget film autobiography of Jackie Robinson, *The Jackie Robinson Story* (1950) showed Robinson breaking the "color bar" of professional baseball in 1947, a bar which had been in effect for nearly forty years. His successes as an athlete, as a man, and as a defender of Anglo-American as well as Afro-American ideals were all reflected in this film. Two other race-pride films, both featuring the Harlem Globetrotters, *The Harlem Globetrotters* (Columbia, 1951), and *Go, Man, Go* (United Artists, 1953), extended the range of film appearances for Afro-American athletes. *The Harlem Globetrotters* also featured Dorothy Dandridge and Bill Walker, and *Go, Man, Go* provided supporting roles for Ruby Dee and Sidney Poitier. Dandridge and Poitier were among a group of emerging Afro-American stars who would find acceptance among general audiences in America. In her film comeback, Ethel Waters became the first Afro-American woman to star in a Hollywood production that was not all-black, *The Member of the Wedding* (1952). Among the other emerging Afro-American personalities in film, Eartha Kitt was introduced in *New Faces of 1952* and Diahann Carroll appeared in her first film in *Carmen Jones*.

The dichotomy of the new atomic age was between the reality that all peoples in the world could be destroyed and the intellectually satisfying reaction to the danger in such idealistic forms as the Universal Declaration of Human Rights (1948). The greater the danger, apparently, the greater the appeal for worldwide brotherhood and unity by America, though not necessarily appealing for brotherhood at home. The Afro-American population grew much faster than did the Anglo-American population after World War Two, but Afro-Americans remained on the bottom of the social scale in the early fifties. Anglo-American support of the Afro-American community seemed to increase slightly in the period following World War Two, prompted in part, unfortunately, by Afro-American baseball star Jackie Robinson coming across as all "Red, White, and Blue" when he testified against Paul Robeson before the Red-hunting House Un-American Activities Committee.

Nearly a century before, John Brown had led his fateful raid on Harpers Ferry in an act designed to challenge his era's discriminatory practices against minorities. In 1953--it could hardly have been done at a more appropriate time--Columbia Records presented Stephen Vincent Benet's *John Brown's Body* with Raymond Massey speaking for Abraham Lincoln. He spoke to a troubled America: "I mean to save the Union if I can and by whatever means I can, under the Constitution . . . . [My wish is that] the last slave should be forever free, here, in this country." A century later slavery as an institution was gone but its successor, Jim Crow, had yet to be entirely rooted out.

Extensive changes in the social order were in the making, however. The first novel by James Baldwin, *Go Tell It on the Mountain* (1953), was published and Ralph Ellison won the 1953 National Book Award in fiction for *Invisible Man*. Ellison thus became the first Afro-American to be awarded a major literary prize for fiction. Ellison's novel discusses James Joyce on identity in one passage: "Stephen's problem, like ours, was not actually one of creating the uncreated consciousness of his race, but of creating the uncreated features of his face." An Afro-American consciousness existed by 1953, but it had not yet been focused. Despite the potential, over a half-century of film images turned out to be an encumbrance which substantially distracted from, rather than contributed to, Afro-American identity.

In the same era, The McCarran-Walter Immigration Act of 1952 followed the McCarran Internal Security Act of 1950, acts which further defined America for Anglo-Americans and provided unprecedented powers for the president in handling internal "emergencies." Both bills were vetoed by President Truman because of their discriminatory nature and both vetoes were overridden by the United States Congress. In 1953, the United States Supreme Court struck close to home with a decision that Washington, D.C., restaurants could not legally refuse to serve Afro-Americans. And in a crucial change in philosophy, the NAACP in 1953 challenged its own previous attempts to enforce the "separate but equal" doctrine by substituting integration of the races as its objective.

Notes

[1] Alan Manning, informal presentation at the Western Regional Popular Culture Association Meeting in Pomona, California, on 1 February 1975.

[2] C. Vann Woodward, *The Strange Career of Jim Crow*, 2nd. rev. ed. (New York: Oxford Univ. Press, 1966), p. 132.

Chapter Nineteen

Korea and Vietnam

America's international concerns shifted from Korea to Vietnam in 1953. The Korean Truce had been signed but Dien Bein Phu had fallen to Ho Chi Minh. Leery of another Asian encounter, the United States Government instead set up a puppet government in South Vietnam under a Roman Catholic brought from a seminary in New Jersey, Ngo Dinh Diem. On the homefront, Artisan Productions made the documentary *Lifting as We Climb* (1953) which highlighted the history of the National Association of Colored Women from its beginnings in 1896, the year of the *Plessy versus Ferguson* Supreme Court decision. On 17 May 1954 the massive civil rights activities of the fifties, sixties, and seventies were set in motion. Led by Thurgood Marshall, the National Association for the Advancement of Colored People (NAACP) fought and won the *Brown versus The Topeka Board of Education* decision in which the Warren Court declared school segregation unconstitutional. The decision to overturn *Plessy*, which had stood as the law of the land for fifty-eight years, shocked many Americans and opened the door to the most significant gains by Afro-Americans to date in the sphere of civil, political, and economic rights and opportunities.

Among the other landmarks of 1954, the television industry instituted a policy, which has yet to be revoked, of banning from its screens D.W. Griffith's *The Birth of a Nation*; "t.v." dinners were popularized; the televised McCarthy Army hearings spelled the downfall of the demagogue and before the end of the year McCarthy was censured by his peers in the U.S. Senate; banned in the United States of America for fifteen years, *Salt of the Earth* was made in Mexico by Americans blacklisted from Hollywood as a result of the House Un-American Activities Committee (HUAC) investigations; Afro-American J. Ernest Wilkens was appointed Assistant Secretary of Labor; the Senate confirmed the first appointment of an Afro-American general in the Air Force, Benjamin O. Davis, Jr.; the Defense

Department announced the achievement of total integration in all branches of the military while the U.S. Navy showed that segregation remained in effect in a documentary it put out, titled *The Navy Steward* (1953), in which "Blacks in the Navy are shown being taught how to serve in the white officer's mess";[1] reaction to the *Brown* decision resulted in the creation of a White Brotherhood in Georgia and the first of many White Citizens' Councils in Mississippi, while other southern states began efforts to dismantle their public school systems; the Voice of America repeatedly broadcast the *Brown* decision throughout the world in thirty-five languages.

The *Brown* decision was not argued by Marshall on the basis that there was inequality in the separate facilities of education, but on the basis that the separation itself was sociologically harmful. It was not until a year after the *Brown* decision that the Supreme Court issued a decree which sought to implement that decision "with all due and deliberate speed." Not for almost sixty years had the Supreme Court ventured such a lucid statement on the rights of the Afro-American minority as it did in the *Brown* decision. It was not so much the decision itself which caused the ensuing furor; rather, the important issue became one of implementation. The South was the most unwilling region, of course, but the North also balked. After 1954, the Ku Klux Klan again emerged with renewed strength in America as a protest against this "second reconstruction." The delays in enforcing the *Brown* decision were temporarily effective. Ten years later, the year in which the first substantial Civil Rights Act (1964) of the twentieth century was passed, only one per cent of Afro-American children were attending school with Anglo-Americans. But other steps were being taken in the sixties, for the sociologist-at-law Marshall was appointed as the first Afro-American Justice of the Supreme Court.

In the mid-fifties, however, the popular mind of the nation itself was not yet in a mood to act upon the *Brown* decision in a unified manner. There were as many differences of opinion within the Afro-American community as within the Anglo-American community concerning the decision. Among the concerns for Afro-Americans were the fact that their children might be entering a hostile environment in integrated schools, that what their children learned there might undermine Afro-American traditions and culture, and the possibility that they would have to give up what it had taken nearly a century to achieve in the way of black colleges and institutes. During his years in office, President Eisenhower, with few very minor exceptions, refused to forceably carry out the Supreme Court's decision because, he said, he believed "that any real improvement in race relations would have to await a change in the hearts and minds of men."[2] That opinion went against the grain of American history which had demonstrated over and over again that only legal action through laws and the enforcement of those laws would bring about such changes. This neutrality on the part of the Executive Officer of the United States left those Americans opposing the decision in a position of command if not control.

In the Afro-American community, non-violent action in the form of sit-ins, sit-downs, and boycotts on the part of the NAACP and the Congress of Racial Equality (CORE) led later to violent adaptations of the same measures by Afro-American groups who expressed the desire to either control America or create a separate black nation within America. The battles of the NAACP to shape the laws of the land were taken up by Martin Luther King, Jr., and others who sought to have the already existing laws enforced. The efforts during the fifties were effective in arousing the national conscience. In their demands for an equal place in American culture, the Afro-American community was uniting behind civil rights groups as never before, and it appeared as if Alain Locke's "New Negro" of the twenties was finally finding substance in America. The state of mind of the Afro-American community tended primarily to back the pacifistic Afro-American leaders like King. Their pacifism was loudly contrasted with the intimidation and violence of southern Anglo-American leaders. Some elements of the Afro-American community, however, reacted by filling the ranks of separatist movements such as the Black Muslins whose strength grew in the large urban centers and prisons. Despite the appeals of the American Community Party, Afro-Americans for the most part balked against that remedy, recalling the experience of the thirties and the prevalence in the early fifties of McCarthyism. In essence, most Afro-Americans were instead still seeking a share of the American Dream.

In his novel, *The Outsider* (1953), Richard Wright rejected both communism and fascism with an existential presentation of the ideological dilemmas of the world outside the self as well as the personal dilemmas that go with free will. The major character, Cross, discovers that no one can exist without an identity and a past, factors which automatically negate free will. Reflecting the early fifties' conflicts in America, the Afro-American Cross was the outsider who understood too much and became alienated from American culture; but at the same time Cross symbolically became the center of knowing, the crossroads, for both the Anglo-American and the Afro-American cultures. Wright himself had spent many years of self-exile in France. Like many Afro-American actors, he was caught at the crossroads between being an American and being an artist. His dilemma was never reconciled for, like James Baldwin after him, and Paul Robeson before him, he left the country for artistic expression only to return frequently to reestablish his roots. A lesser known expatriate who was a contemporary of Baldwin's, John Kitzmiller, made his career in films overseas.

In the period emphasized by this study, Afro-American John Kitzmiller was a forgotten American. Few knew of his numerous film appearances following World War Two in Europe, especially in Italian feature films. In his first film role in 1946, he co-starred with a white actor in *Vivere in Pace* (Italy, 1946), also titled *To Live in Peace*. He played an American soldier during the last year of World War Two in Italy which drew upon his own experience as a G.I. stationed in Italy just after the war. He elected to stay overseas rather than return to America, and the following year he appeared in *Paradiso Nero* (Italy, 1947). His next film appearance again portrayed him as an American soldier in Italy in Alberto Lattuda's *Senza Pieta* (Italy, 1948), also titled *Without Pity*. In this story by Federico Fellini, Kitzmiller is an American deserter involved in an interracial love affair that is as well developed as any in American films prior to 1948. He then played Jack, an American profiteer, in *Tombolo* (Italy, 1949), and appeared in *Ti Ritrovero* (Italy, 1949), and *La Forza del Destino* (Italy, 1950). In Federico Fellini's *Luci del Varieta* (Italy, 1951), titled *Variety Lights* when it was finally released in America in 1965, Kitzmiller played a musician in a vaudeville troupe.

Many more roles in Italian films followed for Kitzmiller prior to 1954 when official policy conerning integration in the United States changed with the *Brown* decision: *Delitto al Luna Park* (1952), *Ultimo*

Perdono (1952), *A Fil di Spada* (1953), *Frini, Cortigiana D'Ortante* (1953), *Legione Straniera* (1953), *La Peccatrice Dell' Isola* (1953), *La Ragazza di Triesta* (1953), *Terra Straniera* (1953), *Desiderio 'E Sole* (1954), and *Non Vogliamo Morire* (1954). His numerous roles continued beyond the scope of this study, but two others are revelant nonetheless: *Onkel Tom's Hutte* (Yugoslavia/Germany, 1965), and *Adieu Uncle Tom* (Italy, 1974).

Mentioned earlier in this study was the fact that after the last Hollywood production of *Uncle Tom's Cabin* (Universal, 1927), a silent film, the introduction of sound made the potential for a black actor in the title role too risky and controversial and no studio or indepedent in America carried on the well-established tradition of seven remakes of *Uncle Tom's Cabin* prior to 1927. That potential was not entirely fulfilled in *Onkel Tom's Hutte*, titled *Uncle Tom's Cabin* when it was released in America in 1969, but it was a far more powerful version indeed because of sound. Afro-Americans Eartha Kitt and Dorothee Gelison were in this version that starred John Kitzmiller as Uncle Tom. Uncle Tom is still the stereotypical tom in many ways, but he is more potent in this film than he could have been in an American production. This film also added to Stowe's book with an uprising by the slaves which results in their freedom.

In *Adieu Uncle Tom*, also variously titled *Farewell Uncle Tom* and *Goodbye Uncle Tom*, Kitzmiller was again prominent posthumously in scenes taken from *Onkel Tom's Hutte*. This film focused more on the conditions of slavery in America and, in effect, helped better justify the inadequately motivated uprising used in *Onkel Tom's Hutte*. In a sense, the expatriate Kitzmiller had come home with these films. In another sense he had not really left America for his roles were often modeled on himself as an American overseas or as an Afro-American battling the racism of Anglo-Americans. His one appearance in an American film was in *Goldfinger* (1964) and it came just prior to his premature death in 1965. Unlike the expatriate experiences of Jack Johnson in Spain in the twenties, Josephine Baker in France in the twenties and thirties, Paul Robeson and Nina Mae McKinney in England and Europe from the thirties to the fifties, and Dorothy Dandridge in England in the fifties, John Kitzmiller had found a better future overseas. Ironically, and also unlike the expatriates who preceded him, his successful career overseas paralleled the years in which the most significant changed in civil rights for Afro-Americans since the Civil War took place in America.

Like some of the films in which John Kitzmiller appeared, a commentary on American ethnic relations set in a foreign country was *Lydia Bailey* (Twentieth Century-Fox, 1952), based on Kenneth Roberts' novel. Afro-Americans Juanita Moore, Martin Wilkens, and Alvin Ailey appeared, and Afro-American William Marshall played the lead role of King Dick. Marshall would go on to another major role as another king, King Glycon, in *Demetrius and the Gladiators* (Twentieth Century-Fox, 1953), but as King Dick he was in Haiti near the end of Toussaint's reign. *Lydia Bailey* suggested parallels to the Korean situation. France had lost Haiti and now Napoleon was returning to reconquer the island; America had "lost" China, according to people like Senator Joseph McCarthy, and had returned to the Asian Continent to establish a beachhead against the ominous forces of communism. Along with the stereotypes of blacks practicing voodoo and being sexually promiscuous, there were some new scenes for the Afro-Americans playing Haitians, not all of which were serious, including a tantalizing scene in which all eight of King Dick's wives had great fun reclothing the Anglo-American lawyer (Dale Robertson) stranded in Haiti by the fighting. While this scene could be included because the setting was Haiti, films using America as a setting were not yet ready for them. In spite of the topic which was itself controversial enough, for instance, the relationship between President Andrew Jackson and his slave lover was entirely covert in a physical sense in *The President's Lady* (Twentieth Century-Fox, 1953). Other scenes in *Lydia Bailey* were a combination of old and new situations. The powerful King Dick, who normally paraded his leadership by wearing a white suit, disguised himself as a servant to the Anglo-American lawyer when they set out to infiltrate the sympathizers of Napoleon. At one point in their perilous journey the Anglo-American, in a parody of blackfacing, dashed mud on his skin to be safe from the white Frenchmen. The bias of the film was definitely in favor of black people justly revolting against white oppressors. A memorable line from King Dick was, it seemed, addressed not only to the Haitians of 1802 but to the Afro-Americans of 1952: "It's more important these days that one remembers that he *was* a slave."

Another revolutionary close to home was portrayed

on film the same year with *Viva Zapata* (Twentieth Century-Fox, 1952), a film in which Afro-American Frank Silvera played Huerta. Silvera was also the investigator into the miracle in Portugal in 1917 dealt with by *The Miracle of Our Lady Fatima* (Warners, 1952). The themes of justifiable revolution and searching for the source of a miracle were indicative of a mood coming to the fore in American in the fifties. Faced with violent as well as non-violent resistance, and the impact of television's extended news coverage, for instance, the tactics of the southern leadership were to become less effective. Southerners were less willing to expose their brutal tactics of using billy clubs and police dogs to both nation-wide and world-wide audiences as boycotts and strikes by the Afro-American community became increasingly newsworthy. On the international scene, "the publicity thus focused upon this weak joint in America's moral armor caused genuine and practical embarrassment to the State Department in the conduct of foreign affairs."[3] On the domestic scene the public outcry against the South's frighteningly fascistic handling of Afro-Americans combined with the sympathy evoked by peaceful Afro-American marches to contribute to the growing momentum of a united Afro-American community set in motion by the NAACP and the *Brown* decision. Some of the barriers between the Afro-American and Anglo-American communities were falling. All of the barriers in the law were under a renewed and increasingly strong attack. Major battles remained to be fought, but the fact that there were many people in America ready to fight them was an encouraging sign.

Hollywood was not among those willing to fight this battle through films. The films which did appear about the *Brown* decision were documentaries made outside Hollywood. The best of these was the dramatized documentary *"With All Deliberate Speed"* (n.d.), which portrayed the making of the decision and how it affected America. The Afro-Americans Lloyd Hollar and Gus Fleming represented Thurgood Marshall and Dr. Kenneth Clark. Other documentaries have appeared like *Confronted* (NET, 1955), which discussed the impact of the decision on schools in the North, and *Segregation in Schools* (CBS, 1955), with Edward R. Murrow narrating on the reaction in southern cities to the decision. Encyclopedia Britannica Educational Corporation's *Separate but Equal* (1971) provided background to both the *Plessy* decision of 1896 and the *Brown* decision of 1954.

It would be hard to imagine how the divergency between fantasy and reality within American culture could be stretched any further than it was in 1954 with the appearance of both *Carmen Jones* and the *Brown versus The Topeka Board of Education* decision. For Afro-Americans, the Supreme Court had made a fundamental turnabout to become an important protector against abridgments of their rights before the new law of the land. But the protection did not extend to the Hollywood fantasies of America's film culture. *Carmen Jones* reinforced the myth begun in 1896, when the first short moving pictures were being made, that the Afro-American image in film meant the film was *about* Afro-American life and culture. Despite the efforts of the civil rights groups, the crises in American culture precipitated by these differences between Afro-American culture and American film culture were, it seemed, to remain present forever.

Notes

[1] Phyllis Rauch Klotman, *Frame by Frame: A Black Filmography* (Bloomington: Indiana Univ. Press, 1979), p. 372.

[2] Nelson Manfred Blake, *A History of American Thought and Life* (New York: McGraw-Hill, 1963), p. 512.

[3] C. Vann Woodward, *The Strange Career of Jim Crow*, 2nd. rev. ed. (New York: Oxford Univ. Press, 1966), p. 133.

Chapter Twenty

An Ailing American Film Culture

America, the nation always in motion, always changing, had put off significant changes for Afro-Americans as long as possible. Films were one important aspect of the slow change in philosophy which occurred between the *Plessy versus Ferguson* decision in 1896 and the *Brown versus The Topkea Board of Education* in 1954. Films were important because their omissions and overwhelmingly negative stereotypes of Afro-Americans were so consistently feeble, and their highlighting of Afro-American life and culture so brief in its rare occurrances, that the Afro-American image had remained nearly devoid of meaning beyond that of its being entertaining. This film image had become so vicious and sterile that after nearly sixty years of exploitation there was little left to mine. In terms of cultural values, Afro-Americans were subject to a sort of censorship over the years. Minority viewpoints were inhibited because Hollywood, as well as the independents, the radio networks, and the television networks, appealed to a general norm to assure an adequate financial return.

The law of the land in 1954 finally caught up with W.E.B. DuBois fifty years before when he challenged the law of *Plessy* and the reigning conservative philosophy of the Afro-American community represented by Booker T. Washington. The half-century battle for integration had culminated in the legal realm with the *Brown* decision. While the decision itself was directed only to education, it had ramifications in political and economic as well as social and spiritual areas which are still being absorbed in the American culture. Two years after the *Brown* decision, Samuel William Bloom concluded from his dissertation research that although the image of the Afro-American in film had improved, Hollywood was following rather than leading.[1] Indeed, it was the Afro-American civil rights groups which supplied the most influential leadership in making the few changes which did occur.

In less than a century, the Afro-American had passed from the slavery of bonds to the exclusion enforced by Jim Crow. In one sense, the attitudes of the Anglo-American public toward Afro-Americans then changed and this changed was reflected in films. By the fifties, particularly through the half-dozen problematic films that challenged the reigning stereotypes, the Anglo-American public came to accept Afro-Americans like Sidney Poitier and Ethel Waters on the screen as stars. But there was still a lack of recognition on the streets of Afro-Americans as people. In other ways, the attitudes of the Anglo-American public had not changed much since the thirties when the premier role for an Afro-American in films was as an entertainer or coon. During the thirties, too, Anglo-Americans were shown in films as predominant in relation to Afro-Americans, and the Afro-Americans were shown most often as holders of menial, unskilled and token jobs. These images reflected what was basically the case in American society, but to add insult to injury Hollywood also disproportionately portrayed large numbers of Afro-Americans as dancers, fun-makers and musicians. These images were at best only partial truths glossing over the humiliating realities surrounding Afro-Americans--realities left to the civil rights groups to cope with. In the context of the movie formulas which made up the film culture, this patter of images was normal. It was a pattern that could only be lamented and not acted against most of the time. The dozens of roles in which Hattie McDaniel or Stephin Fetchit appeared indicate forcibly that the lamentable image of the Afro-American in film was conveyed by inclusion in a negative context. The mammy and the coon were one the wane by the time of the *Brown* decision, but the Afro-American as entertainer has yet to be squared with reality. The Afro-American image in film, overall, was a continuous series of regressions with occasional models to highlight what it could, if not should, have been. This study has emphasized the "inferior" traits in the film images of Afro-Americans while at the same time it has attempted to point out the "superior" attributes of Afro-Americans through the activities of various civil rights groups and outstanding individuals from both within and without the film industry.

There were important implications in what was not shown on the screen as well. In many cases what was most important was what was left out. Afro-Americans were generally excluded from the Hollywood films in important role models such as technicians, teachers, professionals, politicians, and leaders. The independent films by Afro-Americans were exceptional in presenting a sprinkling of Afro-American college students, doctors, scientists, and businessmen. Aside from an occasional documentary, in Hollywood films there was a marked omission of Afro-Americans in science despite the contributions of such Afro-Americans as Dr. Charles Drew and Dr. George Washington Carver, and an equally marked omission of Afro-Americans in the humanities despite the Harlem Renaissance which flourished throughout the period between the two world wars.

If the overall treatment of Afro-Americans in films had been better than it was, then the occasional mistreatment would not have been so noticeable nor so quickly condemned in the present study. The films reviewed in the present study emphasize what was included. The civil rights groups first attempted to censor and then attempted to pose alternatives to these images, both humane and ideal, in the interest of bettering the economic and political situation for Afro-Americans in reality. Despite these efforts to change the stereotypical images on the screen, the images were implanted so deeply that it has been difficult to find significant changes in the popular mind of America. Most often no one thought about the roles in which Afro-Americans were placed because it was a culturally predetermined decision. It was unconsciously accepted as natural and, as such, the roles reflected the attitudes of the era and the milieu in which the films were made.

These images grew up with the culture of the twentieth century. So pervasive were these images that the Afro-American independent filmmakers also relied on them. The essence of these images was present already in the teens: the black butler loyal to his master and the South in Kalem's *A Special Messenger* (1911) or the devoted slave kneeling before Abraham Lincoln in Vitagraph's *The Battle Hymn of the Republic* (1911); the slaves protecting the master's property from the Yankees in D.W. Griffith's *The Informer* (1912) or the slaves harboring a Confederate officer from the Yankees in *In the Fall of '64* (1914); the mammies like Jemima Washington in Pathe's *The Iron Claw* (1916) or the thieving black laundress in Triangle's *Mr. Miller's Economics* (1916); and the sacrifice of the slave's life for his beloved master in *None Can Do More* (n.d.) or the Uncle Tom character in Art Craft's *When Do We Eat*

(1918). The most pervasive Afro-American images in films were established before the end of World War One. Even with the definite stereotyping of roles for Afro-Americans, however, Hollywood could not successfully hold in rein the talents which Afro-Americans brought to their roles: Hattie McDaniels and Ethel Waters as outstanding people and actresses even when strapped to mammy roles, the unsuppressable power of Paul Robeson's presence, the surrepticious "show stealing" of Eddie "Rochester" Anderson, or the quiet dignity of Leigh Whipper and Juano Hernandez.

There is another side to this discussion of Hollywood film images. Afro-Americans wanted to be in Anglo-American movies. Generally, actors went to Hollywood for money and the American Dream as much as for expression. In the case of the majority of Afro-Americans, it was an economic imperative which took them to Hollywood. Many Afro-Americans had talents to offer and needed employment. Hollywood gave them the option of taking whatever roles were offered--scores of them for Louise Beavers, nearly all as maids or mammies--and submitting to such exigencies as speaking so-called Black English, regardless of whether the Afro-American grew up with "Black English" or with "Anglo-American English." This was one technique of many that Hollywood used to devalue the Afro-American image to assure the audience that Afro-Americans remained essentially different, regardless of the socio-economic status or the educational level of the Afro-American playing the part.

Having no part or having the correct part has always been an issue for Afro-Americans. So has the question of whether an Afro-American actor is an actor first or an Afro-American or an American first. Perhaps Afro-Americans could not express pride in the film images of Willie Best or Stepin Fethit, but there was a certain amount of pride in what they accomplished just by securing roles in Hollywood films. In a reversal of the normal exaggeration by Hollywood, the highlights of Afro-American achievement portrayed in films was even lower than what was actually happening in real life. This negligence helped create Afro-American Hollywood rebels. The film rebels were more attractive to Afro-Americans and they formed the most impressive link between film culture and the civil rights groups. The work of Paul Robeson, Lena Horne, Butterfly McQueen, and James Edwards both on and off the screen spoke to one principle: to be an equal one must act as an equal, for it is a reciprocal arrangement. Without a script there can be no act; without an act the script alone is worthless. For these rebels, the Hollywood scripts did not often fit their acts and either they rejected Hollywood or Hollywood rejected them. Whether the civil rights groups then accepted them as spokespeople, as they did with Horne, or left them to speak out on their own, as did Robeson, McKinney, and Edwards, their voices were heard and their points were made.

If film culture mirrors personality, the films in which Afro-Americans have appeared tell about the warps in the American personality. It was an ailing American film culture. Tensions were created by the dichotomy between how Anglo-Americans desired to see Afro-Americans--and how the Afro-Americans desired to see themselves. The Anglo-Americans preferred to see Afro-Americans in light of the film images and the Afro-Americans who thought about it generally preferred to see themselves in light of the civil rights activities. The dichotomy existed but there were nebulous areas in which it did not necessarily hold true: an Afro-American, for instance, may have concluded that in general many Afro-Americans were like those portrayed in films. The Anglo-American influence in the majority of civil rights groups created a similar problem because it raised issues about just who was making the decisions and for whom those decisions were being made in the long run.

Anglo-American attitudes were reflected most powerfully by exclusion, by not bringing into the picture reflections of non-stereotyped Afro-Americans until *Bright Road* (1953), just prior to the *Brown* decision. Few accurate or significant Afro-American historical episodes ever reached the screen, as this study of the black image in films from 1896 to 1954 has shown. Afro-Americans have been excluded from the dreams and the realities of American culture, as well. No matter how much hard work was put in, no matter how much talent was involved, for the Afro-American the opportunities did not exist as they did for Anglo-Americans.

One last image from a film about World War Two is appropriate for what was yet to come. *PT-109* (1963) has black "natives" in the role of entertainers who minister to John F. Kennedy as they sing "Rock of Ages" and row him to safety. For Afro-Americans the rock of ages is America: "Rock of Ages, cleft for me/Let me hide myself in thee." Montague Toplady's hymn was written on the eve of the American Revolution in 1775, but for Afro-Americans America did not change much until 1954 when the sound and the furies of the interplay between civil rights groups and film culture in this study comes to an end. To cite with appreciation William Faulkner's sense of the Afro-American experience, it has been a long battle which is still to be won; but "they've endured." Afro-American James Baldwin pointed out a further dimension of reality in 1953 when he stated that "this world is white no longer, and it will never be white again."[2] No unexpectedly, it is taking American culture and American film culture a long while to catch up with this reality.

Notes

[1] Samuel William Bloom, "A Social Psychological Study of Motion Picture Audience Behavior: A Case Study of the Negro Image in Mass Communication" (Diss., Univ. of Wisconsin, 1956), passim.

[2] James Baldwin, "Stranger in the Village," *Notes of a Native Son* (New York: Bantam, 1972), p. 149.

Bibliography

Books

Archer, Leonard C. *Black Images in the American Theatre: NAACP Protest Campaigns--Stage, Screen, Radio & Television*. Brooklyn, NY: Pageant-Poseidon, 1973.

Baker, Ray Stannard. *Following the Color Line: American Negro Citizenship in the Progressive Era*. 1908; rpt. New York: Harper & Row, 1964.

Baldwin, James. *Go Tell It on the Mountain*. New York: Grosset and Dunlap, 1953.

Baldwin, James. *Notes of a Native Son*. New York: Bantam, 1972.

Bell, Daniel. *The End of Ideology: On the Exhaustion of Political Ideas in the Fifties*, rev. ed. New York: Collier, 1962.

Blake, Nelson Manfred. *A History of American Thought and Life*. New York: McGraw-Hill, 1963.

Bogle, Donald. *Toms, Coons, Mulattoes, Mammies, and Bucks: An Interpretive History of Blacks in American Films*. New York: Viking, 1973.

Braun, D. Duane. *Toward a Theory of Popular Culture: The Sociology and History of American Music and Dance, 1920-1968*. Ann Arbor, MI: Ann Arbor Publishers, 1969.

Brisbane, Robert H. *The Black Vanguard: Origins of the Negro Social Revolution, 1900-1960*. Valley Forge, PA: Judson, 1970.

Brown, Claude. *Manchild in the Promised Land*. New York: Macmillan, 1965.

Burgess, John W. *Reconstruction and the Constitution, 1866-1876*. New York: Charles Scribner's Sons, 1905.

Burroughs, Edgar Rice. *Tarzan of the Apes*. New York: Ballantine, 1975.

Butcher, Margaret Just [and Alain Locke]. *The Negro in American Culture*, rev. ed. New York: New American Library, 1971.

Cantor, Norman F. and Michael S. Werthman, eds. *The History of Popular Culture*. New York: Macmillan, 1971.

Cawelti, John G. *Adventure, Mystery, and Romance: Formula Stories as Art and Popular Culture*. Chicago: Univ. of Chicago Press, 1976.

Chalmers, David M. *Hooded Americanism: The First Century of the Ku Klux Klan, 1865-1965*. Garden City, NY: Doubleday, 1965.

Coombs, Norman. *The Black Experience in America*. New York: Twayne, 1972.

Cripps, Thomas. *Black Film as Genre*. Bloomington: Indiana Univ. Press, 1979.

Cripps, Thomas. *Slow Fade to Black: The Negro in American Films, 1900-1942*. New York: Oxford Univ. Press, 1977.

Davis, David Brion. *The Problem of Slavery in Western Culture*. Ithaca, NY: Cornell Univ. Press, 1969.

Davis, Lenwood G. and Janet L. Sims. *Black Artists in the United States: An Annotated Bibliography of Books, Articles and Dissertations on Black Artists, 1779-1979*. Westport, CT: Greenwood, 1980.

Dixon, Thomas. *The Clansman: An Historical Romance of the Ku Klux Klan*. New York: Grosset and Dunlap, c. 1905.

Douglass, Frederick. *Narrative of the Life of Frederick Douglass, an American Slave*. Ed. by Benjamin Quarles. Cambridge: Harvard Univ. Press, 1967.

DuBois, W.E. Burghardt. *Dusk of Dawn*. New York, 1940.

DuBois, W.E. Burghardt. *The Souls of Black Folk*. New York: New American Library, 1969.

Dunning, William Archibald. *Reconstruction: Political and Economic, 1865-1877*. New York: Harper and Brothers, 1907.

Elkins, Stanley M. *Slavery: A Problem in American Institutional and Intellectual Life*. New York: Grosset and Dunlap, 1963.

Ellison, Ralph. *Invisible Man*. New York: Random House, 1952.

Ellison, Ralph. *Shadow and Act*. New York: Random House, 1974.

Essoe, Gabe. *Tarzan of the Movies: A Pictorial History of More than Fifty Years of Edgar Rice Burroughs' Legendary Hero*. Secaucus, NJ: Citadel, 1973.

Factor, Robert L. *The Black Response to America: Men, Ideals, and Organizations from Frederick Douglass to the NAACP*. Reading, MA: Addison-Wesley, 1970.

Fager, Charles E. *White Reflections on Black Power*. Grand Rapids, MI: William B. Erdmans, 1967.

Foner, Jack D. *Blacks and the Military in American History: A New Perspective*. New York: Praeger, 1974.

Geduld, Harry M., ed. *Film Makers on Film Making*.

Bloomington: Indiana Univ. Press, 1967.
Gulliver, Adelaid Cromwell, ed. *Black Images in Films: Stereotyping and Self-Perception as Viewed by Black Actresses*. Boston: Boston Univ. Afro-American Studies Program, 1974.
Haskell, Molly. *From Reverence to Rape: The Treatment of Women in the Movies*. Baltimore: Penguin, 1974.
Hatch, James V. *Black Image on the American Stage: A Bibliography of Plays and Musicals, 1770-1970*. New York: Drama Book Specialists, 1970.
Henderson, Robert M. *D.W. Griffith: The Years at Biograph*. New York: Farrar, Straus and Giroux, 1970.
Hornsby, Alton Jr. *The Black Almanac*, 2nd. rev. ed. Woodbury, NY: Barron's Educational Series, 1975.
Jackson, Kenneth T. *The Ku Klux Klan in the City, 1915-1930*. New York: Oxford Univ. Press, 1967.
Jacobs, Lewis. *The Rise of the American Film: A Critical History*. New York: Teachers College Press, 1968.
Jarvie, I.C. *Movies and Society*. New York: Basic Books, 1970.
Jerome, V.J. *The Negro in Hollywood Films*. New York: Masses and Mainstream, 1950.
Johnson, James Weldon. *The Autobiography of an Ex-Coloured Man*. New York: Hill and Wang, 1960.
Johnson, Lemuel A. *The Devil, the Gargoyle, and the Buffoon*. Port Washington, NY: National Univ. Publications, 1969.
Kaufmann, Stanley, ed. *American Film Criticism: From the Beginnings to Citizen Kane*. New York: Liveright, 1972.
Klotman, Phyllis Rauch. *Frame by Frame: A Black Filmography*. Bloomington: Indiana Univ. Press, 1979.
Kovel, Joel K. *White Racism: A Psychohistory*. New York: Pantheon, 1970.
Lacy, Dan. *The White Use of Blacks in America*. New York: Atheneum, 1972.
Lahue, Kalton C., ed. *Motion Picture Pioneer: The Selig Polyscope Company*. New York: A.S. Barnes, 1973.
Landay, Eileen [pseud. for Eileen Rosembaum]. *Black Film Stars*. New York: Drake, 1973.
Leab, Daniel J. *From Sambo to Superspade: The Black Experience in Motion Pictures*. Boston: Houghton Mifflin, 1975.
Lee, Ray and Vernell Coriell. *A Pictorial History of the Tarzan Movies*. Los Angeles: Golden State News, 1966.
Lindsay, Nicholas Vachel. *The Art of the Moving Picture*, rev. ed. New York: Macmillan, 1922.

Locke, Alain LeRoy, ed. *The New Negro: An Interpretation.* New York: A. and C. Boni, 1925.

Macdonald, Dwight. *Against the American Grain.* New York: Random House, 1962.

Mapp, Edward. *Blacks in American Films: Today and Yesterday.* Metuchen, NJ: Scarecrow, 1972.

Mass Violence in America: Hearings on the Ku Klux Klan, 1921. Government Printing Office, 1921; rpt. New York: Arno Press and New York Times, 1969.

May, Henry F. *The End of American Innocence: A Study in the First Years of Our Own Time.* New York: Alfred A. Knopf, 1959.

Maynard, Richard A., ed. *The Black Man on Film: Racial Stereotyping.* Rochelle Park, NJ: Hayden, 1974.

Maynard, Richard A. *The Celluloid Curriculum.* New York: Hayden, 1971.

Maynard, Richard A. *Propaganda on Film: A Nation at War.* Rochelle Park, NJ: Hayden, 1975.

Mellon, Joan. *Women and Their Sexuality in the New Film.* New York: Horizon, 1973.

Memmi, Albert. *The Colonizer and the Colonized.* Intro. by Jean-Paul Sartre. Boston: Beacon, 1970.

Miller, Ruth, ed. *Blackamerican Literature: 1760-Present.* Beverly Hills, CA: Glencoe, 1971.

Morley, Christopher. *Morley's Magnum.* Philadelphia: J.B. Lippincott, 1942.

Moulton, Powers. *2500 Jokes for All Occasions.* New York: New Home Library, 1942.

Murray, James P. *To Find an Image: Black Films from Uncle Tom to Super Fly.* Indianapolis: Bobbs-Merrill, 1972.

Myrdal, Gunnar. *An American Dilemma: The Negro Problem and Modern Democracy.* New York: Harper and Row, 1962.

The Negro Family: The Case for National Action. Washington: U.S. Government Printing Office, March 1965.

Newby, I.A. *Jim Crow's Defense: Anti-Negro Thought in America, 1900-1930.* Baton Rouge: Louisiana State Univ. Press, 1968.

Niver, Kemp R. *D.W. Griffith's The Battle at Elderberry Gulch.* Ed. by Bebe Bergsten. Los Angeles: Locare Research Group, 1972.

Noble, Peter. *The Negro in Films.* London: Skelton Robinson, ca. 1948.

Nye, Russel. *The Unembarrassed Muse: The Popular Arts in America.* New York: Dial, 1970.

Okoye, Felix N. *The American Image of Africa: Myth and Reality.* Buffalo, NY: Black Academy Press, 1971.

Ortega Y Gasset, José. *The Revolt of the Masses.* New York: W.W. Norton, 1932.

Patterson, Lindsay, ed. *Black Films and Film-Makers: A Comprehensive Anthology from Stereotype to Superhero.* New York: Dodd and Mead, 1975.

Pines, Jim. *Blacks in Films: A Survey of Racial Themes and Images in the American Film.* London: Studio Vista, 1974.

Porges, Irwin. *Edgar Rice Burroughs: The Man Who Created Tarzan.* Provo, UT: Brigham Young Univ. Press, 1975.

Powers, Ann. *Blacks in American Movies: A Selected Bibliography.* Metuchen, NJ: Scarecrow, 1974.

Report of the National Advisory Commission on Civil Disorders [*The Kerner Report*]. New York: Bantam, 1968.

Rhodes, James Ford. *History of the United States: From the Compromise of 1850 to the End of the Roosevelt Administration*, vol. 9. New York: Macmillan, 1928.

Robinson, Edwin Arlington. *Collected Poems of Edwin Arlington Robinson.* New York: Macmillan, 1929.

Rosen, Marjorie. *Popcorn Venus: Women, Movies and the American Dream.* New York: Avon, 1974.

Sampson, Harry T. *Blacks in Black and White: A Source Book on Black Films.* Metuchen, NJ: Scarecrow, 1977.

Scott, Emmett J. and Lyman Beecher Stowe. *Booker T. Washington: Builder of a Civilization.* Garden City, NY: Doubleday, Page and Co., 1916.

Silva, Fred, ed. *Focus on The Birth of a Nation.* Englewood Cliffs, NJ: Prentice-Hall, 1971.

Simmons, Charles W. and Harry W. Morris, eds. *Afro-American History.* Columbus, OH: Charles E. Merrill, 1972.

Sklar, Robert. *Movie-Made America: A Cultural History of American Movies.* New York: Vintage, 1976.

Sloan, Irving J. *The American Negro: A Chronology and Fact Book.* Dobbs Ferry, NY: Oceana, 1965.

Sochen, June. *The Unbridgeable Gap: Blacks and Their Quest for the American Dream, 1900-1930.* Chicago: Rand McNally, 1972.

Stowe, Harriet Beecher. *Uncle Tom's Cabin.* New York: Washington Square Press, 1966.

Tindall, George B. *The Emergence of the New South, 1913-1945.* Baton Rouge: Louisiana State Univ. Press, 1969.

Washington, Booker T. *Up from Slavery.* New York: Dell, 1975.

Williams, John A. *The Man Who Cried I Am.* New York: New American Library, 1967.

Wise, Gene. *American Historical Explanations: A Strategy for Grounded Inquiry.* Homewood, IL: Dorsey, 1973.
Wister, Owen. *Roosevelt: The Story of a Friendship: 1880-1919.* New York: Macmillan, 1930.
Woodward, C. Vann. *The Strange Career of Jim Crow,* 2nd. rev. ed. New York: Oxford Univ. Press, 1966.
Wright, Richard. *Native Son.* New York: Harper and Row, 1940.
Wright, Richard. *The Outsider.* New York: Harper and Row, 1965.
X, Malcolm and Alex Haley. *The Autobiography of Malcolm X.* New York: Grove, 1966.

Articles, Dissertations, and Presentations

Achebe, Chinua. "The African Image in the West." Talk at Bowling Green State Univ. (Spring 1976).
Adams, Randall. "*The Exorcist* as a Popular Culture Artifact." Paper presented at the Western Regional Popular Culture Association Meeting, California State Polytechnic Institute (1 February 1975).
Baker, Donald G. "Black Images: The Afro-American in Popular Novels, 1900-1945." *Journal of Popular Culture,* 7 (Fall 1973), 327-346.
"Black Gable, The." *Time* (23 August 1976), p. 64.
Bloom, Samuel William. "A Social Psychological Study of Motion Picture Audience Behavior: A Case Study of the Negro Image in Mass Communication." Diss., Univ. of Wisconsin, 1956.
Bloomfield, Maxwell. "Dixon's *The Leopard's Spots*: A Study in Popular Racism." *American Quarterly,* 16 (Fall 1964), 387-401.
"Burden, The." *The Crisis,* 9 (December 1914), 94-95.
Burke, William Lee. "The Presentation of the American Negro in Hollywood Films, 1946-1961." Diss., Northwestern Univ., 1965.
Carter, Everett. "Cultural History Written with Lightning: The Significance of *The Birth of a Nation.*" *American Quarterly,* 12 (Fall 1960), 347-357.
Colle, Royal D. "The Negro Image and the Mass Media." Diss., Cornell Univ., 1967.
Cripps, Thomas. "The Myth of the Southern Box Office." In *The Black Experience in America.* Ed. by James Custer and Lewis Gould. Austin: Univ. of Texas

Press, 1970.
Cripps, Thomas R. "The Reaction of the Negro to the Motion Picture *The Birth of a Nation*." *The Historian*, 25 (May 1963), 344-362. Also anthologized in *The Making of Black America*, vol. 2, ed. by August Meier and Elliott Rudwick (New York: Antheneum, 1969).
Davis, Jackie. Speaker for Happiness of Womanhood (HOW), before Paul Vanderwood's "History Through Film" class, San Diego State Univ. (25 October 1973).
"Farm Security Administration: Before the War, 1935-1941." Smithsonian photograph exhibit displayed at San Diego State Univ. (February and March 1975).
Fearing, F. "Films as History." *Hollywood Quarterly*, 2 (1947), 422-427.
Fredomways. Special Issue: The Black Image in the Mass Media. Vol. 14, no. 3 (1974).
Friedman, Norman L. "Theory Number Two: Studying Film Impact on American Conduct and Culture." *Journal of Popular Film*, 3 (Spring 1974), 173-181.
Gilmore, Al-Tony. "Jack Johnson: The Man and His Times." *Journal of Popular Culture*, 2 (Spring 1973), 496-506.
Greider, William. "Don't Pay the Purists No Mind, Honey." *The Guardian Weekly*, 122 (6 January 1980), 17.
Harlan, Louis B. "Booker T. Washington and the White Man's Burden." *American Historical Review*, 71 (January 1966), 441-467.
Jahnke, Karl R. "The Black Image in American Popular Song, 1890-1910." Seminar paper for course in "American Racism" at San Diego State Univ. (10 April 1975).
Johnson, Abby Ann Arthur and Ronald M. Johnson. "Forgotten Pages: Black Literary Magazines in the 1920s." *Journal of American Studies*, 8 (December 1974), 363-382.
Kagan, Norman. "A Primer Black American Cinema." *Cinema*, 6 (Fall 1970), 2-7.
Kepley, Vance Jr. "The Film Medium as History: The Social and Political Implications of D.W. Griffith's *The Birth of a Nation*." Senior thesis in history at the Univ. of Illinois (May 1973).
Kroll, Jack. "John Wayne: End as a Man." *Newsweek*, 93 (25 June 1979), 44-47.
Leab, Daniel J. "The Gamut from A to B: The Image of the Black in Pre-1915 Movies." *Political Science Quarterly*, 88 (March 1973), 53-70.
Lemons, J. Stanley. "Black Stereotypes as Reflected in

Popular Culture, 1880-1920." *American Quarterly*, 29 (Spring 1977), 102-116.
Lesage, Julia. "Feminist Film Criticism: Theory and Practice." Paper delivered at the Midwest Women's Film Conference in Madison, Wisconsin (June 1973).
Lewin, Harlan. "The Feature Film as Data for the Study of Politics: The Documentary Function Unfulfilled." Paper prepared for delivery at the Annual Meeting of the American Political Science Association in Chicago, Illinois (7-11 September 1971).
Lyons, Timothy J. "Hollywood and World War One, 1914-1918." *Journal of Popular Film*, 1 (Winter 1972), 15-30.
Manning, Alan. Informal presentation on television in the fifties at the Western Regional Popular Culture Association Meeting in Pomona, California (1 February 1975).
McClure, Arthur F. "Hollywood at War: The American Motion Picture and World War Two." *Journal of Popular Film*, 1 (Spring 1972), 123-135.
McCreary, Eugene C. "Film and History: Some Thoughts on Their Relationship." *Societas*, 1 (Winter 1971), 51-66.
Menig, Harry. "A Guide to the Will Rogers Film Festival." Paper accompanying the film festival at the American Studies Association National Convention in San Francisco, California (18-20 October 1973).
Moss, Carlton. "The Negro in American Films." *Freedomways*, 3 (Spring 1963), 134-142.
Nelsen, Anne K. and Hart M. Nelsen. "The Prejudicial Film: Progress and Stalemate, 1915-1967." *Phylon*, 31 (Summer 1970), 142-147.
Nesteby, James R. "Cawelti's Methodology and Popular Culture Studies." *Magazine of the Faculty of Arts* [Sana'a University, Yemen] (Fall 1979), pp. 81-84.
Nesteby, James R. "Tarzan and Cultural Imperialism in Arabia." *Journal of Popular Culture* [to appear in vol. 15 (1982)].
Nesteby, James R. "Tarzan and the Ku Klux Klan: Anglo-Americanism in the Twenties." *Journal of English*, 6 (September 1979), 79-109.
Nesteby, James R. "Tarzan of Arabia: American Popular Culture Permeates Yemen." *Journal of Yemeni Studies*, vol. 3 (Summer 1980).
Nesteby, James R. "The Tarzan Series of Edgar Rice Burroughs: Lost Races and Racism in American Popular Culture." Diss., Bowling Green State Univ., 1978.
Nesteby, James R. "The Tenuous Vine of *Tarzan of the*

Apes." *Journal of Popular Culture*, 13 (Spring 1980), 483-487.

Opubur, Alfred E. and Adebayo Ogunbi. "Ooga Booga: The African Image in American Films." *Other Voices, Other Views: An International Collection of Essays from the Bicentennial*. Ed. by Robin W. Winks. Westport, CT: Greenwood, 1978, pp. 343-375.

Osofsky, Gilbert. "Progressivism and the Negro: New York, 1900-1915." *American Quarterly*, 16 (Summer 1964), 153-168.

Petry, Daniel. Informal talk about his film, *Buster and Billy*, with Paul Vanderwood's "History Through Film" class at San Diego State Univ. (Spring 1975).

Pierson, George W. "The M-Factor in American History." *American Quarterly*, 14 (Summer 1962), 275-289.

Quarles, Benjamin. "What the Historian Owes the Negro." *Saturday Review*, 49 (3 September 1966), 10-13.

Reddick, L.D. "Educational Programs for the Improvement of Race Relations: Motion Pictures, Radio, The Press, and Libraries." *Journal of Negro Education*, 13 (Summer 1944), 367-389.

Reisman, Leon. "Cinema Technique and Mass Culture." *American Quarterly*, 1 (Winter 1949), 314-325.

Rollins, Peter C. "Film and American Studies: Questions, Activities, Guides." *American Quarterly*, 26 (August 1974), 245-265.

Rollins, Peter C. "Will Rogers: Symbolic Man and Film Image." Paper presented at the American Studies Association National Convention in San Francisco, California (19 October 1973).

Rudwick, Elliott M. "The Niagara Movement." *The Journal of Negro History*, 43 (July 1957), 177-200.

Slotkin, Richard. "Dreams and Genocide: The American Myth of Regeneration Through Violence." *Journal of Popular Culture*, 5 (Summer 1971), 38-59.

Smith, Barbara. "Reader's Forum: Black Women in Film Symposium." *Freedomways*, vol. 14 (1974).

Soyinka, Wole. Talk on African literature at San Diego State Univ. (14 April 1975).

Wilson, Ray (Local Chairman, National Socialist White Peoples Party) and Carroll Waymon (Afro-American Professor of Education). Debate before Paul Vanderwood's "History Through Film" class at San Diego State Univ. (10 October 1973).

Wilson, Woodrow. "The Reconstruction of the Southern States." *Atlantic Monthly*, 87 (January 1901), 1-15.

The author, James R. Nesteby, is an underpaid, overworked, humorless, stuffed-shirt professor.

It would be gratifying at times to admit in print to such a clichéd assertion. But I am presently a Fulbright Lecturer in American and British Literature at Aleppo University in Syria and enjoying it. Prior to this award, I lectured in American and British literature for the University of Maryland in Heidelberg, Germany, and, years ago, for Sana'a University in Yemen. As an ABD (all but dissertationese), I did a rewarding stint as assistant director of the National American Studies Faculty of the American Studies Association in Philadelphia. Wordy but not fancy, this record, for nowadays professors only get paid when gainfully employed, and that I have been.

My graduate work: English and Popular Culture at Bowling Green State University and American Studies at San Diego State University. As an undergraduate I experienced an experimental education on an island called Mackinac. Mackinac College did not survive the turmoil of the late sixties, but its well-deserved influence does survive through students and professors from around the world, including I, me, or myself--whichever persona a former student, now professor, should use.

When not overseas, I make my home in Southern Illinois, near Metropolis, a town with two commonly acknowledged attributes: It's across the Ohio River from Paducah, Kentucky, and it's the foster town (some over-achievers here wish they could say "metropolis" or even "city"), of our country's favorite savior--upholder of all that we wish we could believe in--Superman. In my mind, Metropolis has a third and a fourth attribute: It's the birthplace of the pioneer Afro-American filmmaker, Oscar Micheaux, and, while not the most sensational community in America, it is Heartland, U.S.A., just up the river from where Huck and Jim wished to land their raft. Both Paul Vanderwood and Jimmy Baldwin also appreciate this.

Saved for last is the revelation that I've published a handful of articles and a couple of books, most of which I pray are worthwhile. They're certainly not profitable. For some people, though, that's not enough. They want to know what an author is working on. After giving essentially the identical answer for too many years, I despair of such implicit promises. However, to avoid disclosures about marital, familial, financial, and other "als," I'll say with no sincerity intended that I plan to finish a book called *Tarzan and American Racism*. I also plan to persevere on another about the mythical island-continent of Caspak.